The child and the book

The child and the book:
a psychological and
literary exploration

NICHOLAS TUCKER

CAMBRIDGE UNIVERSITY PRESS

CAMBRIDGE
LONDON   NEW YORK   NEW ROCHELLE
MELBOURNE   SYDNEY

Published by the Press Syndicate of the University of Cambridge
The Pitt Building, Trumpington Street, Cambridge CB2 1RP
32 East 57th Street, New York, NY 10022, USA
296 Beaconsfield Parade, Middle Park, Melbourne 3206, Australia

First published 1981
Reprinted 1982
First paperback edition 1982

Printed in Great Britain at the University Press, Cambridge

British Library Cataloguing in Publication Data
Tucker, Nicholas
The child and the book.
1. Childrens literature – History and criticism
I. Title
028.5   PN1009.A1   80-49883
ISBN 0 521 23251 1 hard covers
ISBN 0 521 27048 0 paperback

Dedicated to Mathew, Emma and Lucy,
with love

Contents

Acknowledgements

Having originally studied both literature and psychology, I have always been aware of possible connections between the two. However it was only when I started working with children as an educational psychologist, and later had a family of my own, that I began to become interested in the relationship between children and some of their favourite books. In fact, I have been writing about children, their literature, or both together for the last fifteen years, but from all the newspapers or journals I have written for, I would particularly like to thank Beryl McAlhone, one-time editor of *Where*, who from early on encouraged me to specialise in this area. Thanks are also due to Paul Barker, editor of *New Society*, Elizabeth Thomas, at one time of the *New Statesman*, and to various other editors and friends on *The Times Literary Supplement*, *The Times Educational Supplement*, *Children's Literature in Education*, and other publications who have allowed me to quote from articles of mine that first appeared in their pages. I should also thank the BBC for use of material formerly broadcast by myself at different times.

There are many others I am grateful to, whether children's writers, librarians, teachers, students or simply parents, for their constant willingness to talk over some of the points discussed in this book at various conferences or meetings over the years, nor would I want to forget the part my own children have taken in all this. Family reading has always been something that we have done together, and still try to keep up, despite increasing distractions. The children's comments as we have gone along have often been very enlightening, so it is only just that I now dedicate this book to all three of them, without whom it might still have been written, but with so much less point or pleasure for myself.

Introduction

Books published about children's literature up to now have generally concentrated upon only a few possible approaches. There have been a number of very adequate historical surveys of children's literature, for example, while other studies have chosen instead to concentrate on present-day children's books and their authors. Another popular type of study takes a more pedagogic attitude towards this subject by discussing particular ways of getting books across to children, and there are also several good surveys available of what seems to be children's most popular reading-matter at various ages.

All these different approaches can be valuable in their way, and I have learned much from many of them. But in this book I shall be considering instead a different and previously rather neglected topic: exactly *why* are certain themes and approaches in children's literature so popular with the young, and what do possible answers to this question tell us both about children and about many of their favourite books? Can the discovery of common factors in the plots or characters of popular children's books, for example, help reveal recurrent, predictable patterns in children's imaginative needs and interests? Or looking at this relationship from another angle, can various studies in developmental psychology also sometimes explain why some literary approaches have always seemed more acceptable to the young than others?

Throughout this book, therefore, I shall be discussing children's literature in its more developmental aspects, and examining ways in which it grows with and keeps close to children over the years in correspondence with their own changing imaginative and intellectual outlook. In this sense, I shall usually be more concerned with assessing particular books or authors for their potential psychological appeal rather than for their literary merit. Even so, the discussion of the psychological appeal of any particular book often brings one very

1

close to making literary judgements too, since literary sensitivity when writing for the young can also be described in terms of the skills with which an author responds to various psychological and imaginative needs within his or her audience. Children, for example, sometimes need stimulation in their literature to help them to move away from certain lazy, immature ways of thinking; a good author, consciously or unconsciously, provides this stimulation by writing about characters and situations in a way that is both fresh and convincing and which, in the light of a child's developing understanding, can also point the way forward towards greater insight. In other moods, however, children may simply want confirmation in their books of certain common, set ways of thinking, and here they often prefer the undemanding fantasies provided for them by literature which frequently has very little literary merit as such, but which I shall also be discussing here.

Trying to discover some of the nature and effects of the interaction between children and their favourite books is by no means easy, though. One simple-minded approach to the problem has always been to ask children themselves through various questionnaires or surveys, what exactly their books mean to them. Turning a powerful searchlight of this sort onto complex, sometimes diffuse patterns of reactions is a clumsy way of going about things, however, and children can be particularly elusive when interrogated like this, with laconic comments like 'Not bad' or 'The story's good' adding little to any researcher's understanding. But this taciturnity is not surprising: as Charlotte Brontë pointed out over a hundred years ago in *Jane Eyre*, 'Children can feel, but they cannot analyse their feelings; and if the analysis is partially effected in thought, they know not how to express the result of the process in words.'[1] A recent, very thorough review of research on children's responses to reading came to the same conclusions. 'If the child is allowed to choose what he wants to read, and allowed further to make his own undirected response to such reading, the nature of that response will be subjective rather than objective — felt rather than thought.'[2]

Attempting to guess at the appeal of any book to children, therefore, will necessitate both psychological and literary detective work, and not a little honest speculation. I shall also be using results from past reading surveys when these seem useful, though, together with autobiographical memories of childhood reading from various sources which can provide the intimate detail missing from more

2

impersonal types of discussion. Such memories can sometimes be quite idiosyncratic, but they can also be very revealing when it comes to trying to describe the various emotions occasionally engendered by books at different ages. As I have already said, however, this sort of evidence will also be coupled with a broader discussion of young readers' typical literary preferences drawn from other, less subjective sources. Even so, many of the conclusions I shall be making will have to be tentative, given that individual responses to the experience of reading are often diverse in a way that will always defeat any attempt to be overprescriptive.

The same risk of overstatement must also be resisted when discussing the nature of children's more general emotional and intellectual needs, in so far as these are relevant to explaining certain common preferences for different types of children's literature. Not infrequently, any individual's particular psychological development may not always seem to follow the patterns that psychologists have come to think will be most likely, but here it should be remembered that psychology is always more concerned with probabilities rather than certainties, and so tends to look for *trends* in behaviour rather than for cast-iron rules. There is also the problem, in any book concerned with child psychology, of choosing which psychological theories to follow, given that there are still various quite different ways of looking at things within developmental psychology itself. In my case, however, I shall be guided by two major theoretical approaches, both of which provide explanatory frameworks which have, despite some criticism and modifications, proved generally useful since their inception.

Where children's emotional responses are concerned, I shall be discussing ways in which literature sometimes appears to reflect and relieve various common unconscious or only semiconscious fears and desires whose presence, in the reader, is in my view best explained and described by psychoanalytic theory. Psychoanalysts believe for example, that very charged material can often find its way quite safely into fiction when it is suitably disguised from the reader by appearing in make-believe form acted out by different, imaginary characters. In this way, therefore, it need not arouse the anxiety, guilt or denial commonly experienced when individuals are *directly* confronted by various personally taboo feelings or fantasies. But recognition of possible personal meanings and relevancies in certain powerful stories can still occur, it is thought, at an unconscious level.

3

Literature that is rich in otherwise suppressed individual fantasies therefore, may often have a strong appeal for particular readers, even though they may not understand what this appeal consists of. In the opinion of Freud, whose own writings on this topic still read well, fiction that allows for the expression of unconscious fantasy in this way acts as a useful safety-valve to the individual. But although I shall be using some of Freud's insights, prospective readers of this book need not fear that they will therefore soon become lost in a forest of symbols. Instead, I shall only be drawing on broad psychoanalytic approaches towards understanding certain strong, sometimes hidden emotions in the reader, and their possible reflection in literature.

While psychoanalytic interpretations of literature have been current for some time, other complementary or contrasting psychological explanations for the appeal of literature have been neglected. Cognitive psychology, for example, has always stressed that the major intellectual task facing children is their constant need to make sense of everything that is happening around them, and here the dominant figure over the last fifty years has been the Swiss psychologist, Jean Piaget. His approach is also important in explaining the appeal of stories to children. Their fiction, after all, usually portrays a simplified, cut-down version of reality which young minds may find particularly easy to understand, but this is not to say that children necessarily read books chiefly for intellectual stimulation or explanation. In any novel, it is always the story itself that must initially appeal to readers, thereby arousing a curiosity about what is going to happen next that can only be satisfied by getting to the end of the book. But readers will also require a version of events that they can both grasp and sympathise with if a story is going to hold their attention. For this reason the way in which children's literature manages to accommodate itself to various essentially childish modes of comprehension will be one of the main themes of this book.

Although Piaget's work is well known among psychologists, it has had less impact than it deserves in discussion of the reading response, and by drawing freely upon it I hope I can do something to make up for this previous neglect. Even so, the most eminent of psychologists will always have their detractors, and Piaget has at one stage been labelled, by communist psychologists from China, as a 'bourgeois empiricist'. The criticism here is that Piaget only tested and questioned Westernised children brought up in a particular and often favourable social and economic climate; his results, by this argument, could hardly be termed a universal psychology of childhood.

It is strange that Piaget has been picked on in this way, since his work — more than most — has led to an enormous amount of cross-cultural psychological research, much of which has corroborated his original theories. It is true, however, that Piaget has always been most interested in discovering the intellectual *strategies* that individuals at various ages have in common, when it comes to trying to understand the total environment in which they find themselves. But the analysis of how different environmental or personality factors may then affect the development of particular ideas or attitudes arising from such common intellectual strategies, has never been his special concern. For example, Piaget describes — as we shall see — all young children as going through an omnipotent, egocentric stage, where they think the world revolves around their every wish. At the same time, they tend to see the workings of the universe in terms of what Piaget has described as 'immanent justice', whereby everything is thought to work out according to sound moral law, with rewards for the good and punishment for the bad.

There has been plenty of experimental work since supporting these broad conclusions, but it has, on the whole, been left to other psychologists to point out that harsh reality, or indeed the typical thought-patterns of certain cultures, can sometimes put a stop to such amiable fantasies much sooner in the case of some children than others. An American psychologist Jerome Bruner, for example, has recently drawn attention to what has been called 'the culture of poverty', where those born into an economically and socially deprived society may soon cease to view life in such a purposive, patterned way. Instead, they may quickly come to share the prevailing, depressed view of many of those around them, where individual success is seen more in terms of sheer luck than as having anything to do with particular effort — a typical attitude of personal impotence produced by overwhelming economic and environmental disadvantage.

This gap between common intellectual strategies, and cultural or individual expectations which may differ widely from each other, obviously makes it impossible to try to describe anything like a universal literary response, so far as the possible personal ramifications for each individual are concerned. In this book, however, and following Piaget, I shall chiefly describe the more typical ways in which children seem to approach and make sense of their stories at various ages, leaving particular details — of how individuals or whole cultures can then sometimes react to such stories quite differently — to one side. But although responses to literature will always differ in some ways, there will be times as well when regular and fairly predictable similarities in reactions to certain aspects of fiction can tell us a good deal about both people and books. Apart from what Piaget has to suggest on this score, it is also true that all human beings seem to respond to certain similar fantasies, which find echoes in literature throughout the world. The existence of archetypal plots and fantasies in literature, therefore, argues for some sort of uniformity in what can best capture and spur on the imagination, and when such themes also occur in children's literature, I shall sometimes try to provide possible reasons for their particular appeal. Where any more specific claims about the interaction of literature and children are concerned, however, I have confined my argument in this book to British children's literature, and its likely readers both now and in the past. What overlap or divergence such reactions may have with children's typical responses from quite different cultures though, is a question which must be left for another type of study.

There is also another possible charge of 'bourgeois empiricism' that could be levelled against anyone like myself who tries generalising about children's responses to literature. Since children's books are written, published and very often purchased by adults, how can one be sure that one is not describing an interaction with literature that children merely get to like, rather than like to get? Anyone at the time who tried to describe children's literary preferences in the early nineteenth century, for example, could say little about the popularity of limericks, because Edward Lear's *A Book of Nonsense* had yet to prove that such popularity actually existed. Can one be sure that one's own literary establishment will not also produce new material one day that will prove very popular, and to that extent help lead to new theories, or at least to some modification of older ones, on why certain books can so quickly become favourites with so many children?

This argument could certainly prove dangerous for critics who generalise only about respectable children's literature, where adult influence has always been fairly evident and sometimes obtrusive. But if any discussion also includes popular literature for children, such as nursery rhymes, fairy stories and comics, as I have tried to do here, then the results should give some idea of what children have always seemed to like, very often despite rather than because of adult approval. At the same time, the last hundred years has seen a general liberation of children's literature from much of its old, semi-pedagogic role, and sometimes popular books for children this century have been almost as disliked by adults as they have been welcomed by most young readers. Continuing adult attempts at interference, however, have on the whole not been successful; although the works of Enid Blyton, for example, have been banned from more public libraries over the years than is the case with any other adult or children's author, she still remains very widely read.[3] So while one can never be certain that there are no more developments in children's books just around the corner to reveal some new dimensionto young readers' imaginative needs, one can — by sticking to tried favourites — be fairly sure of generalising about fiction that has already proved its popularity with a great many children.

As it would have been impossible to try to analyse the appeal of every favourite book or comic for children, however, my final choice of fiction to discuss has been somewhat arbitrary. I have, though, tried to deal mainly with books representative in various ways of the different fictional genres that have always seemed popular with children, written by authors drawn from the living and the dead but with the emphasis equally on best-sellers from the immediate and occasionally the more distant past. This is not simply because I once used to enjoy such books myself and so have some direct experience of their appeal, though this may have something to do with it. There is also the point that former best-sellers that continue to attract young readers today obviously must have a popularity that transcends temporary trends, and therefore have something worth discussing in more detail here. Some of the novels written for children now will also one day be seen as classics for their time and continue to win new readers. But because one can never quite tell which of them are going to remain of permanent interest, I have accordingly usually decided to stick with tried and tested books, even when they sometimes now seem rather dated. There are other ways, too, in which I have been forced to limit my discussion of the otherwise vast and sprawling field of children's literature, when it is taken as a whole. Apart from nursery rhymes, for example, I shall not be discussing the appeal of poetry nor that of general non-fiction. In fact, poetry is sadly little read by children today, and while non-fiction can sometimes be very successful with young readers, 77 per cent of them, according to Schools Council researches, still prefer reading fiction, which is why I have chosen it as the best potential area for any examination of overall imaginative responses to literature.[4]

There is, however, another type of potential ambiguity intrinsic to any discussion of this whole topic, including my own, and this arises over the precise definition of what we choose to term as 'children's stories', and whether they can always be easily distinguished from so-called 'adult fiction'. Although most people would agree that there are obvious differences between adult and children's literature, when pressed they may find it quite difficult to establish what exactly such differences really amount to. Adult books, like the novels of Ian Fleming, are often read by children, just as grown-up readers may sometimes want to turn again to classics like *The Wind in the Willows* or *The House at Pooh Corner*. There are also books, from *Alice in Wonderland* to the sagas of Tolkien or Richard Adams, which have always attracted a wide readership from the moment of publication. Could it therefore be that there are no valid differences between children's and adults' literary taste and that children's literature as such is an artificial device thought up by adults more or less to keep the young in their place?

There is an element of truth in this sort of assertion, but not much more. Certainly, adults do not always want to read books that take full account of their maturity, and there is much written for them that appeals, and always has appealed, to children as well. Attempting to discourage children from occasionally reading this sort of adult literature can often be a quite mistaken policy. Equally, mature readers who somehow feel inhibited by age from trying authors who write ostensibly for a younger audience, may find themselves missing a whole range of literature which would once have been enjoyed by adults, but which now, for reasons of literary convention, has become unfashionable for older readers. In this context, it has sometimes been said that if Malory or Dickens were alive today, they would probably be writing for children, so preoccupied has the adult reading market now become with fiction that thrives on the close study of personal relationships in preference, say, to epic or picaresque forms of literature.

Even so, while some common ground exists between adult and child reading, just as it does when it comes to watching popular programmes on television, there are also distinctive differences between the reading needs of the young and old, and therefore between the types of literature they get. Adult readers may not always, or indeed ever, wish to read up to the level of their intelligence or experience, but so long as they have the potential for doing so, some of them will require literature which lies beyond the intellectual and emotional grasp of a child. In the same way, children may sometimes want literature that is so simple that none but the most determinedly regressive adult reader would ever find it satisfying; it is rare, for example, to see any grown readers still enjoying Enid Blyton's *Little Noddy* stories.

Beyond such extremes, however, there are also other differences between the literary tastes and needs at least of experienced adult readers and those of the average child. Where intellectual skills are concerned, for example, children — crudely defined here as those beings between school age and puberty, so omitting babies and older teenagers from the argument — will prefer books that deal with concrete events rather than with abstract discussion, and which have an emphasis upon action in preference to introspection. At the same time, such action must then be treated in ways that do not make too many demands upon still immature intellectual skills. Scott Fitzgerald once wrote that 'The test of a first-rate intelligence is the ability to hold two opposed ideas in the mind at the same time, and still maintain the ability to function', and Piaget would probably agree from his own researches, which suggest that this ability is altogether too difficult for children up to the age of seven or so, and after that only in a context of thinking about actual, concrete objects. The next stage, when it is possible to hold two contradictory, abstract ideas together in one concept, such as the notion of a good—bad character, or an act that may be both positive and negative in its implications, will generally have to wait until most children are at least around the age of eleven.

It follows, therefore, that younger children will not on the whole welcome ambiguity in their literature. The type of moral judgement they can most easily share and understand will tend to praise or condemn characters for their surface acts alone, without wanting to consider more subtle explanations, either in terms of motivation or else in the suggestion of an altogether more complex scale of values. Older children, it is true, eventually get past this particular stage of making very simple, absolute moral judgements, but usually arrive at an only slightly more complex level, where conventional morality will still be preferred to more radical ideas that sometimes challenge tradition and the majority view.

A young audience, therefore, always has a tendency to go in for snap moral judgements, often based upon preconceived, immediate emotional reactions towards certain acts or situations and this, in turn, limits a children's author in any attempt to develop a more complex view of things. Instead, there may be pressure to simplify causal connections, substituting in part a more predictable, morally coherent world picture for the confusion of reality itself. This is something that a great writer like Tolstoy could refuse to do, for example in his deliberately inconsequential descriptions of the battle scenes in *War and Peace* (where he seems to have followed the advice of the Duke of Wellington, who warned his contemporaries not to write about Waterloo since he personally did not know what had really happened there, and was sure that no one else did). In fact, one of the appeals of fiction for all ages is that it can present the reader with a pattern of events that is in itself more comprehensible than the jumble of happenings that seems to make up real life. But while Tolstoy or Henry James can write for an audience capable of understanding the necessarily indeterminate complexity of much human experience, a children's writer will usually have to offer a more comprehensible world of cause and effect, simplified towards a minimum of explanation.

Writing of William Cobbett's return from his first trip in America, Chesterton describes his hero's 'terrible discovery that terminates youth, even if it often gives a new interest to life: the discovery that it is a strange world, that things are not what they seem and certainly not always what they profess to be'.[5] Before reaching this particular stage of knowledge, however, children will tend to see the workings of the universe and of human affairs in terms of what seems to them like good, common sense and an overall moral coherence. This is not to say that they want all their stories to end happily, although this is often the case. Rather, there is a strong wish, usually reflected in children's literature, that stories should always be quite clearly rounded off, with justice more or less seen to be done, even if this works against characters with whom children may generally sympathise. One reason, perhaps, why younger readers often find *Alice in Wonderland* rather frightening could be because of its moral anarchy, where events are always so arbitrary and unpredictable.

10

It could, however, also be argued that adult readers of fiction also usually prefer a firm moral framework to most of their stories, with few really able to tolerate fiction in which the good repeatedly suffer and the bad flourish, or where it is impossible to draw moral lines between any of the characters. But even so, some more sophisticated literary approaches which practised adult readers can usually understand quite quickly — such as satire, which often superficially exhibits a moral aimlessness as a cover for criticism of society — will still very much puzzle younger readers. The failure to detect irony lies in the reader's inability to understand the author's intention, often signalled by a particular use of language bordering on parody of whichever person or institution is being satirised. In Swift's *A modest proposal for preventing the children of poor people from being a burden to their parents or their country*, for example, the satire is underlined by the use of a particular scientific-economic jargon to advance the idea that pauper children should be eaten by the rich. An intelligent, practised reader will soon notice the difference between this type of voice and the tone of Swift's other writings, and even from a cursory knowledge of history will realise that the whole idea is a macabre absurdity. Children, however, have neither the literary skill nor the historical perspective for this sort of analysis; they are, anyhow, naturally susceptible to sarcasm, becoming easily confused over the way that the surface meanings of words can also convey a contrary interpretation. Once again, this difficulty is not always confined to children. In research on the reading comprehension of college of education students, for example, older readers were sometimes seen to let their immediate reactions to a text swamp more critical and accurate understanding, often becoming quite confused between what authors appeared to write and their actual intention.[6] There was also the eighteenth-century Irish bishop who was reported to have found that *Gulliver's Travels* 'was full of improbable lies, and for his part he hardly believed a word of it'.[7] But if older readers occasionally have difficulty spotting irony or other finer variations in literary tone, children can be expected to have far more severe problems when faced by this sort of subtlety.

So although readers of any age can often find themselves wishing for a conventional treatment and happy resolution when caught up in a particular piece of fiction, selective adult readers are better equipped to reject this type of wish-fulfilment in writing where it would be clearly inappropriate given the development of the rest of the novel. What may seem like realism in fiction for younger readers, however, often amounts only to a reflection in print of the reality — to them — of their own typical, personal idealism, where they still mainly believe in what they *want* to be true. For this reason, it is hard to imagine pre-adolescent readers being able to see any point worth making in some of the gloomier plots associated with writers like Zola or Gissing, and more than one adult has told me how perverse and depressing they once found Thomas Hardy's *Jude the Obscure*, when first read in their youth at a time when their own more positive view of the world made this type of pessimism seem almost totally alien.

Some children's writers, as we shall see, do hint from time to time that things are more complex and less morally logical than such a view would suggest, while others go along with various optimistic fantasies more or less in their entirety. But no successful children's writer could ever hope to get away with a morally nihilist vision of things in their books; children would not accept or even understand this attitude — one reason, possibly, why Hans Andersen's more depressing short stories have never really caught on with the young. Something of the same point was made recently by a modern children's author, Russell Hoban, whose book *The Mouse and his Child*, also contains some very dark moments. It is about some clockwork toys up against a horrifying, cruel gangster rat in the brutal world of a giant rubbish tip. Very much against the odds, however, and somewhat out of the character of the rest of the book, they finally defeat and reform their enemy, and re-establish themselves in a derelict doll's house that has become a symbol of home and safety. As Russell Hoban writes, 'I believed that the winning of the doll's house was truly a victory and I believed that victory might be a permanent thing. That's why the book is a children's book.' But as he adds, 'Now I know that the winning of a doll's house may be a proper triumph for clockwork mice in a story, but for human beings in real life it won't do. Nor can any victory be permanent.'[8] But this sort of gathering pessimism would be out of place in a children's book, perhaps one reason why the promised sequel to his novel seems now to have been put aside.

A children's author must also be more selective when it comes to communicating with his or her audience. The endless paragraphs of a Proust, the convoluted sentences of a Henry James, or the sophisticated, literary English of a Meredith will not get through to children.

Such stylistic features may baffle many adults too, of course, yet the determined, practised adult reader can enjoy such writing, and the particular effects it is able to convey, in a way that one would never expect to find amongst children, except perhaps for the odd, super-precocious child who always exists to confound any such generalisations. But on the whole, children usually seem to prefer a style that does not present too many difficulties, using a high percentage of direct speech and a less complex vocabulary. Such a style favours the description of plot rather than character, since it does not lend itself easily to psychological analysis, save of the most rudimentary sort.

Even so, children will not always necessarily prefer consistently plain, direct English in their stories. As we shall see, young readers can also be exceptionally sensitive to the sound and overtones of words, and good writers should always try to cater for this response. This is not just a question of incorporating a number of fine-sounding archaic words or particular quirks of dialect into a text, though this often can be effective. It can also be that certain words or phrases that may seem fairly prosaic to an adult can sometimes come across in a particularly exciting way to children. As Joan Aiken — an excellent contemporary stylist for children herself — has written about her own childhood reading, the very oddest terms picked up randomly from children's books can occasionally seem to

have an extra glamour and luminosity — I found this with a lot of terms in American books, pickled limes in *Little Women*, and mysterious creatures called patter-rollers in *Uncle Remus*. And quite apart from the interest and mystery of unknown words, children find them beautiful. It was the lavish language, expressions such as cynical immorality and blatant indecency that I relished in *Stalky & Co.*[9]

In fact, the way children respond imaginatively to the sound of words, as opposed to their content, is probably the single most unpredictable topic to try to understand in the whole field of children's literature. The young Compton Mackenzie, for example, used to think of words in terms of colours and shapes. 'Thus the grace before meals *For what we are going to receive* always presented itself as an oblong chocolate-brown affair whereas the grace after meals *For what we have received* appeared a round mustardy-yellow affair.'[10] Faced by this sort of idiosyncrasy, no children's writer can ever hope to know exactly how a young audience is going to react to the prose in their books, but in general authors should always take extra care to produce their best when writing for this formative age. When very young readers are concerned, though, authors should also try to avoid making things unnecessarily hard. At the most basic level, for example, it is often valuable to keep subject and predicate close together; a sentence like 'The girl standing beside the lady had a blue dress', for example, was once misinterpreted by some 59 per cent of the seven year old readers to whom it was put. When it was re-presented as 'The girl had a blue dress and was standing beside the lady', however, all but the poorest readers understood it the first time round.[11] This difficulty with intervening clauses can be paralleled, perhaps, in the way that children at this age also sometimes have difficulty with too many sub-plots or flash-backs to different times in their stories. In both cases, when a reader's concentration is limited it can be unwise for authors to attempt to spread themselves too widely, either in one sentence or over an entire plot.

There may also be some emotional as well as intellectual limits over what younger children can take in their fiction. Most children, for example, quite like stories where they can test themselves out against some of their own fears, rather as adults often enjoy horror films, but with young readers there is a greater possibility of going too far. Just as small children are more open to belief in any sort of story, including tall ones, since they lack the scepticism that comes with age and experience, so too can their rational defences become more easily broached and flooded by powerful, fearful images. Auto-biographies, particularly from before this century, often described with bitterness certain stories or pictures that seemed designed to terrify children into good behaviour. Dickens, for example, writes feelingly about the horror stories that his nurse used to tell him with full dramatic effect every night, however much he begged her not to. E. Nesbit was also tortured by fear as a child. In one of her stories, *The Aunt and Amabel*, she describes Foxe's *Book of Martyrs*, one such frightener from her youth, as 'A horrible book — the thick oleographs, their guarding sheets of tissue sticking to the prints like bandages to a wound . . . it was a book that made you afraid to go to bed: but it was a book you could not help reading.' It could equally be argued that adult readers can also be upset by frightening stories, but there is still, on the whole, a difference in susceptibility to very horrific material between the old and at least some of the very young. But argument about where any particular 'cut-off' point arrives in the treatment of horror or fear for a child audience will always flourish in such a generally indeterminate area.

In *The Lucifer Stone*, for example, a recent, unremarkable novel for children by Harriet Graham,[12] the boy hero is at one stage lowered down the shaft of a disused mine by the murderous villain, in order to search for the usual hidden treasure. The child is nearly killed, but escapes and the crook is finally arrested, just as any young reader would have learned to expect. While reading the book, however, I was reminded of a recent, well-publicised case, where Leslie Whittle, a young girl, actually was lowered into a disused shaft, but in her case murdered. This whole horrifying episode, which occurred well after *The Lucifer Stone* was published, has already been made into an 'X' certificate film, and could conceivably form the basis one day for an adult novel, rather as in John Fowles' disturbing book, *The Collector*. But such a plot would never be suitable in a book for younger readers, who were already reported to be upset by news bulletins about Leslie Whittle's murder, sometimes suffering nightmares as a result. The convention, therefore, that novels like *The Lucifer Stone* should end happily is not there simply because adults want to shelter the young for no very sound reasons. Many children simply have different capacities for accepting extreme fear or depression in literature; although some have an appetite for horror, others become disturbed by strong material. This is not the same as suggesting that all fearful literature should be banned, however — something that has never been practicable.[13]

There are other limitations that young readers impose upon the writer's choice of theme or treatment by virtue of their own immaturity and lack of knowledge. Novels that deal with experience chiefly confined to adults, for example, will not attract young readers if this experience is also described in an adult way. Even Jean-Paul Sartre, for example — a very precocious reader when young — describes in his autobiography the experience of reading and re-reading the close of *Madame Bovary* as a boy, totally unable to understand why Charles Bovary became depressed after he had found love-letters addressed to his wife, or why he looked at her former lover so darkly when they happened to meet again. The very situation of Emma Bovary, who sustains herself on unreal fantasies taken from romantic novels, and then disastrously tries to make her personal life follow suit, is also difficult for children to comprehend, since they themselves will not yet have enough experience of life to help them understand the essential falsity of Emma's illusions.

At adolescence, literature for young readers becomes less distinguishable from adult reading, however, and even before this stage there will always be some adult novels quite well adapted to the needs of many children. The undemanding, best-selling romantic novel, for example, has always dealt with the triumph of virtue over vice, often assisted by venerable conventions which seem to indicate the type of accompanying moral order in the universe so sympathetic to a child's actual beliefs, such as omens which turn out to be true, and fortunate coincidences which ensure that justice is always restored in the last few pages.

Some of the greatest fiction has also, at least initially, been built on similar romantic, immediately attractive structures, such as the Cinderella plots of Jane Austen or the moral symmetry of Shakespeare, where evil always gets its deserts and the good are usually left at the end to restore the situation. But best-selling authors can only succeed if they manage first to win and then to hold the interest of a great many diverse readers, and one way of doing this has always been to begin with very basic plots or situations that everyone, children included, could normally find it easy to identify with at the immediate level of undemanding personal fantasy. Once any reader's sympathy and curiosity have been aroused through coming to believe in the story and caring about its characters, then of course authors can afford to develop a more subtle approach in what they are doing. Many great nineteenth-century novels, however, still chose to finish with orthodox, happy endings, and child readers who had stayed with them up to this point may have enjoyed such conclusions as much as anyone else. They would probably have missed a good deal before, though, where the novelist may have been developing a more complex picture of things, belied by any conventional, super-optimistic conclusion.

Once novelists around the turn of the last century began to cater specifically for children, essentially adult classics were gradually abandoned by many younger readers in favour of books written closer to their particular requirements. Children no longer had to raid more sophisticated, wordy literature for what it could still offer them, such as favourite passages of adventure in *Robinson Crusoe*, a gratifying concentration upon a child hero in *Lorna Doone* and *The Water Babies*, or the basic fairy-tale plots of Charles Dickens with heroes setting out to make their way, sudden reversals of fortune, and generous benefactors standing in for fairy godmothers.[14] The fact that some children used to turn to adult classics — often published in especially abbreviated versions — for want of more appropriate reading for themselves, however, has led to the erroneous belief still sometimes found today that complex books like *Gulliver's Travels* or *Moby Dick* are in some ways children's literature — to be reprinted in their entirety each year in cheap editions and bought by unknowing adults for a generally unreceptive offspring.

A few adult classics, however, continue to straddle both age-groups successfully, and here the case of *Huckleberry Finn* is particularly interesting, as it was written, like *Tom Sawyer*, in the tradition of the boy's adventure story, and is still sometimes referred to as such. So it is, in a sense; children, like adults, are quite able to follow the course of Huck's adventures down the river, marvelling at his narrow escapes, and enjoying the fun and games initiated by Tom Sawyer in the last few chapters. But while they may get an inkling of Mark Twain's larger purpose in this novel, some of it will also necessarily elude them because of their inevitable lack of experience and knowledge. Such points may pass by many adult readers too, but once again there is at least greater potential amongst older readers to understand the more subtle things Mark Twain was suggesting.

For example, the irony of the church service preaching brotherly love, in a Kentucky community that supports feuding as a way of life, may escape young readers simply caught up in the exciting events of the story. More important, though, will be the reader's ability to see Huck's dilemma — whether or not to betray the runaway slave Jim — in something like its historical perspective. A modern child reader, in all probability, can see no moral problem for Huck: a slave on the run is now a romantic, heroic figure, and even to think of giving one up would be viewed as nothing less than evil. Huck has to work this out for himself, however, and his pain and effort in doing so can only be understood in terms of his own contemporary culture — something that children now are ill-fitted to comprehend, both through their ignorance of history, and also because of their greater inability to empathise with others who may once have thought very differently.

The ambiguous tone of Mark Twain's view of his own childhood environment, and his criticism of modish high-mindedness co-existing alongside an occasionally idle, vicious and coarse community, all suggest a far deeper, more comprehensive moral vision than anything found in the breezy and nostalgic simplicities of *Tom Sawyer*. Children can enjoy both works, but there is a complexity to *Huckleberry Finn* that a young reader will appreciate more when returning to the book as an adult. The fact that children can get at least something out of such classics does not, therefore, mean that no real distinctions exist between complex literature of this sort and books more clearly geared to a child's limited comprehension.

Even in novels where children may be the main characters, child readers may still not understand them if the author treats such characters with the complexity, say, found in Henry James's *What Maisie Knew* or in L.P. Hartley's *The Shrimp and the Anemone*. This does not imply that these authors have created false pictures of childhood; rather, that a young audience has a better chance of understanding either child or adult characters when they are both cut down to a more stereotyped level of description and explanation.

When adult readers themselves want the relaxation of more undemanding literature, they too turn to books which older children may also be able to enjoy. The lone detective, cowboy, soldier or general adventurer in adult fiction, for example, who brings villains to justice against stiff odds, may satisfy the same daydreams of personal power and independence that children enjoy in their own literature. Elsewhere, Agatha Christie has been fairly called the Enid Blyton of the detective story, since her books also create an imaginary world where the reader's curiosity, once aroused, can always rely upon everything finally working out logically and satisfyingly, with none of the inconclusive messiness of the real world. Yet even quite easy adult best-sellers can still be too difficult or remote for most young children because of other factors such as a more sophisticated vocabulary, offhand allusions to contemporary affairs or general knowledge, and more recently, fantasies about prolonged and successful sexuality.

On the whole, therefore, children before adolescence will prefer literature that focuses more on child or child-like characters, and their typical feelings and preoccupations, just as adults will usually choose to stay with stories concentrating on their own age-group and interests. Nevertheless, juvenile comics still sometimes manage to hang on to some older readers, and at the time of the 1955 debates on horror comics in this country, one newsagent claimed that his customers for this material included two colonels and some army majors.

It would be wrong, however, to see adult interest in children's literature solely in terms of nostalgia or regression. Around adolescence the difference between child and adult literature becomes so indistinct that it can make perfectly good literary sense for the adult reader to turn sometimes to children's authors of the quality of Alan Garner, Philippa Pearce, Leon Garfield, William Mayne, John Masefield, Walter de la Mare, Jane Gardam and many others. To this extent, it is true that some, but not all, of the distinction between adult and older children's literature is artificial, depending in some measure on what is thought appropriate, both for adult and child reading at the time. For example, it has recently been claimed, that

While there was a time when the best adult fiction was timeless in nature and dealt at the core with Everyman, that is no longer true. Decade by decade, new books for adults have become more personal, more singular. It is a long and narrowing road from *Moby Dick* to *Portnoy's Complaint* . . . Everyman has gone out of fashion for adults. What separates us has come to seem more pertinent than what draws us together. But Everyman is present still in the best children's stories, just as he always has been.[15]

Children, however, with their essentially moral imagination, still demand big themes in much of their literature: dealing, for example, with heroism, personal salvation, or good and evil, and at its best, adult readers also sometimes want to share such literature without any necessary sense of literary slumming at all.

In general, though, it does seem possible to agree upon a number of differences which normally obtain between a great deal of typical child and adult literature, given that these demarcations occasionally become blurred around adolescence or in the case of a few remarkable books like *Alice in Wonderland*. In this present study, therefore, I shall be attempting to describe the changing nature, as I see it, of children's reactions to juvenile literature both as child readers get older and as their books become more complex. Such a broad subject, however, can only in itself be approached broadly, which is why I have not sought to include any neat little tables of information about, say, the relative popularity of different types of appeal, or the most important effects resulting from reading literature. This is because I do not believe that such tables are always very helpful, since as I have already said, there can be so many different ways in which a reader responds to stories — for one child, it may even be that a particular book becomes a favourite because of quite extra-literary associations like an attractive binding, or because it happens to be a present from a cherished source. This type of ambiguity may irritate those in search of a few, reliable measures both for a book's worth or for a child's likely response to it, but one of the distinctive aspects of literature is that it does not lend itself to arbitrary rules of

19

thumb, and books about children's literature that attempt to be over-prescriptive seem to me to do themselves, children and books something of a disservice. Even one child's reactions to a book can be ambivalent, let alone the response of a mass readership. Children, for example, tend to share fantasies of personal omnipotence together with an awareness of their own vulnerability. Accordingly, as we shall see, their favourite literature often reflects their need for security and order, but elsewhere the same or different books can also respond to children's frustration at their own impotence, by offering them compensatory fantasies where powerful or mischievous characters defy authority and break most of the conventional rules. Similarly, children in real life can both love and sometimes resent their parents, and so can be attracted towards stories that mirror both positive and negative feelings towards mother or father figures. Where they themselves are concerned, children like to find idealised reflections of their own good self-images in literature, yet they may also sympathise with other characters who stand in for some of their own less mature or acceptable feelings or fantasies. As for books, these can be used as pleasant diversions from reality, but at other times may inspire positive action or imitation. Children reading books can on occasion imagine that they are actually in the plot, accompanying the action as an unseen observer, or even as a friend of the main characters. At other times, however, children read while also having their minds on different things at the same time, and so only half-attending to what is happening.

But if literary responses are always going to be impossible to describe in anything like their essential variety, I still believe that enough is now known about child development to allow for at least some generalisations about how young readers are most likely to think and feel at certain ages in various particulars, and to what extent this sometimes affects their choice of favourite literature. Apart from the last two chapters, therefore, which deal with more general issues, I have otherwise decided to follow broadly chronological lines in this study by concentrating upon aspects of the changing relationship between children and literature from infancy to adolescence. This does not mean, though, that I think all this may be used as some kind of recipe book, whereby children of the right age may always be happily matched up to the appropriate story. Certainly I hope this will sometimes happen, but since individual reactions to literature are often extremely subjective, each child will always to a certain extent also find his or her own path through books, reading them in ways that will in some senses remain mysterious. So while particular age-groups will be suggested after each chapter-heading as especially suitable for the sort of literature I shall be discussing in that section, these guidelines are only very rough. As it is, sometimes individual readers will react to quite difficult books very early on, and may also retain great affection for more babyish titles during their teens. In addition, an effective adult narrator can sometimes make quite demanding literature accessible to a wide range of children by using all the arts of the story-teller, such as the editing of difficult passages, extra expressive forms of narration, and answering questions as they arise.

The changes in literary preferences that I shall be discussing, therefore, will always be necessarily inexact but still, I hope, worth describing to the extent that they correspond, as I shall try to indicate, with certain important aspects of children's more general psychological growth and development. At the same time, I shall also be considering other, related issues to do with children and books that arise directly from this type of study, such as the possible uses of imagination, whether there can be such a thing as unsuitable literature for the young, and what sort of children are most likely to turn to reading as a major source of pleasure.

Finally, discussion of which books often seem most appropriate for children of different ages may also help resolve some of the confusion that has always surrounded the practical criticism of children's literature. As it is, adult critics approach children's books from a bewildering variety of angles. Sometimes authors are censored for 'writing down' to children; elsewhere other novelists may be criticised for being beyond the reach of the average child. But such criticisms would be more significant, so far as I am concerned, if those making them more often seemed to have some clear basis for assessing what type of writing children should be more or less capable of understanding at various ages. Good critics, of course, can get this right through a mixture of intuition and practical experience with children; others, however, can sometimes be found making very unreal statements about the requirements of the normal child reader.

To be fair, there may indeed never be any certain answers to these and other problems, but I shall try in this book to suggest some new and, I hope, more helpful ways of thinking about these questions by collating a variety of sources, both literary and psychological, which although relevant to each other have not previously been brought together. In so doing, I am still very aware of the times when I have only been able to scratch the surface when it comes to trying to explain the appeal of certain books for children. My main purpose in writing this book, though, is in no sense any attempt to explain away literary responses in the young altogether. Rather, by looking at certain genres of children's literature and the possible responses to them at different ages, I shall hope to throw some light on more general reasons why various books may once have appeared quite so special and meaningful. After providing this type of background, however, any discussion or tentative explanations of more personal reactions towards the story, language, characters or atmosphere of certain favourite literature must inevitably be left to readers of this book, if they so wish, to try to work out for themselves in the light of their own individual memories and experience.

1 · First books (ages 0–3)

In the very beginning, books will mean nothing to a new baby, at the stage when even the most everyday events of life will still be sufficiently bewildering. As William James once wrote, 'The baby, assailed by eyes, ears, nose, skin and entrails at once, feels it all as one great blooming buzzing confusion.'[1] Writers since have sometimes unconsciously improved on this statement by substituting the word 'booming' for 'blooming', but either in its original or in its amended form, this quotation gives a good idea of the total flux into which children are born.

The child, however, is by no means a passive agent in the face of such confusion. It is now, in fact, a commonplace in developmental psychology that even small babies can soon be actively occupied in learning about their environment by a continuous process of assimilating and adjusting to new experience, so that their first reactions eventually become organised into ever-more coherent patterns of thought and behaviour. At some time, picture-books too can start playing their part in this type of exploration by providing children with simplified and therefore more easily manageable images of the outside world. Faced, for example, by vivid, new experiences, like a visit to the seaside or to the zoo, children — at least on the first occasion — are quite likely simply to turn their backs and play quietly on the sand, or else notice the sparrows around the elephants' house rather than the elephants themselves. This will be because dramatic, unprecedented new experiences of this sort may initially be too difficult for children to comprehend, in terms of fitting them into their already existing stock of patterns and images of the outside world. But cut down to more manageable proportions in picture-books, illustrations of the same things sometimes seem more acceptable. For Jean-Paul Sartre as a very small child, illustrations in the *Grand Larousse* represented men and beasts *'in person'*, whereas in real life, 'You met vague shapes which more or less resembled the archetypes without attaining to their perfection: in the Zoo the monkeys were less like monkeys and, in the Luxembourg Gardens, men were less like men.'[2]

To start with, however, a small baby is taken up entirely with his or her immediate reactions to things, and may not, as yet, have the power to think about objects when they are not there. While babies will be glad to play with a favourite toy, for example, they may not possess a symbolic image of that toy in their own mind's eye to enable them to remember it in its absence. If children under one year old appear to enjoy some picture-books, therefore, it will probably not be because they can recognise what their illustrations are trying to represent to them, but because of other factors, such as the special context in which they may be looking at these books — curled up happily on a mother's lap, perhaps, and then presented with something that they may enjoy principally because of its bright colours and interesting shapes. By around the age of one, however, most infants are able to differentiate between photographs of their mother and father and photographs of other baby and adult faces, and by one-and-a-half years they will generally have developed the ability to recognise familiar objects in picture form. Once this stage has been reached, further development can be quick, even for children with no previous experience of looking at pictures. Given that early illustrations are sometimes in monochrome, often smaller in scale, and frequently inexact, stylised representations of familiar objects, this early ability to recognise pictures is no mean achievement, and has indeed been taken by some as evidence of an innate human skill.

In these early years children seem to find some particular artistic styles easier to understand than others. Pictured objects, for example, can be seen more clearly if they stand out distinctly from their backgrounds — something that rarely happens in the smudgy printing and faded colours of rag-books, however ingenious the basic idea of a washable literature for 'children who wear their food and eat their clothes.'[3] Glossy, stiff-board books which can be wiped down with a damp cloth are a sounder investment against sticky fingers and the whole range of destructive affection which children can bring to their first books, provided that the pictures within them are appropriate. Small children, for example, will find it easier to recognise pictures of whole objects. In one experiment, some nursery non-readers were shown a picture of a girl playing the piano.

'It was a view from a three quarters above angle, with only the girl from the waist up, and the keyboard of the piano visible. All the children had seen a piano — one was played every day, in fact, in the nursery class they attended — but only one out of 20 recognised the piano in the picture with absolute certainty.'[4]

Other infants actually worried whether the girl had any legs at all, just as close-up shots on television, which have the effect of severing the head from the body, can sometimes bewilder or even frighten smaller children.[5]

Objects that overlap other depicted objects in pictures can also sometimes cause difficulties to the untrained eye, and so, too, can the profusion of detail in illustrations at a time when children find it easier to be presented with simplified images of things, with only one or two salient characteristics emphasised in order to put the exact nature of the object beyond doubt. The cartoon art of Walt Disney or Dr Seuss, for example, can suggest complicated machines such as bicycles or typewriters simply by concentrating on their most obvious features, just as small children themselves will often draw houses consisting only of a square, two windows, a door and a smoking chimney. Artistic conventions for conveying perspective in pictures may also be misunderstood at this age, where someone shown walking in the distance may simply be thought of as a small man, rather than as a large man seen from far away. In fact, ideas of relative size are better suggested to small children through direct comparisons with other objects in the illustration drawn upon the same plane. When a picture of a slug on its own was once made to fill a whole television screen in close-up, many children imagined it to be the same actual size as the sea-lion that was shortly made to follow it during the same programme.[6]

While children are still learning to read pictures, therefore, they tend to like more simplified types of artwork, and for this reason realism in pictures, in the sense of accurate perspective, close attention to detail and naturalistic colour, may only be preferred around the age of seven or so. But even when artistic styles are easy and undemanding there may still be complications for small children in other ways, for example with pictures where there is a lot going on at once. As it is, younger children usually have the ability to focus either on the details of a picture or on its overall theme and shape, but they cannot always fuse these two perceptions into one, comprehensible whole. Faced, therefore, by illustrations where the main action is spread between different characters, or over different parts of a page, children — with their still uncoordinated and sometimes confused eye movements — may not always be able to scan such pictures systematically in order to build up a total impression of what is actually happening. Instead, they may focus their attention randomly, thereby occasionally attributing a quite undue importance to details that have little significance to the main action.

Knowing something about what sort of artistic styles small children prefer is often helpful, therefore, but even so there will always be other strong reasons for children liking one picture-book rather than another, even though its illustrations might fail most of the psychological checkpoints so far mentioned. Pictures which remind children of their parents or themselves may always be popular, for example, and there can be many other reasons why children may like a particular picture-book despite rather than because of its artistic style. One book, for example, may always be associated with something pleasurable, like a birthday, another may be linked with something less agreeable, while a third may contain lavish examples of a child's favourite colour. There is always the possibility, in this way, of truly idiosyncratic judgements within the very young of the type of passionate illogicality that once persuaded a little girl of three-and-a-half that while the number 4 looked 'soft', number 5 appeared distinctly 'mean'.[7]

So although children themselves will always be the final and sometimes unpredictable arbiters of what they like in picture-books, some particular topics are usually fairly popular with them for their own good reasons. Ever since primitive picture-books first became common in the early nineteenth century, for example, there has been a steady trend in books that illustrate normal street sights and occupations; just right for children who accompany their mothers outside, and who later want to recall and name some of the things they have seen. The traditional way of picturing adults at work has always been to show them at their cheeriest and most healthy, even when it was once a question of the very poor doing unpleasant or degrading jobs.[8] This tendency to portray adult life at this stage through 'Arcadian spectacles' can still be found in many picture-books and comics today.

Other popular themes in early picture-books include animals, sometimes shown as groups of babies and parents, again with an obvious relevance to the child. There are also many books that start inducting children into the mysteries of adult skills, such as learning

26

the ABC, counting, or even the first intimations of how things work. Easy picture stories may also now get through to children, and here one of the masters of the art of writing and illustrating for the very young is the Dutch artist Dick Bruna. In his books, figures always stand out flat and square against the clear, uninterrupted colour surface that makes up their background, and are drawn in thick, black contour lines which render their basic shapes impossible to miss — no danger of overlapping detail or confusing, common contours here. Elsewhere, essential detail is kept to a minimum: a child's grief, for example, is portrayed by a down-turned mouth, two round tears and hardly anything else. The texts, in turn, are usually as spare and easy to follow as the illustrations.

Popular as they are, however, a diet of picture-books that only consisted of titles by Dick Bruna and his imitators would be scant fare for a child, and even in his own country the Dutch librarians' association decided not to recommend his versions of *Hop o' my Thumb* and *Cinderella*, on the grounds that the brevity of the texts could not do justice to these rich, traditional tales. There is also a need at this age, therefore, for a different type of literature which extends the imagination and perceptual skills beyond their present confines. In fact, even quite small children are interested in more than simply recognising familiar objects and confirming already existing skills; a two-year-old boy was reported, for example, as staring much longer at a picture of a man with three heads or with his head upside down than at a picture of a more ordinarily arranged person.[9] It is also true, at least for children around the age of seven or so, that there is usually a distinct preference for artistic styles which are developmentally superior to those which children themselves are adopting in their own drawings at the time.[10]

In this way, children should both have books that they can start managing for themselves, where they can understand at first glance at least a number of the pictures, and also books which may have more need of an adult interpreter, to go through the pages, explaining some problems of style as well as content and — in short — helping a child to follow a more complex visual text. This sort of book also has more chance of growing with a child, without becoming discarded later as something now quite infantile and therefore beyond interest. But whoever the artist and whatever the story, no picture-book can ever afford to get too far away from a child's immediate interests and levels of understanding, however much an enthusiastic parent may want to push a particular title. The best picture-books, perhaps, are those that manage to strike a compromise between what children can follow with ease, and what they can understand by making a slightly greater imaginative effort. Or as a great artist for children himself once wrote, 'There is a receptive impressionable quality of mind, whether in young or old, which we call childlike. A fresh, direct vision, a quickly stimulated imagination, a love of symbolic and typical form, with a touch of poetic suggestion, a delight in frank gay colour, and a sensitiveness to the variations of line, and contrasts of form.'[11]

Whatever the picture-books a child gets, however, the intimate experience of sharing them with a parent is probably the most basically satisfying of the lot. From this safe vantage point, children can look at pictures that have the effect of slowing down normal experience, so that a child can take an isolated image on the page and then absorb or discuss it at leisure, gradually learning its most obvious characteristics. Next time the child looks at that book, the same object will still be there, and in that way a tiny part of the child's life will already have become more predictable, and therefore more potentially manageable. At the same time, children will also learn how to interpret certain artistic conventions: that an upturned line means a smile when it is on a face, for example, while a down-turned line means the opposite. However obvious this particular convention may be to adults, it is sometimes not understood by children left to themselves until the ages of six or seven, and drawings of facial expressions depicting other emotions than joy or sadness, like pain, anger, fear or surprise may not be understood until even later.[12] No wonder comics, normally read without attendant adult help, tend to portray such emotions so very expressively; artwork that was more understated might simply not be comprehended by younger readers.

At the same time, however, the child will be doing far more than learning how to recognise certain artistic conventions. By looking at illustrations that symbolise objects and events in the outside world, children will start developing their own reactions, and also share those of their parents, towards experience already familiar to them and other experience still to come. The scenes and figures of any picture-book can always have a double significance, therefore, both for what such things mean objectively, and also for what they come to signify to the child, in terms — for example — of safe or dangerous, pretty or ugly, nice or nasty, silly or sensible, funny or serious or any other of the host of value judgements with which we monitor the world, but which children have to learn from afresh. In fact, the child's early view of things is always an intensely purposeful, even moral one, forever concerned with judgements like good or bad, useful or useless, and this way of perpetually placing objects in the outside world into a personal relationship with the self is as much an effort after meaning as finding out what things are called, what they do, and how they work. When children have the chance to learn about their environment, perhaps from the leisurely reading of a picture-book with a parent, as well as elsewhere, they can start feeling slightly less a stranger in a generally unpredictable universe; a gift from early literature which foreshadows some of the greater things still to come from books in the future.

Nursery rhymes

As well as enjoying pictures, children will also react to the sound and rhythm of language itself — long before they are interested in books or stories. This is not surprising: while the vocabulary and conceptual grasp needed to follow even a short story through to the end is quite considerable, children from the very earliest age are attracted simply by the sound of the human voice, which they soon learn to distinguish from other noises surrounding them. 'Baby-talk', addressed to the child, and once despised by stern commentators on baby-care, is in fact found in most cultures as an important way in which mothers simplify language, so helping their infants to acquire the first stages of speech and comprehension. (Baby-talk directed at much older children, or even at adults, is of course a rather different matter!) Most mothers soon find out that the smallest baby likes being talked to, sometimes smiling or laughing in response, and when speech or song is combined with gentle rocking, this can also be particularly soothing, hence the ubiquity of the lullaby in human society.

The importance and later beneficial effect of this early verbal stimulation through language can hardly be exaggerated. Long before children can speak for themselves, they can react non-verbally to adult speech, and indeed can sometimes be very effective in initiating verbal stimulation from their parents. Later progress in this vital area of language comprehension and acquisition is quickest when children

29

have already had this chance to respond to adult speech. But children will learn language and other ways of relating to adults much less easily when they are simply plonked down in front of endless television programmes, since broadcast speech is not usually related to any particular needs or meanings in their own behaviour.

Simple songs and rhymes in the parents' repertoire can also play a part in helping to sustain this first, important relationship built up between adults and babies through shared pleasure in language, games and other popular routines. In fact, nursery rhymes — still the best-known of these early songs and games — themselves grew up from spontaneous interactions between mothers and children many years ago, and in this way various 'unrelated snatches of worldly songs, adult jests, lampoons, proverbial maxims, charms, and country ballads' have all made their way into nursery lore. But as Peter and Iona Opie go on to explain, 'The mother or nurse of former days did not croon her ditties because they were songs for children, but because — with her sleeves rolled up and arms in the wash-tub — they were the first verses to come into her mind when her children had to be amused.'[13]

The fact that rhymes of such diverse origins gradually became associated with the nursery in this haphazard and unorganised way is of great significance for their enduring popularity ever since. When no one is consciously thinking 'This must be valuable', or planning in any detail what exactly to do next, the result can be an exchange between parent and child that finally settles through trial and error into something very satisfying. With nursery rhymes, mothers always seem to have sung the songs that first came to mind and babies, over the years, have selected their favourites, making sure, by their enthusiastic reactions and retentive memories, that such rhymes were preserved. The various reasons why babies and infants may always have liked particular rhymes may be to do with certain common needs and enjoyment which adults, however hard they try, can only partially guess at, and as the Opies have written elsewhere, 'We find that almost the only factor the verses have in common is that they are memorable.' In this way, a casual song or rhyme, sometimes from very lowly origins, can gradually slip into the culture simply because it has enduring qualities which infants can recognise from the start. *Old King Cole*, for example, was originally a drinking song, but when enough mothers had enjoyed singing it, and enough infants had demanded an encore, it eventually became a nursery-rhyme classic.

In the last two centuries nursery rhymes have gradually been collected together, illustrated and published, and today there are more in print than ever before. This has meant that they have stopped developing, since anthologists now tend to copy selections from previous nineteenth-century editions, rather than try to assemble what might be the nursery rhymes of our own times. For some children, traditional nursery rhymes may still be the first literature they experience, with so many anthologies around now to shore up what was once a thriving oral culture. Other children do not always hear these rhymes, however, and although there have been reports ever since 1800 that children are no longer in touch with traditional lore, it does seem that television and the radio today have begun to interfere quite radically with the transmission of nursery rhymes between the generations.[14]

If this is so, many children may be getting instead some of today's substitutes for nursery rhymes, such as particular advertising jingles, snatches of pop songs or football chants, and these too can also be popular in the same way as traditional nursery rhymes used to be. It may be a long way, it is true, from the verbal richness of a rhyme like *Sing a Song of Sixpence* to *We All Live in a Yellow Submarine*, but it will be equally natural for a young mother not brought up herself on nursery rhymes to reach instead into her own mental stock cupboard for literary and musical bits and pieces like this when the time comes, just as all parents – even the most devoted followers of nursery rhymes – may also find themselves occasionally singing or quoting from obscure and half-forgotten songs of their youth.

Even so, given that traditional nursery rhymes are not the only type of material especially suitable for small children, they are still very popular amongst many families, and continue to offer excellent clues to children's more general literary interests at this early age. Children's liking for these rhymes cannot be explained simply in terms of adults thrusting their own favourites upon them. A few writers, particularly in the last century, attempted to ban nursery rhymes altogether, or at least put various improved versions into circulation. Some of these were later taken up by anthologies, whilst the cruder, older rhymes were often quietly dropped. Yet many of the old, traditional versions continued to persist, if not at home then at least in street or playground, often despite adult interference or disapproval. Those would-be nursery rhymes that have been deliberately written for, and perhaps at, children, have rarely survived in the same way; those that have are often the most mercilessly parodied by children themselves — victims include Mrs Hale's *Mary had a Little Lamb* and Jane Taylor's *Twinkle Twinkle Little Star*. But in general, as Cecil Sharp once wrote about folk-song, 'The individual invents, the community selects', and where nursery rhymes are concerned, the community here represents children as well as adults. In an oral tradition, a rhyme that few children liked or cared to remember would simply disappear, and in this sense, surviving nursery rhymes are to an extent those selected by a child audience, sometimes over very many years. Once these rhymes went into print, the position changed slightly, but favourite nursery rhymes still belong to an oral tradition, and books that contain few of these, and perhaps too many improvements or innovations, may also eventually fail through lack of demand.

At the first stages, the swing and beat of nursery rhymes particularly appeal to the young, with simple verses satisfyingly rounded off by terminal rhymes, and double rhymes sometimes concealed elsewhere. This basic appeal continues, whether the actual finished product makes any sense or not, even after the child can better understand the meaning of language. Who cares, for example, that *Hickory Dickory Dock* or *Eena Meena Mina Mo* are both relics of old counting systems, when it is the alliteration and staccato rhythms that may be their chief attraction? This early preference for sound, rather than meaning, sometimes has comic results. A nineteenth-century opponent of nursery rhymes, Samuel Goodrich, once made up his own rhyme, simply to prove what idle nonsense the whole genre amounted to. This was it:

> Higglety, pigglety, pop!
> The dog has eaten the mop;
> The pig's in a hurry,
> The cat's in a flurry,
> Higglety, pigglety, pop!

But while all the rest of Goodrich's huge output of improving literature for young readers is now forgotten, this rhyme can still be heard today, and was the subject of a recent illustrated book by the brilliant American artist, Maurice Sendak, some hundred years after it was so casually composed.

The initial reaction by a child to the sound of nursery rhymes has often been best described by poets, including Dylan Thomas:

The first poems I knew were nursery rhymes, and before I could read them for myself I had come to love just the words of them, the words alone . . . I did not care what the words said, overmuch, nor what happened to Jack and Jill and the Mother Goose rest of them; I cared for the shapes of sound that their names, and the words describing their actions, made in my ears; I cared for the colours the words cast on my eyes . . . I fell in love — that is the only expression I can think of — at once, and I am still at the mercy of words.[15]

No wonder, then, that it has always been adults rather than children who have particularly concerned themselves, from time to time, with the possible hidden meanings of the more cryptic nursery rhymes. Some of the far-fetched interpretations that have resulted from this interest have been assembled together and then magisterially rebutted in Iona and Peter Opie's *Oxford Dictionary of Nursery Rhymes.*[16]

Take this rhyme, for example:

> Rub-a-dub-dub,
> Three men in a tub
> And who do you think they be?
> The butcher, the baker,
> The candlestick-maker,
> Turn them out, knaves all three.

There have been some ingenious explanations about what these three worthies are doing in the tub in the first place, and why there is a sudden burst of indignation against them in the last line. The Opies, as usual, have the answer: the original rhyme apparently referred to three half-submerged country *maids* in a tub, a primitive form of striptease in country fairs, to be ogled at through a peep-hole by the butcher, the baker and the candlestick-maker — yesterday's equivalent of the tired business man. Later on in oral history, when the original story had become more mangled, it was these characters who were made to appear in the tub and not the maids, but children themselves do not need this or any other explanation to enjoy the rhyme. So long as a story is clear-cut and eventful, questions of motive, causation and consequence can wait. By the same token, it does not matter to them why a goose should want to throw an old man downstairs, or what exactly 'Pop! goes the weasel' might imply (a matter still disputed among scholars). If there is action, a good rhythm and a suitably child-centred vocabulary, then any further explanations may be unimportant. For Dylan Thomas, again, nursery-rhyme words

Made their own original associations as they sprang and shone. The words, 'Ride a cock-horse to Banbury Cross', were as haunting to me, who did not know then what a cock-horse was or cared a damn where Banbury Cross might be, as, much later, were such lines as John Donne's 'Go and catch a falling star, Get with child a mandrake root', which also I could not understand when I first read them.[17]

All nursery-rhyme language, in fact, tends to be clear and forceful — the 'memorable speech' that W.H. Auden once chose as the best definition of true poetry. Without this quality, these rhymes would not have lasted; as it is, they are indeed those 'smooth stones from the brook of time, worn round by constant friction of tongues long silent', Andrew Lang's flowery but still useful description. It would be tedious to go through the rhymes in order to prove this point; simply allow a few typical lines to come to mind at random, and listen to the direct, pungent quality of the introductory couplets, the alliteration or concealed rhymes that link Humpty with Dumpty, or the irresistible rhythms that drive along 'Trit trot to Boston', or 'Hinx, minx, the old witch winks', together with the constant repetition that soon turns such lines into popular catch-phrases. For G.K. Chesterton, 'Over the hills and far away', was one of the most beautiful lines in English poetry, and it has been frequently borrowed by other poets, including Gay, Swift, Burns, Tennyson and Stevenson.[18]

At a more mundane level, advertisers and other propagandists still make use of nursery-rhyme forms for getting across messages in an easily memorised way. Of course, nursery rhymes have no monopoly of catchy, rhythmic phrases; pop songs, refrains from favourite story books, and the child's own inventions can all compete, but even so it would be hard to name any other body of literature possessing greater verbal immediacy, and which is remembered so long after other memories from childhood have faded.

There are many other attractions in these rhymes for children, again sometimes long before any real sense of the words comes through. Knee-riding, toe-tickling and dandling games can all be found among the most popular rhymes, along with those favourite games where the child is presented with a mock fall, as in that savage little rhyme, *Rock-a-Bye-Baby*. This contains a good example of the concealed aggression often found towards the end of lullabies, inevitable perhaps when a mother's patience is beginning to wear thin. Because babies have a horror of falling, this rhyme has always proved popular, in the sense that play in the young often centres around a potentially fearful situation, reduced by a game with someone one can trust into something of more manageable proportions. Other rhymes accompany other games, usefully catalogued by the Opies in *The Oxford Nursery Rhyme Book*.[19] There are rhymes, for example, to show the features, pick out fingers and toes, and with which babies can perform perhaps their very first, simple dance, as in *Ring-a-Ring O' Roses* — often erroneously considered to be a relic from the plague years, and as such, possibly the best-known out of a great many nursery-rhyme misattributions.[20] All these games, and the rhymes that suggest and then accompany them, are more than simply pleasant pastimes for the child. Play is also a serious business — a means of discovering the environment, beginning with the baby's own body, and going on to investigate other familiar things and people. A baby will also often want its parents close at hand, and nursery rhymes that a mother can sing to and play with her child have their place, as we have already said, in helping to build up and maintain this early physical contact, so important to both parties in the establishing of their relationship. In fact, the games and easily memorised nonsense and half-sense of nursery rhymes embody and hand down some particularly effective ways of amusing and stimulating the very young, concentrating as they so often do on simple, easily-memorised phrases and rituals. Any activities involving pleasurable repetition, when an infant can soon learn to predict what is going to happen next, can also be important in the growth of general confidence.

When an infant develops speech, nursery rhymes can have another type of function. Consider first some of the problems facing a young child trying to make sense of the buzz of adult conversation, where, as Thurber once wrote, fathers may be for some mysterious reason held up in their office, someone else may be all cut up as a result, a third adult may reputedly be under a cloud, while the young listener to these inexplicably bizarre happenings may be described as 'all ears'. Even if the surface meaning of adult speech is understood, adult phrases in different contexts may still mean something quite different, to be greeted with shouts of laughter if children try using them inappropriately. Children are also limited in their understanding by their own short span of concentration. Any necessary link between cause and effect may only be spotted if the two happen close together, and even here only when actual, concrete processes are involved — more abstract reasoning must wait until later. Finally, small children will only have their own limited experience of life on which to model their perceptions and conjectures: the inevitable egocentrism from which every human being must learn to develop, and which, to begin with, leads us to imagine that all other objects in the world, animate and inanimate, are very likely to have similar needs, thoughts and feelings to our own.

In this bewildering universe, however, many nursery rhymes have been scaled down over the centuries towards direct and easy comprehension. They are almost always brief and to the point, simply presenting the bare outlines of situations, usually without further explanation or justification. Events within them may be familiar or utterly bizarre, but they are all usually treated in the same brusque, take-it-or-leave-it way: a quick run-through of some often quite arbitrary events, rounded off by rhyme and metre into something that gives the impression of logic and inevitability. There is still always the chance of misunderstanding, of course: G.K. Chesterton once described a little girl who had 'an insomnia of insane terror', after hearing the rhyme about *Little Bo-peep*, and confusing the lamb's *bleating* with the idea of *bleeding*. But although nursery rhymes usually have rustic settings that have now disappeared for most children, their actual vocabulary is still fairly easy to follow, making its point with the minimum of verbal frills. One word often buttresses another, so providing double clues, such as 'cold and frosty', 'come with a whoop and come with a call', or a coat that is 'flimsy and thin'. Again, the words themselves often describe objects or people who are frequently doing things that children can recognise even from their own short experience, such as losing and finding, eating, punishing or being punished, playing or quarrelling, falling down, stealing, getting up and going to bed, cooking, and hanging out the clothes. When adult characters are involved in these rhymes, they too tend to behave like children, and so become easier to understand. Courtship, for example, may be conducted through the medium of strawberries and cream, and kings and queens may spend their time happily cooking and then eating jam tarts or bag puddings. It is, of course, no accident that there are so many references to food in nursery rhymes; it is after all something of paramount importance to the young, and nursery rhymes reflect this interest, whether through describing characters who eat too much, too little, or variations in between.

There are many other ways, too, in which nursery rhymes infantilise the adult world. A queen, for example, is more comprehensible to the young as a gracious hostess for pussy cats than as a constitutional monarch, and both Queens Victoria and Elizabeth II have at one time been asked by children about the whereabouts of the little mouse who lives under the chair.[21] This simplifying tendency has sometimes attracted its critics. An American writer has objected to the way these rhymes 'brainwash' girls into ideas of marriage and motherhood at an early age. Statistical evidence, of a sort, is produced to show that while 'little' appears in the title of ten rhymes about feminine characters, it only appears seven times where males are concerned. In addition, the phrase 'old woman' appears thirteen times in one nursery-rhyme anthology, but 'old man' only once, while in terms of punishment, boys — it is claimed — come off much more lightly than girls.[22] The whole argument about sexism in literature and its possible effects will be dealt with later; for the moment it would seem unfair to attack nursery rhymes in particular on this score. Oversimplified sexual stereotypes are probably inevitable at the very beginning of understanding, and can also be found in the early games children play, where they may continue to act out traditional roles — mother with baby, father going off to work — even if the evidence of their own homes suggests a different pattern. More subtle understanding must usually wait until later, when the child is better equipped to think in terms of finer distinctions, but even so, nursery rhymes still feature some lively females, who do their own work, disobey some of the rules, and are not always as easily married off as their critics have sometimes implied. As for the famous and in these days sometimes detested rhyme, *What are Little Girls made of?* (sugar and spice, as opposed to the slugs, snails and puppy-dog tails that are the constituents of all true little boys), this has always struck me as a tease; a deliberate provocation of both its male and female audience, rather than any serious attempt to influence anyone. It would not be a definition of little girls that would be accepted by the mothers of Polly Flinders, Sulky Sue, Hannah Bantry or some of the other young women found in nursery-rhyme disgrace.

Another common factor that both nursery rhymes and children's games share is a pervasive violence. According to Geoffrey Handley-Taylor, one of a long line of would-be nursery-rhyme reformers, at least one hundred nursery rhymes contain 'unsavoury elements'. These include eight allusions to murder (unclassified), twenty-three cases of physical violence (unclassified), down to three cases of death by drowning, one case of death by devouring, and one case of scorning prayer. More generally, 'Expressions of fear, weeping, moans of anguish, biting, pain and evidence of supreme selfishness may be found in almost every other page.'[23]

There are many possible explanations for the popularity of this sort of violence, whether in rhymes or in those spontaneous children's games of teachers and pupils, or even mother and family, where great whippings may be enacted by children portraying characters who in real life would be horrified by these practices. All this may be a useful safety-valve, and it is certainly better to air negative feelings about parents or other siblings, who may unconsciously be identified with various villains in nursery rhymes than to attempt to suppress such emotions altogether. But whatever the motive for enjoying it, slapstick humour, whether in film, circus, story or game, is usually a certain winner with the young, and nursery rhymes also cater for this taste, just as they reflect children's other volatile emotions and mood swings. Anger and tears, passion and reconciliation, crime and punishment are never far away in an infant's life, and also appear in nursery rhymes, sometimes rapidly and dramatically following each other either at the turn of a page or at the beginning of the next line. Children can be really fascinated by depictions of such larger-than-life, explosive emotions that they may have some inkling of from their own tantrums and affections; when they hear about other nursery-rhyme children who sometimes behave badly, there will probably be an element of recognition too.

A further distinctive feature of nursery rhymes is their frequent reference to death. It is only in this century that this emphasis may seem strange; death would once have been very much part of every-day life, from the casual slaughter of mice, rats, rabbits and kittens to the annual excitement of pig-killing. Members of the family would also die at home, rather than shut away in a hospital. Today, how-ever, both sets of grandparents may well outlive a child's own youth, and death amongst siblings is rare.

But the immanence of death in a child's life before 1900 still does not explain why the subject should also interest a modern child in circumstances where death is kept more distant. It is not simply a question of only finding the topic in nursery rhymes and fairy stories; in children's own games, once again, they will also frequently play at being dead, or choose to imitate shoot-outs or other sudden death scenes from television Westerns. Nightmares may also centre around fear of dying from quite an early age, and a general interest in death is also something that can crop up in various other ways in infantile conversation, sometimes a little disconcertingly (young son: 'When are you going to die?' as a casual enquiry to an old man passing by in the street).

Any topic of such importance to adults, however, is bound to surround itself with a mystery that naturally stimulates children to try to discover more about it. It has also been suggested that dreams and games about death form part of the psychic inheritance of mankind — Jung's 'collective unconscious' which for him is the ultimate source for all the fantasies about birth, copulation and death found in every human culture. At another level, death is also an immensely puzzling concept for children, and thus likely to be something they will constantly return to in their efforts to make sense of their own environment. As Piaget suggests, children begin by imagining that all things in the world — animal and material — have a will and life of their own. Thus everything is seen as existing in terms of its particular motivation for living, but this notion of a well-regulated, thriving universe receives a jolt when the child becomes aware of the difference between life and death, and the idea that some things die for no apparent reason, at least so far as any child can understand. 'From this moment', Piaget writes, 'the idea of death sets the child's curiosity in action, precisely because, if every cause is coupled with a motive, then death calls for a special explanation. If the child is at this stage puzzled by the problem of death, it is precisely because in his conception of things death is inexplicable.'[24]

In Piaget's view, the concept of death, for a child, is nothing less than the origin of all genuine intellectual curiosity. Another psychologist, Arnold Gesell, takes a different view, believing that death has no meaning at all for a child of three, and that puzzlement over the topic does not really begin until five or six years old. The idea that death is final may have to wait until a child is around seven years old, but children much younger than this will still be drawn to the topic, perhaps as a way of externalising anxiety about the possible death or disappearance of their own loved ones, perhaps as a crude beginning of what is after all the major concern of all philosophies: trying to discover the meaning of a life that is doomed one day to cease.

In all events, nursery rhymes — by frequently taking up a topic that is more often ignored in contemporary children's literature — prove once again how close they are to children's particular and most immediate interests. Rhymes like *Ding, Dong Bell*, *Humpty Dumpty*, *A Frog he would A-Wooing Go*, and many others, have only survived because small children are interested in them, and will later sing them for themselves. *Ding Dong Bell* has, on occasion, been accused of not so much responding to an interest in death as actively suggesting how to go about killing something, with animal welfare officers claiming that children have tried to drown kittens apparently under its influence. Whether this sort of argument against literature is always fair, however, will be discussed later.

From death to sex: James Reeves has pointed out that a great many folk-songs, from which numbers of nursery rhymes have been drawn, are shot through with erotic imagery.[25] As in Shakespeare's plays, references in certain contexts to ploughing and reaping, gathering flowers, hunting and shooting, all have sexual overtones that would once have been clearly understood. In this tradition, one could include a charming if lesser-known nursery rhyme:

> Sukey, you shall be my wife
> And I will tell you why:
> I have got a little pig,
> And you have got a sty.[26]

Other nursery rhymes have been far more explicit, although these have on the whole tended to disappear from anthologies. Even so, children are still left with rhymes to do with kissing and courtship, another very popular interest with the young, as one can see in their own games. If violent nursery rhymes sometimes satisfy, consciously or unconsciously, a certain sadistic streak in adults who sing them to the young, as well as in the children who listen to them, then amorous nursery rhymes may have a more agreeable function. The nursemaid or young mother who originally sang about her 'bonny brown hair' may have been thinking about herself as much as the child she was entertaining.[27] At another level, nursery rhymes that deal, however lightly, with any relationship between male and female cannot help being interesting, if only for what they may symbolise for the young. Relationships between father and mother and the sexes in general are something that small children will soon become aware of, and as such form another part of the environment that they will want to explain to themselves. Once again, nursery rhymes offer a lively and occasionally outspoken commentary on the male—female relationship in many of its aspects, often more vividly than is the case in other kinds of children's literature.

The point has already been made that nursery rhymes offer children experience with the very shortest of stories — ideally suited for limited concentration and a generally inadequate understanding of cause and effect. There are, in fact, few long nursery rhymes; even if an original source were a lengthy folk-song or ballad, what usually survives, in terms of an oral culture, is only the first couplet or so. Some rhymes tell no story at all:

> There was an old woman,
> Lived under a hill.
> And if she's not gone,
> She lives there still.

As an eighteenth-century commentator once remarked, 'Nobody will presume to contradict this.'[28]

On the other hand, nursery rhymes can also tell more organised stories, when children are ready for them. To begin with, there are those accumulative rhymes, like *The House That Jack Built*, where each logical step follows with remorseless repetition; losing the story-line in these circumstances would almost be something of a personal triumph. Next, the child can move on to slightly more developed sagas, *Jack and Jill*, for example, or *Little Boy Blue*, and as the child gets more verbally adept, longer rhymes such as *Babes in the Wood*, something more like the length of a short story. By this time, children may have moved to a state where they can follow a continuous narrative; quite an achievement, when it is remembered how hard they may have recently found it to put their own thoughts in order, or repeat things back in logical sequence. Nursery rhymes are made particularly easy to remember and repeat, however, by virtue of their form — it is not quite so difficult to anticipate the next event in a narrative if it rhymes with the line before, or follows a strong rhythm.

Once children have mastered the narrative principle that runs through most rhymes, they can then move on to something even more sophisticated, where language begins to detach itself from the here and now in order to play games with its audience. There are rhymes, for example, that stand reality on its head, as in tall stories like the *Derby Ram*, with its wool that reached to the sky, so providing nests for eagles. Then there are other rhymes where logic is twisted in the direction of the shaggy dog story:

> A man in the wilderness asked me,
> How many strawberries grow in the sea?
> I answered him, as I thought good,
> As many as red herrings grow in the wood.

There are more jokes to try upon oneself, and later on upon others,

41

such as riddles, tongue-twisters, and various verbal catches. Some can be quite subtle:

> Three children sliding on the ice,
> Upon a summer's day,
> As it fell out, they all fell in,
> The rest they ran away.
>
> Now had these children been at home,
> Or sliding on dry ground,
> Ten thousand pounds to one penny
> They had not all been drowned.

This is very much in the spirit of that favourite playground chant, 'One fine day in the middle of the night', something else for children to come back to in their own minds when they are better able to see beyond the surface meaning of words, which initially may have been taken quite literally. The ability to understand verbal jokes like this involves important, analytic skills; irony in prose, for example, is never easy for children to understand, with its contradiction between the spirit and surface meaning of a text. Some nursery rhymes offer early opportunity for practice in this sort of general comprehension, sometimes at quite a high level of complexity.

Finally, there are those hypothetical rhymes that invite children to suspend their knowledge of reality, and try to imagine what it would be like if things were very different; for example, if all the world were paper, or all the seas were one sea. There are even invitations to ponder on the hypothetical uses of language itself: 'If ifs and ands were pots and pans'. Having originally stated that children turn to nursery rhymes in the early stages because they are so easy to understand, it may now seem contradictory to suggest the popularity of rhymes which are also about extraordinary situations. But they too have their function, in helping children to test out their knowledge of normality by making such impossible claims that even a small child will spot the difference between what can and cannot be. There is also another important point to be made about this type of nonsense: in nursery rhymes, as in all forms of early intellectual stimulation, the child may sometimes welcome variety as well as predictability. Piaget in particular has suggested that the young have both a lasting desire to understand and be able to predict the course of familiar events, and also a natural curiosity that will want to investigate anything new. This continuing need to investigate and then assimilate variations in the environment into bigger and more complex mental maps is, according to Piaget, the basis for all motivation to learn.

In the case of nursery rhymes, there is indeed a fascinating mixture of the bizarre and the familiar. Some rhymes have very mundane functions, for example, like helping a child to learn the alphabet, counting, the days of the week, months, and seasons, and even, with some help, the difference between left and right. ('Which finger did he bite? This little finger on the right.') They can also hand down traditional wisdom, such as the amount of sleep or play each person needs, when to change from winter to summer clothes, and even some primitive weather-forecasting techniques: 'red sky at night; shepherds' delight'. It does not matter if some of this advice is more traditional than accurate; it will still have the effect of appearing to reduce uncertainties and complexities into manageable forms. The same might be said about those rhymes that give hints on etiquette or sound morals, although fewer of these are now included in anthologies. Other rhymes, while not preaching any morals, also describe forthright little stories, where everything tends to follow pat, with the good rewarded and the bad punished.

But because nursery rhymes were very rarely written especially for children, they also sometimes contain a breadth of vocabulary and subject matter unlikely to be found in more self-conscious writing for the young. Within them, homely phrases can sit next to wild non-sense, and a simple concept such as 'a horse' can be extended into dun-horses, cock-horses, mares, colts, foals, donkeys, asses and ponies, who in turn may amble, trot, gallop, prance or even dance, all interesting variations on a basic movement which children can try out, if they are lucky, on the knee of an obliging parent. As for moods and feelings, a horse — in nursery-rhyme land again — may be petted and fed for all its hard work, but also be the object of its rider's anger, where it may be whipped, slashed, lashed, beaten or walloped for its pains; all splendidly mouth-filling words to be married to the ever-interesting topic of violence. A child may not recognise all these terms, but this blending of the everyday with the lesser-known is just the sort of verbal variety that a growing intelligence can find most stimulating.

Nursery-rhyme scenery also provides a mixture of the strange and the everyday, with its references to a now remote way of life, made up of bird-scarers, milkmaids and shepherds, alongside more immediately recognisable bakers, cobblers and butchers. Charms to make cows 'let down' their milk, old wives' tales and other country lore may not seem relevant to a town child today, but still carry a certain fascination. Elsewhere, exotic or bizarre nursery-rhyme characters can seem familiar because of some of their mischievous, child-like ways, and critics have often objected to this cast of all-too human, fallible individuals. In nursery rhymes, for example, children may be either good or horrid, or if they are like the girl with a curl in the middle of her forehead, both at the same time — another complex notion for a child to tackle, used to more simple divisions into either 'good' or 'bad'. Sometimes characters go to bed like lambs, to receive the benediction of that amiable voyeur, Wee Willie Winkie, or else they may be encouraged to leave their sleep and come out to play when the moon is bright and full. This inherent unpredictability has always made it hard for moralists to put up a consistently good case for nursery rhymes. One author, for example, has claimed that 'Some of the rhymes teach children proper behaviour, kindness, modesty, truthfulness and obedience; others make virtues seem worth while because they are rewarded, whereas misdeeds are scorned or punished.'[29] Unless one is referring to an extremely selective anthology, however, there are too many contradictions in nursery rhymes to support this argument. What sort of morality punishes Tom for stealing a pig, but smiles on King Arthur for doing the same to three pecks of barley meal?

Children themselves are not models of consistent, equable behaviour; one reason, perhaps, why they may find it easy to respond to the equally inconsistent attitudes and adventures found in nursery rhymes, where characters may vary in mood between compassion and insensate rage, greed and self-denial, reasoned logic and consuming madness, or the sentimentality of *I Love Little Pussy* with tough, brutal attitudes elsewhere. This same, potentially stimulating unpredictability can also be found in the various depictions of animals in nursery rhymes, who may sometimes be dressed in the height of fashion, like the three young rats with black, felt hats, or else come closer to the birds or beasts of everyday life, passively awaiting the next milking, or laying eggs to order. Cats and dogs are equally adaptable, wearing petticoats, playing the fiddle and visiting the queen on one page, and frightening mice, sipping milk or lying quietly by the fire on the next. Even household objects have this fluid, quick-changing quality: a shoe can simply be lost, as they often are with the young (especially just before school), but may also

44

house a large and almost certainly unplanned family. At the same time, adult characters range from homely farmers and tradesmen to exotic kings and queens across the sea, rather as references to dishes and spoons mix with tales of gold and silver, and unicorns appear on the same pages as pigs.

No other kind of literature can rival this span of subject and treatment. Certainly, it is not something one can expect to find in carefully graded story-books, with their limited, selected vocabulary, simple grammatical forms and everyday settings, where all adult characters tend to wear a smile, and adventures usually centre around the details of day-to-day suburban living. Children have a need for this type of writing as well, but the appeal of nursery rhymes, with their mixture of the familiar and the exotic, the simple and complex, the respectable and subversive, is something rather different. In addition to all these attractions, however, there is also perhaps the most important appeal to children of all: the pull of poetry itself. Children love rhyme and metre from very early on; infants can convulse each other, for example, by inventing their own crude rhymes for each other's names, and will sometimes chant in natural rhythms when they are playing, again without prompting from outside. Add to this apparently natural pleasure the well-tried humour, mystery and excitement of nursery rhymes, and one is left with a powerful formula. Take, for example, a particularly haunting rhyme:

How many miles to Babylon?
Three score miles and ten.
Can I get there by candle-light?
Yes, and back again.

As the Opies have written, the mysterious cadences of these few lines have appealed to many, including authors such as Stevenson and Kipling. Some explanations for the text have been put forward; is Babylon a corruption of 'Babyland', perhaps, or could the whole thing refer to a dream journey, at night? But these conjectures, although interesting in themselves, are irrelevant when it comes to explaining the popularity of this verse. Like all nursery rhymes, it has only lasted so long because it has always appealed to children as poetry, and once heard a few times has proved hard to forget. As it is, children today often hear little enough poetry in their lives, but those who come across nursery rhymes will still be encountering easily the best collection of poetry for the young ever to get into print.

2 · Story and picture-books (ages 3–7)

As they grow older, children begin to understand the rudimentary laws of cause and effect more clearly, and so are better able to describe what is actually happening in illustrations, whereas before they may simply have been happy to recognise and enumerate the main objects in their pictures. This development, of course, will also make it easier for a child to follow a picture-book story, making sense of what is going on by recalling previous pages. A picture-book like Pat Hutchins's *Rosie's Walk*,[1] for example, which sustains one single joke from the first page to the last, can now be understood and enjoyed. Each time Rosie — the innocent hen — is about to be despatched by the fox, some fluke happening intervenes so that it is finally the fox who meets disaster. For this delightful book to make its full effect, readers must recognise what the fox is up to, and then become aware of the regularity and nature of his failures. A smaller child might still see this story in terms of disconnected episodes; the older infant, by contrast, should have the ability to pick out its pattern of events.

Even so, picture-book stories for the bottom of this age-range will still have to be fairly simple, focusing on one main character, with much of the plot bolstered by regular patches of repetition, as in those folk-tales like *The Little Red Hen* where everyone has their own typical and oft-repeated refrain. Stories that attempt to spread the main action into sub-plots will probably remain too complex. Nor should the length of early fiction go much beyond the small concentration span of a young reader, which is best suited to short stories, told in a minimum of language and with plenty of pictures which both inform the text and allow for a succession of convenient mental resting places.

A rough distinction can be made between picture-books where illustrations complement a generally rather spare text, and story

46

books in which illustrations play a more subordinate role to a longer text. Where picture-books are concerned, for example, children should now be able to start taking on more sophisticated art styles than those principally discussed in the previous chapter, though artistic style as such will always be less important than content when it comes to attracting and interesting a young audience. One experimenter found some time ago, for example, that while boys tended to like pictures of ships, girls seemed to prefer illustrations of fairies and angels.[2] Time may have changed the nature of such traditionally stereotyped reactions, but the point remains: children do not, on the whole, evaluate illustrations in terms of how they have been executed by the artist. This is not to say that artistic style is unimportant; merely that on its own it cannot save a book which in a child's mind seems to be dwelling on unappealing topics.

Popular subjects for this age, in fact, range from the world of everyday objects, like pillar-boxes, trains, shops and tradesmen, to some of the more dramatic or unusual countries, experiences and characters that lie beyond a child's immediate knowledge. The static objects of previous picture-books may now sometimes be treated as animated characters in their own right, whether they be steam-shovels, motor-cars, household goods or toys. Children can very easily accept this type of fantasy, since the idea of universal animism seems fundamental to all human imagination. The young, however, may for a time take this notion quite seriously, unlike adults who usually revert to ideas of animism only in odd moments, such as the occasion when the wonderfully irascible Sir William Eden, father to a future prime minister, hurled the family barometer when it was set fair into the rain-soaked garden with the cry, 'See for yourself, you fool!'

Once a suitably attractive topic has been found, however, the art of the picture-book then rests on the interaction between illustrations and the text, and the way in which the results can both find favour with children, and also lead them on to new levels of response. One artist, for example, can play safe and simply create stereotyped characters and scenery, and while children may quickly feel at home among easily recognisable visual clichés, it may be less easy for them to grow in understanding with such books. Another artist, meanwhile, will produce pictures that are immediately eye-catching, perhaps glowing with bright colours and alive with interesting shapes, but which are out of keeping with their accompanying text. A story

swamped in this way can come a poor second, with its meaning dis-
torted rather than enhanced for the child. Even a brilliant artist like
Arthur Rackham cannot always escape this charge: his illustrations
for nursery rhymes and fairy-tales portray a type of crabbed,
grotesque ugliness that rarely exists in those sections of the text
upon which he is concentrating. This may not affect the illustrations
as works of art, as the increasingly high prices paid for original
Rackham pictures seem to indicate, but this lack of congruence is
still an occasional weakness in Rackham as a book illustrator. Yet
there are also other examples, as in his work for *The Wind in the
Willows*, where he does remain faithful and sensitive to the text, with
illustrations which both mirror particular scenes and also convey
some of the essence of their story.

Even so, capturing the true spirit of any text is always going to be
a somewhat subjective process, dependent on the different ways in
which different people may react to the same story. Not surprisingly,
therefore, the most successful picture-books have often been produced by author—illustrators, where text and picture have the greatest
chance of working together in harmony under the controlling imagination of a single creator. As Edward Ardizzone, one of the best
author—illustrators, has written, 'The professional writer . . . not
being visually minded, cannot leave out enough; he must elaborate;
he cannot visualise how the picture will tell the story. And this, I
think, is why the best picture books have been created by artists who
have written their own text. It is a one-man job.'[3]

One can see the truth of this comment by looking at some of the
picture-books that Ardizzone has illustrated for other authors. *Titus
in trouble*[4] for example, a story written by James Reeves and illustrated by Ardizzone, begins thus: 'Titus lived in London in a narrow
street beside the River Thames. It was a hundred years ago and more.
There were sailing ships on the water right at the end of the street.'
In one of his own illustrated stories, however, Ardizzone could have
got away with just one sentence of text here, since his accompanying
picture shows quite clearly the narrow street, the sailing-ship on the
water, and the fact that all this was set in past times. In picture-
books where the story should not go much beyond 2,000 words in
order to hold a child's concentration successfully, the economy that
can arise when pictures complement rather than repeat a text is a
valuable one, not least because it is giving the young reader the
chance to learn to use pictures as an essential part of a story,

rather than merely as an attractive elaboration of the already obvious.

This possibility of reader involvement is another characteristic of the successful picture-book, and important for children still unskilled in reading words, but more competent now in their understanding of certain types of illustration. Pictures that do everything for a reader, by bringing out and emphasising all the most obvious points in a style that can immediately be understood, can of course be very useful and indeed sometimes loved by children, but they do not really cater for the imaginative cooperation of a child. As Ardizzone has written, once again, 'One should not tell the reader too much. The best view of a hero, I always feel, is a back view.' These back views, in his own work, can certainly be most expressive, from the determined rounding of Tim's shoulders in the picture-books given over to his adventures, to the uneven, spindly shape of his well-meaning but unreliable friend Ginger. This sort of understatement, as well as getting over the idea of a certain artistic shorthand by inviting readers to fill in the missing detail for themselves, also allows for greater possibilities of reader identification: since children never see Tim's face in detail, it is easier for them in fantasy to imagine that it could, on occasion, look the same as their own. In this way, such pictures run less risk of actually standing between children and their imaginative realisation of a text — something that becomes more likely when over-explicit illustrations are used. As the little girl once said, when she refused to look at an illustrated version of a favourite fairy story, 'You see, I already know who the princess looks like — me!'

Edward Ardizzone, of course, is not the only successful author—illustrator for children, and some of his audience has sometimes found him hard to take, passing comments like 'too dark', 'too thin', or more libellously, 'careless' and 'not finished' — evidence of the growing preference for surface realism in illustrations that begins to show itself as children get older. But any artist who tries to extend children's visual imagination away from the immediate and the obvious risks this type of dismissive reaction, both from some children and from adults. Maurice Sendak, for example, was once blamed by an editor for drawing truncated, ugly children in his books, with oversize heads and short legs and arms. As he replied himself, 'I know the proportions of a child's body. But I am trying to draw the way children *feel* — or rather, the way I imagine they feel.'[5]

49

Such artists may indeed occasionally baffle children and parents, but when they do get through to their audience, they can be extremely stimulating, able to lodge in the visual memory long after other, more orthodox illustrations have lost their savour.

Different artists, of course, convey other meanings and impressions according to their own particular skills and habits. Randolph Caldecott, for example, can extend a simple nursery rhyme over a whole picture-book, by bringing in odd, suggested detail to create new overtones to an already familiar story. Another artist, Wanda Gag, shows how drawing in black and white can be as memorable and atmospheric as any coloured illustration, and other illustrators have experimented with pictures that run into texts, texts which run into pictures, and borders to pages that elaborate on the main story by including within them a selection of symbolic, emblematic detail. Some artists have produced pictures which, for one child, were 'so beautiful it hurts'; others have concentrated on capturing the essence of the familiar, from illustrations of apples to a cat yawning. There are also funny picture-books, to make a child laugh, and some more fearful illustrations, which can be useful if they make previously unconscious and worrying fears visible, and therefore more under control. Very frightening illustrations, however, may sometimes be too powerful for a young audience, and are therefore best avoided.

The whole picture-book world, in short, has a wealth of experience to offer children, and every time a child goes from one book to another, there will always be the possibility of finding out something more about colour, form, texture and movement.

Experience in learning to interpret illustrations gained this way can be useful as well as pleasurable. As it is, even school-age children often show surprisingly unsophisticated responses to illustrations: it may take a child up to seven years of age, for example, before he or she understands that the size of a character in a picture is not always a determinant of age, so that a baby, if it is drawn large-scale in the foreground of a picture, may still be thought to be older than its parents pictured in small scale in the background. This difficulty in understanding linear perspective in illustrations, something that was also mentioned in the case of very young children in the previous chapter, can frequently be found too in adults from different cultures looking at pictures for the first time. Readers with experience in looking at picture-books, however, learn to make some fairly complex inferences at quite an early age, with illustrations sometimes offering them a better opportunity to work things out for themselves than will be the case with verbal information simply on its own, which can be difficult to hold in the concentration for long. Experimenters have found, for example, that children even as young as three years old are sometimes quite successful when asked to infer the likely emotions of certain characters in a visually presented story. But when the same situation is presented to them verbally, without the help of pictures, there is a tendency to focus simply on the outcome of the plot, rather than on anything to do with its characters' possible feelings or motivation.[6]

This is not to say that small children cannot still be confused by more complex pictures. Younger children, for example, are often puzzled by illustrations where there is some incongruity between small detail and the apparent, total situation — for example, where a child is pictured as both beaming happily and about to be injected with a hypodermic needle. Pre-school children tend to insist that the child in the picture is still frightened — only older children, around six years old, could begin to discount the first, overall impression conveyed by this situation, instead using the evidence of the child's smile to suggest that the child and the doctor in the picture might only be playing.[7] But the more opportunities there are for children to look at pictures, where they can really pore over detail in their own time, the more will their interpretive skills have the chance to increase, whether this involves infants looking at fairly simple picture-books or even much older children of secondary-school age who can still enjoy reacting to the more sophisticated humour found in picture-books by modern artists such as Raymond Briggs, Quentin Blake, or Goscinny and Uderzo, creators of the famous *Asterix* comic books.[8] In this sense, picture-books offer the child of most ages, but particularly when he or she is small, an arena where they can grow in confidence and understanding quite quickly, with or without some adult help. When so much in a young child's life seems distant and puzzling, picture-books — which can both slow down and simplify experience by presenting it in static, often more readily comprehensible terms — may be, quite literally, just the sort of thing a very young audience is looking for.

Story-books and comics

Like picture-books, many of the slightly longer story-books that children will enjoy at this age also tend to concentrate on familiar, day-to-day events, as in the *Topsy and Tim* series, a pleasant if undemanding sequence of illustrated stories by Jean and Gareth Adamson. In one typical example, *Topsy and Tim's Monday Book*,[9] an ever-grinning milkman delivers his goods in the rain, 'wearing a big, black shiny cape'. This change in the weather means that the twins must put on their Wellington boots, but Tim has a tantrum and objects to this (Topsy, by contrast, rarely shows any bad temper, and is instead a model for the type of decorum that used to be described as 'typically feminine'). In due course, Tim gets his feet wet and has to dry off at his nursery school, eventually returning to home and conformity wearing the despised boots. And so such stories tend to go on, forever turning around moods, characters, scenery and plots that would be immediately recognisable to small children, themselves similarly taken up with daily mini-dramas arising from playing, shopping, eating, and relationships with animals, pets, toys, parents, grandparents and first teachers.

In fact, such books often have a useful role to play not simply in commenting on the present, but also sometimes in helping children prepare for the future. A child just before starting full or part-time education, for example, will be very interested indeed in hearing stories about schools or various other experiences in the future that also tend to crop up in story-books for this age. Some publishers, however, now produce 'situation' books for smaller children, which aim at preparing them for some quite specific changes in their lives, from the arrival of a new baby to the experience of moving house. Again, the potential appeal and effect of this literature will be indivisible from the way it is introduced to children, and the state of their own existing feelings beforehand. It seems unlikely that a child's jealousy over a new baby could be averted simply by reading a book that seeks to explain away such emotions before the event, although bringing feelings to the surface may be no bad thing, so long as parents can then deal with them adequately. A report in *The Lancet* once referred to forty young children admitted to hospital for squint operations.[10] In nine cases, the parents had not prepared them at all, saying things like 'I couldn't bring myself to tell him — I was so afraid.' Four mothers had actually told lies, giving their children the idea they were going to the cinema, or some other sort of treat. Not surprisingly, many of the children were badly disturbed by the whole experience. A simple picture-book about going to hospital could conceivably have helped here, both with children anxious about what was going to happen to them, and with adults feeling awkward about introducing the topic themselves.

Other parents have reported finding story-books that introduce the idea of adoption useful for reading to their own adopted children.[11] Once again, no book on its own could lead to a young reader's 'happy acceptance of being adopted', but these parents found that literature could help in getting something across in a way that both they and their children found acceptable. So long as such parents, or any others, do not then go on to think that children's books are important *only* because they can sometimes be put to such practical uses, then there seems every reason to encourage this particular approach to literature.

Some of the blandest literature available for this age-group can be found in infant comics. Although most people associate any sort of comic for children with slapstick humour or melodramatic adventure, those aimed at infants between the ages of four and seven usually contain neither of these popular ingredients. They also tend to be more expensive than other comics, designed, in fact, as 'parent-buys' for small children who may either not have their own pocket money, or who may not be allowed out to shop on their own. The fact that their main audience may rarely have a hand in purchasing these comics may help explain their very safe and unadventurous contents — sometimes more popular with parents than with offspring, who often prefer something more lively. Some items within them, though, are popular enough with young readers, although this liking does not usually rival the more positive enthusiasm engendered by comics for older children.

Small children, for example, tend to be very rule-oriented, not so much in the conduct of their lives, but in the way they seek to order the confusion around them. Rigid social rules help this tendency because they offer convenient, arbitrary measures of approved behaviour: a child may believe in them not because they make particular sense, but simply because they are there, almost as if they have an independent existence of their own. The frequent moralising to be found in so many infant comics may not, then, simply represent the heavy tread of the authoritarian adult forever getting at children — small children may actually like such an approach. An example is Fleetway's *Teddy Bear* comic, now deceased but still typical of other publications currently available for this age-group.

Every week one moral precept used to appear prominently in the middle of a page, boxed in by a decorated border, like the religious slogans that used to hang over the beds of the pious. Each homily began with the words, 'Teddy Bear says . . . ' and was accompanied by a picture of the comic's name character, wearing a bow-tie and a complacent smile. Typical sentiments expressed included: 'Try not to put too much food in your mouth at once'; 'Try to remember not to leave your Christmas toys lying around'; and 'Always thank Mummy and Daddy for a lovely present.'

Other comics of this type prefer to stick in the moral at the end of a story, occasionally using a different-coloured type to emphasise beautiful thoughts like, 'This story teaches us that even if we are not clever, we should always keep on trying to do well.' There is also the tendency to personify human failings in the names of some typical characters, as in Bunyan's *The Pilgrim's Progress*, with Cousin Never-hang-his-coat-up Puss Cat, or Cousin Never-wipe-his-feet Puss Cat.[12] In general, humanised animals are very popular in these comics, as in all literature for children at this age.

The settings for these stories tend to be as blandly domestic as in the *Topsy and Tim* book series, with Sonny and Sally of Happy Valley, or Sally Sweet of Sunshine Street. Very little anger, insolence, or violence is ever allowed to mar this dream world, where Mummy is always immaculately groomed and Daddy enjoys all the comforts of a well-appointed home. The normal expression for child and adult is a fixed, glassy smile — even for the dustman as he humps a heavy load, in a series called 'People we see'. If there is to be something about gypsies, then it may be on the lines of 'Gay Gypsies', a title from one recent comic, where any possible ambiguity was soon quali-fied by the sub-heading, 'Many gypsies live in gaily painted caravans.' Slight infantile mischief is occasionally on view, but is soon nipped in the bud by Mummy 'smiling firmly' and saying 'No'.

Infant comics also carry pages of things for a child to do, like pic-tures to colour or dolls to cut out and dress. There are, as well, weekly puzzles — for instance dots that have to be joined up in order to create a 'mystery object' which a bright child can sometimes identify even before putting pencil to paper. There may also be mazes, memory tests and pictures with deliberate mistakes, together sometimes resembling a battery of early intelligence tests. Such games do, in fact, offer the child an opportunity to experiment with early perceptual and motor-coordination skills. At the same time, the strip-cartoons provide a picture of a safe, domestic world, where readers can recognise familiar landmarks and respond to a type of didacticism which may have something in common with their own thought habits. In one story, for example, 'Nurse Susan' and 'Doctor David' run a dolls' hospital with some of the strict rules over visiting hours or 'proper' behaviour in the wards, typical of children's imaginary games at this authority-minded stage of development. But while it could be argued that infant comics cater for small children's needs in some respects, no one could suggest they cover a wide range of interest or emotions. There is occasional wish-fulfilment within them, for example where humanised animals drive their little cars and generally enjoy technology reserved for adults in our culture. This particular little fantasy of competence in a safe, suburban setting usually appeals to children, just as in real life they enjoy the chance to 'drive' those dummy cars, buses or trains on the fixed tracks of fair-grounds. But in general, the image of childhood presented here is passionless and often sentimental.

While children may often be quite happy to accept this bland image of themselves, there will also be a need for literature with more bite, particularly when it comes to stories that recognise the less socialised, more aggressive sides to childhood. As it is, there are even occasional tantrums in the otherwise tranquil life of Topsy and Tim, and other books, like Leila Berg's *Little Pete* series, or Dorothy Edwards' *My Naughty Little Sister* books, constantly take up the ever-popular theme of children's occasional anti-authority behaviour. In real life, children are of course very dependent on authority figures, but in time they must also learn to become more independent of them. Accordingly, their own attitudes can combine certain residual desires to have their own way in everything, left over from early egocentricity, with a consciousness of their actual vulnerability and ineffectiveness. Anti-authority themes in literature, therefore, may reflect small children's occasional anger at being continually controlled and manipulated by those bigger than themselves, just as more positive feelings towards authority may be represented by idealised parent-figures in fiction, always there in an emergency.

Books at this age may also be used by children to experiment with other violent, exciting fantasies, all in the comparatively safe area of the imagination. Ardizzone, once again, has said that his very lively stories about Tim began in response to his children aged six and four demanding 'a story with lots of danger in it', and the results include shipwreck, fire at sea and pirates all in a tough world quite beyond the intervention of Tim's parents, who can never seem to keep any reasonable track of him. These early dreams of independence are understandable in their popularity, and are perhaps the forerunners of best-sellers to come in later years, which still exalt the hero in rather the same way, forever in retreat from both the comforts and the constraints of settled, suburban living. Although Ardizzone's adventure stories were at first rejected by various pre-war publishers, there has been general recognition since that children may need tough little stories as well as bland material in their books, and ideally should always have access to both.

There are other infantile feelings and fantasies, however, which can sometimes be more safely ventilated under the disguise of reading about the adventures of humanised animals. Small children, for example, commonly think — at least up to the age of seven — that what happens in a book is something quite real. To hear a story, for example, about a mother who is killed by someone, could bring about almost intolerable anxieties and depression, at a time when children are still very dependent upon their parents. Yet at the same time, on occasions when they themselves feel seriously thwarted, children too can sometimes have murderous thoughts about some of their nearest and dearest, and may anyhow want occasionally to experiment with feelings of separation and mourning as a way of testing themselves out, just as they often experiment — in play or in the imagination — with other fears or anxieties. They can, therefore, be expected to be particularly interested and involved in books like Jean de Brunhoff's *Babar the Elephant*, where a mother does meet her death, but not a human mother, so that this horrifying yet fascinating and perhaps secretly exciting fantasy is presented to children in a way that most of them can more or less accept without becoming too personally involved or guilty in the process. Very much the same thing can also be found in Walt Disney's earlier, long films, which frequently revolved around the loss or separation from the parent, as in *Dumbo*, *Bambi* and *Pinocchio*, though for smaller children the animal or puppet disguises in these films are sometimes not enough to enable them to distance the action from some of their own worst fears for themselves. The results then are those infantile sobs in the dark so often heard when these particular films are shown.[13]

At a milder level, books like Russell Hoban's *Frances* series also help ventilate other painful emotions, such as jealousy of a younger sibling, again under the general disguise of writing about a day in the life of a family of humanised badgers. But while these books and others touch on problems or emotions which a child may want to explore in the imagination, it would be absurd to see this as the only function of fiction for this age. The best story-books have always explored a whole range of interests and emotions, such as the tales of Beatrix Potter, which are still excellent examples of the type of fiction that so many younger children enjoy. Unlike books constantly searching for a surface realism, these stories have not dated whereas the fashions, milk-floats and telephones of *Topsy and Tim* will soon look antique, and in fact have already been changed in more up-to-date editions from 'frilly frocks and tartan knicker suits to anoraks and striped T-shirts'.[14] But inhabited rabbit burrows and dressed up young animals belong to no particular time or place, and more importantly, Beatrix Potter writes about feelings and adventures that are part of every child's imagination — something that makes her an arresting as well as an entertaining writer for the young. Rather than try to discuss every writer who has appealed to children in this younger age-group and the possible reasons for their popularity, I shall focus particularly on Beatrix Potter's stories for all they can tell us in general terms about younger children's imaginative responses, and the ways in which an author can set about attempting to satisfy them. Not that Beatrix Potter's stories are always so successful: *The Tale of Little Pig Robinson* is untypically verbose, while an almost forgotten work, *The Fairy Caravan*, is nearly unreadable. Her best books, though, still show no signs of losing any of their appeal to children. Sales figures alone can only be a crude indicator of a book's popularity, since it is adults who make such purchases, but adults will not go on indefinitely buying books for younger readers which are meant to give pleasure but no longer do so. To this extent, Beatrix Potter's high sales over the last fifty years tell their own story.

However vivid an imagination a writer for young children may have, this must be expressed in a prose style that is simple, direct and memorable. In this respect, it is no accident that Beatrix Potter was always an admirer of and something of an expert on nursery rhymes, bringing out two mini-volumes of her own, *Appley Dapply's Nursery Rhymes* and *Cecily Parsley's Nursery Rhymes*. These collections mix some of her own rhymes along with other versions discovered by her in the British Museum library. In her stories, she often quotes from old nursery rhymes; it is not fanciful to suggest that within her own writing she absorbed some of their smooth rhythms and direct vocabulary. When she finished a particular work, she would always keep at it, polishing the prose and cutting out redundant phrases. The very format of her books, with their small pages, each passage of text facing a picture, ensured that there were few words to spare in any story, and in the correspondence with her publishers there are many reminders of the care she took with her prose style. Sometimes this would show itself in her spotting a faulty rhythm. In *The Tale of Tom Kitten*, for example, she originally wrote a slightly clumsy sentence, 'There were very extraordinary noises during the whole of the tea-party somehow.'[15] This was later changed to the superior, 'Somehow there were very extraordinary noises over-head; which disturbed the dignity and repose of the tea-party.'

'Dignity and repose' is not a phrase one would normally find in an infant's vocabulary, but Beatrix Potter knew what she was about. So long as the general context is clear, the odd expressive phrase, however unfamiliar, can always enliven an otherwise fairly basic vocabulary, which in any unrelieved form can soon become monotonous. This also applies to her famous use of 'soporific' in *The Tale of the Flopsy Bunnies*, with its meaning immediately made clear in the next sentence: '*I* have never felt sleepy after eating lettuce, but then *I* am not a rabbit.' As she once wrote to her publishers, who were sometimes alarmed by her adventurous vocabulary, 'Children like a fine word occasionally',[16] and so of course does a true author. Discussing *The Tale of Benjamin Bunny* she once wrote, 'I would like the book to end with the word "rabbit tobacco", it is rather a fine word.'[17] Sometimes her publishers worried whether a word even existed or not, complaining about an expressive sentence like, 'Once they heard a door bang and somebody scuttered downstairs.'[18] In reply Beatrix Potter agreed that she could not find 'scutter' in the dictionary, but if she were not allowed to use it, would 'scurried' do instead? Fortunately, her publishers allowed her to keep 'scuttered'; a marvellous word for expressing the furtive, scrabbling noise made by rats as they hurry along.[19] Elsewhere, she pushed her luck by the deliberate use of faulty grammar — something that might disturb pedants even now, when successful authors regularly receive worried correspondence about their supposed 'bad English', often regardless of its context. In her case, Beatrix Potter wanted to end *The Tale of Little Pig Robinson* with the lines, 'He grew fatter and fatter and more fatterer'. When her publishers demurred, she wrote back, 'Of course there is no such word; but it is expressive! If you don't like it, say "fatter and fatter and more fat". It requires three repeats to make a balanced ending'.[20] Once again, she got her way.

Sometimes she stretches her love of occasional fine language to the limits of a young reader's tolerance. Her favourite work, *The Tailor of Gloucester*, strictly speaking needs to be read with the help of a specialist dictionary in order to understand or even pronounce technical terms like 'padusoy' (silk from Padua), 'lutestrings' (lustred or watered silk) and 'robins' (an old-fashioned term for trimmings). But as she writes in the text, 'Stuffs had strange names and were expensive in the days of the Tailor of Gloucester.' In fact, her fine illustrations give a good idea of such wealthy brocades, in contrast to the poverty of the tailor, and the effect would not be so vivid without the use of a few exotic, antique words. The same cannot be said about all her other obscurities, however, such as the references to 'seed-wiggs' in *The Tale of Ginger and Pickles*, along with one of her rare descents into baby-talk in the same story, where 'The handbills really were most "ticing".' Yet the sort of latitude Beatrix Potter felt able to take in her stories, combined with her professionalism when it came to scrutinising the result, is almost always a source of strength. Although she was always cooperative with her publishers, she was never economically dependent upon the sales of her books, and indeed drifted into writing by accident. *Peter Rabbit* began life in illustrated letters sent to a child recovering from a long illness. These letters were kept, but it was eight years before Beatrix Potter asked for them back in order to put her little book together. A number of classic children's books have originated in this casual way, and for good reason. As Beatrix Potter herself once said, 'It is much more satisfactory to address a real live child; I often think that that was the secret of the success of Peter Rabbit, it was written to a child — not made to order.'[21] Other writers, such as Kenneth Grahame, Jean de Brunhoff and J.R.R. Tolkien, also told or wrote their stories for their own households before they thought of publication. Just as adults can drop their defences and reveal a more spontaneous, imaginative side to themselves when playing with children, so *literary* play, in the sense of telling stories to children just for fun, has often produced its share of really original, creative writing, where enjoyment has initially been its own reward, rather than dreams of a publisher's advance or anxious cogitation over what the children's market can take at a particular time.

But although many children's authors, when questioned, will maintain that they write primarily to please themselves and perhaps a few children in their circle too, this was particularly true of Beatrix Potter before she became famous. For much of her life she was a lonely, isolated person. Pet animals, and the lakeland countryside where she spent her holidays, were lifelines to a more fulfilled existence than her boring life in London could ever offer. She used to sketch her own pets to amuse and console herself long before she ever thought of publication, sometimes giving her much-loved animal models names like Hunca Munca and Mrs Tiggy, later of course to be incorporated into her stories. Not surprisingly, this affection is also evident in the way she later illustrated her books, with the same animals lovingly depicted in all their various poses, set against a background where the sun always shines and colours merge gently into each other. Everything is neat, ordered and flourishing, adorned by flowers and set against a lyrical back-drop of mountains. This is nature at its most idyllic: a cosy and charming domestic setting.

These stories eventually enabled Beatrix Potter to make good contacts with children in a way that might otherwise have been difficult for her, given that she was brought up to be a rather stiff, repressed type of personality. As one of her young admirers wrote about her later, she was always 'someone to be reckoned with, someone who would demand a great deal of one in the way of character, and be unsatisfied with less than the best. We had kind aunts, and charming aunts, and silly aunts, but she was someone to look up to and live up to.'[22] But it is not simply the prettiness and warmth of her stories that have always got through to children; there have also to be interesting, exciting adventures too, and here Beatrix Potter sometimes uses dark as well as lighter shades, also appealing to children but in a different way. For example, she often turns in her stories to what her biographer has called:

the simple traditional pattern of the fairy tale. Instead of giants and ogres and bad fairies, there are Mr Tod and Samuel Whiskers to beware of. The results of too great innocence or rashness, in fairy tales or Beatrix Potter's stories, are much the same. The stories point no moral, unless it be that the helpless and the simple, if they are not very careful, may make a meal for somebody else.[23]

The appeal of this basic plot of pursuit and prey for young children is not hard to imagine. They too are simple and comparatively helpless; they too are aware of danger, and this is true whether children are neglected or as protected as it is possible to be. From early on, they all have some terrors that cannot be explained in any rational way, such as fear of the dark and all the natural or supernatural creatures that can be imagined to inhabit it. Sometimes these terrors can be fanned by various cultural influences: a fairly widespread fear of wolves, for example, was reported among children around the time Disney first animated the story of the three little pigs on film, with its famous hit song, *Who's Afraid of the Big Bad Wolf?*[24] But parents who have tried to bring up their children without any fearful imaginative experience from outside have usually not managed any better than those who have tried to rule out all fairy-tales, since fear, like fantasy, comes from within as well as from outside the reader.

In many Beatrix Potter stories, the theme of danger gives both tension to the plot, and a sense of relief at the happy ending. There are no tragedies in her books, but a succession of very near escapes in a number of them. In most ways she was no sentimentalist, showing the cycle of predator and preyed upon with the 'gentle detachment' Graham Greene once ironically but accurately ascribed to her.[25] Yet she also recognised that her audience liked optimistic conclusions in its stories: once children had identified themselves with the animal heroes of her tales, it would be too harsh and depressing to show them coming to a sticky end. Instead, she sometimes pictures her characters living dangerously in a world which can be full of fearsome surprises. Although main characters survive, offstage personalities do not always fare so well. Peter Rabbit's father, no less, was baked in a pie for Mr McGregor, and other animals, from baby rats and mice to butterflies and grasshoppers (roasted with ladybird sauce) are also devoured at some stage in a story.

Other writers for children often gloss over these glimpses of a harsher reality in their adventure stories, but Beatrix Potter was not interested in this type of evasion. As a naturalist, she was used to all aspects of animal life, herself quite able to skin a dead specimen and then boil it down to preserve the skeleton. At the same time, her taste in traditional stories was equally uncompromising; when she wrote her own unpublished version of *Little Red Riding Hood* in 1912, both Granny and the young heroine fall to the wolf without rescue, the story finishing bleakly with 'And that was the end of little Red Riding Hood'. Later, in *Sister Anne*, her version of the Bluebeard story, there is a particularly macabre little song about the

61

conversion of human bones into a violin. A few similar moments of darkness also occur in some of her own original stories for children, such as the famous, graphic description of 'Something between a cave, a prison, and a tumbledown pig-stye' in *The Tale of Mr Tod*, where 'There were many unpleasant things lying about, that had much better been buried; rabbit bones and skulls, and chicken's legs and other horrors. It was a shocking place and very dark.'

Moments of fear have their place in stories for the young, however, so long as they are successfully contained by a plot that ends on a reassuring, consoling note. For young readers, the expression of some of their own nameless, common anxieties on the printed page may help render them more controllable, though as always not all children will react in the same way. For some, the fear evoked in the moment when, say, Peter Rabbit is caught in a net, or the sorrow conveyed by his sobs when he twice gives himself up for lost, may be altogether too strong to enable them to enjoy the story. In the same way, the death of Ginger in *Black Beauty* may remain as an ever-poignant tragic memory to some children later on, even after other human deaths in fiction have been forgotten, while Abraham may be as much detested for despatching an innocent ram in the Old Testament as for thinking of doing away with his own son.

The fact remains, however, that humanised animals still tend to give authors more imaginative licence when it comes to placing them in various, sometimes extreme situations. While some young readers may still be equally upset over the fate of such animal characters, for other children, possibly brought up in the country, the killing of marauding rabbits or whatever may seem more of an everyday matter. But the popularity of Beatrix Potter's books, especially those about pursuit and the preyed upon, does suggest that this theme is of particular importance to small children, and that she deals with it in a way that her young readers generally seem to find acceptable. Not that she always writes about the fears that haunt children; some of her other stories are as tranquil as anyone could wish. But in nearly all of them she deals with issues of particular meaning to children, such as the relationship between parent and child, seen in many variations throughout her stories, or the constant way in which food is made to play an important part, even to the extent that heroes and heroines may sometimes be the intended main meal themselves.

In all her stories, in fact, Beatrix Potter describes a half-human, half-animal world, populated by partly-clothed animal characters who have courtesy titles and surnames, and visit each other exactly as humans do, but who also mix the gentilities of polite conversation with offhand references to a more savage state. This type of ambiguity enables her characters to flit between human and animal roles, according to the needs of the plot. Peter Rabbit, for example, is first established very much as an animal, surrounded by his family 'Underneath the roots of a very big fir-tree'. On the next few pages, however, everyone is given a more human shape, with Mrs Rabbit, in her voluminous dress and pinafore, helping to dress her children and then setting off through the wood 'to the baker's'. Peter himself, who like his mother walks on two legs, soon gets into trouble, and loses his shoes and his jacket – a crime whose seriousness will not be lost on young readers, still living in an atmosphere where domestic offences may always seem more significant than most others. Without his clothes, Peter returns to the animal state, running on four legs and twice evading attempts on his life.

Perhaps it would have been too frightening to show a humanised rabbit just about to have its back broken by Mr McGregor's enormous, nailed boot, however, and at that stage, readers may feel relieved to see Peter looking like an animal again. One of the constant themes of folk and fairy stories, also found in children's own nightmares, is the idea that there may be terrifying adult figures around with murderous intentions towards the young. There are various explanations for these fantasies; psychoanalysts, for example, may see them as an indirect reflection of a child's own aggression. As children get older, it is suggested, and beyond the age of immediate temper tantrums, they increasingly want to deny to themselves that they still have occasionally angry and even destructive feelings towards their loved ones when thwarted, and this they can attempt to do by projecting such feelings on to other, imaginary figures. In this way, children avoid the guilt and anxiety that can arise through awareness of their own capacity for destruction, at least in the imagination, towards those they are also dependent upon. But the adult figures who may best come to represent this projected hostility – from ogres to the rheumatic Mr McGregor – can still be fairly terrifying, and occasionally haunting characters in the imagination. In *The Tale of Peter Rabbit* the central situation – as we have seen – is made not quite so frightening for young readers through the use of characters who at the moment of greatest danger look more like animals than human beings. But despite the animal disguise, the plot here is still near enough to some of children's most terrifying fantasies or nightmares in their own lives to make it of great, even sometimes compulsive interest for them; truly, a story that may be demanded over and over again.

Children can, of course, still identify with a character like Peter Rabbit when he is behaving more like a true animal, but perhaps with a different part of themselves. Peter as a humanised rabbit is no match for Mr McGregor, and young readers identifying with the diminutive, childlike figure suddenly confronting his enemy round the end of a cucumber frame, will quite justifiably shudder for his safety. Peter the rabbit, however, without his clothes — which at one stage almost fatally entangle him in a gooseberry net — is a more resilient quarry, scuttling away on all fours with all the speed of his kind. Here, Peter may represent for his young readers the toughness and freedom from constraint so commonly symbolised by wild animals in fiction. Children can identify their own fantasies of independence with the adventures of such characters, just as they can thoroughly enjoy the way that Peter makes a fool of his stern, adult enemy. Throughout Beatrix Potter's stories, in fact, her animals are allowed a licence not normally given to human characters — at least not without extra explanation or moralising. Her animal characters, for example, often steal, destroy, or invade each other's territory and even devour the young of other species. ('Yes, it is infested with rats', said Tabitha tearfully. 'I caught seven young ones out of one hole in the back kitchen, and we had them for dinner last Saturday.') This type of sentence does not make *The Tale of Samuel Whiskers* into a nursery equivalent of *Titus Andronicus*; cats *do* eat baby rats, after all, just as larger rats sometimes make away with kittens. But the way that very human-looking animals are still free to break various important human taboos makes stories about them especially interesting to children, themselves still prey to primitive fantasies in their own imagination.

There are many other advantages in using animal characters. Like children, they too are generally at the mercy of adult humans — another reason for identifying with them, especially those warm, furry animals that accept and sometimes return an infant's strong affections. They are also easy for everyone to identify with in other ways, since they transcend social class, skin colour and, to a certain extent, age. When they are introduced into a story, their existence can simply be stated, 'Once upon a time there were four little rabbits.'

Beatrix Potter always took great care over the opening and con-
cluding sentences in her stories. With animal characters, she could
start off directly and end abruptly, without need for all the tying up
of loose ends or other extra detail that audiences expect where
human characters are involved (though fairy stories, for different
reasons, can also get away with this type of brevity).

All Beatrix Potter's striking effects, however, are achieved in an
atmosphere that conveys the assurance of the familiar, with stories
usually set in the same rustic scenery, and characters who sometimes
move from one book to another. Danger is often present, but not
tragedy, meals of various sizes are enjoyed at regular intervals, and
parents always care for their offspring, rewarding the obedient but
never failing to punish the mischievous.

This type of predictability is echoed even in the physical shape of
her books, so easy for young hands to hold and manipulate, and
with their identical format, pictures on every page, and coloured end-
papers showing other familiar and possibly favourite characters from
different stories. All this can have a strong appeal to young readers,
looking for order in their environment, including their early literature. But within these regularities, there is still variety to stop a child
becoming bored. The tales range from the simple, almost mono-
syllabic *The Story of a Fierce Bad Rabbit*, to the extended prose of
The Tale of Samuel Whiskers, and the plots vary from danger and
suspense to descriptions of the blameless, uneventful life of Mrs
Tiggywinkle.

Beatrix Potter is not the only writer to appeal to small children,
but she is one of the best. In her books, she provides interest and
excitement, and even in her illustrations there may still be hints for
the wideawake of danger to come, such as pictures of the just visible
trout nosing his way towards the unaware Jeremy Fisher, or Peter
Rabbit's tell-tale ears sticking out of the watering-can where he is
trying to hide from Mr McGregor. For older readers, there is also the
gentle irony of these stories and the easy prose style; important for
tales which are frequently read aloud. Within them, moralising,
lengthy conversations, or detailed descriptions that hold up the
development of a clear story line are always avoided.

When a child has come to the end of Beatrix Potter's stories, however, or to other books of equivalent length and difficulty by authors
such as the Revd W. Awdry, Leila Berg, Wanda Gag, Rumer Godden,
Joan Robinson, Alison Uttley and many others, then it will be time

to move on to fiction with more plot to master and new literary conventions to recognise. Even so, between the ages of three and seven, children who have regularly come across books may already have learned a good deal in one way or another both from and about early fiction. In some cases, where a particular prose style is found to be especially congenial, children can get to know some stories almost off by heart. Later on, however, they will learn how to digest and remember only what seem like the most significant points of any story. If a child is asked whether he or she likes a piece of fiction during this stage, the questioner is quite likely to get in response a summary of the story itself. But this is, in fact, an early form of literary criticism, in that children are thereby demonstrating the extent to which any story may have got through to them and captured their interest, so that afterwards they are still able, or not, to recall most of it successfully. Any idea that comments can be passed *about* a story will normally have to wait until later; for the moment, stories will largely be confused with accounts of real happenings to someone, to be discussed or recalled in general terms by children, perhaps, but not to be thought about or judged as works of *fiction*. This acceptance of the essential truth of fiction will generally extend to fairy stories as well.[26] These stories are again an enormously rich source for the exploration of children's imaginative responses to literature, and as such deserve a chapter for themselves.

3 · Fairy stories, myths and legends

This chapter does not begin by suggesting a typical age-range during which children may most enjoy fairy-tales, since so much depends upon the story in question. In fact, there have always been arguments over the age at which children should be exposed to any fairy story, and though the terms of this dispute have changed over the years, controversy about timing and suitability still remains. For many early nineteenth-century critics, fairy-tales were self-evidently bad because they 'fill the heads of children with confused notions of wonderful and supernatural events'.[1] Although it is now common to deride such views, one should also remember that critics like Mrs Trimmer were writing against a background of widespread superstition, where witches and fairies were still often believed in as quite real. When such stories were passed on to children, in the case of middle-class homes very often by uneducated nursemaids, they might well come across not as fanciful tales but as real-life possibilities.

When belief in fairies and their tribes was finally pushed into odd country corners in nineteenth-century Britain, it then became possible to have a splendid revival of fairy-tales, with little idea that they might still deliberately foster ancient superstitions, and these stories have always retained huge popularity with children ever since. Yet some doubts remained. Although adults could now be trusted to take these stories with a pinch of salt (a true fairy-tale gesture in itself), others worried that children would not always be able to accept them with equal detachment. Notable amongst these was the Italian educationalist Maria Montessori, herself in revolt against the Froebel type of nursery education where exposure to fairy stories was considered an essential part of the kindergarten curriculum. For Montessori, fairy stories were suitable for children around the age of seven, but at the age of four could do serious or even permanent damage. Her main argument was that small children lack sufficient experience to be able to sort out fantasy from truth; early exposure to fairy-tales, therefore, may simply be confusing or even worse. There is little supporting evidence for some of her more alarming predictions, however. It is quite true that small children can become very disturbed by terrifying stories, which should certainly be avoided, whether in fairy-tales or elsewhere. As for the other bad influences upon the young discussed by Montessori, while a child may indeed have once jumped out of a window in misplaced emulation of Goldilocks, some children have always made injudicious jumps from heights, whether they have read particular stories or not. By the same token, one should also consider how many infants may have been saved from disaster by following more prudent examples gleaned from fairy-tales. As in Montessori's similarly fierce attack upon parents who foist the notion of Father Christmas on to their children, there seems a lack of balance in an argument that can seriously contemplate 'permanent damage' as one likely result, when one considers other competing and surely more fundamental social, economic and emotional influences also affecting the young.

Even so, there are good reasons for reserving at least the more complex fairy stories for late rather than early infancy. Small children do have a haphazard memory for order and logic, and may get lost in the elaborate conventions and extended plots of some fairy stories. Nursery rhymes offer the reader a quick dip into fantasy, often concentrating on situations which children soon recognise from their own experience. Fairy-tales and legends, however, stem from more complex myths that have meaning for older readers as well, and which sometimes demand a more sustained effort of concentration and imagination.

Some balance is always likely to be needed, therefore, between the amount and complexity of fantasy with which a child is presented at any age and other literature which concentrates more upon the here and now. But this need for balance has often been forgotten, as in the atmosphere in Russia after the revolution, when fantasy in literature was frowned upon. On one occasion when Kornei Chukovsky — himself a poet — tried to defend traditional fairy stories, he was told by an official, 'These are no use to us. We would rather have books about diesels and radio.'[2] One can understand how any new political order would want to make a clean sweep of traditional attitudes, whether in literature or elsewhere, but ultimately this attitude underestimates children themselves, as well as some of their favourite stories. As Chukovsky points out, most children enjoy playing with mud pies, but are generally too sensible to try to eat them as well. It is true that they may sometimes confuse explicit fantasy with literal truth, but if they are denied fantasy in their literature, they may simply go on to invent it for themselves. There is a nice story, told by Chukovsky, of a Russian educationalist who tried to protect her son from 'unrealistic literature', only to find that he was spinning the wildest fantasies for himself, involving a red elephant, a friendly bear and a hearth-rug that could also turn into a ship. At table he would converse with an imaginary companion, in this case a baby tiger, and insist that he himself, and even more gallingly, his mother, had the occasional capacity to transform themselves into little birds. As Chukovsky concludes, 'Although his mother observed that he literally bathed in fantasies as in a river, she continued to "protect" him from the ill effects of books of fairy tales.'[3]

On this argument, fairy stories simply recognise rather than suggest typical childhood daydreams. On the other hand, there can also be an over-reaction in favour of this need for fantasy — something criticised by another famous educationalist, Susan Isaacs, writing at the same time as Maria Montessori.

As soon as we came to realise what a rich fantasy life the young child has, and how inevitably he looks out upon the world from the centre of his own personal feelings, we have behaved as if he did this all the time, and wanted nothing *but* fairies and fantasies ... The events of the real world are, indeed, often a joy to the child, as to us, just because they offer an escape from the pressures of fantasy.[4]

Or as G.K. Chesterton put it,

When we are very young children we do not need fairy tales. Mere life is interesting enough. A child of seven is excited by being told that Tommy opened a door and saw a dragon. But a child of three is excited by being told that Tommy opened a door. Boys like romantic tales; but babies like realistic tales — because they find them romantic.[5]

There is, therefore, something to be said for this point of view too, and it is interesting that both Chesterton and Montessori mention the age of seven as the best time for enjoying fairy-tales, since this also echoes the researches of Arnold Gesell, who found after exhaustive questioning of American children that they tended to like fairy stories and legends most at this age. By this time, after all, a child should have the intellectual competence to concentrate on a slightly longer story, and with practice should be able to predict most of the common patterns of action and behaviour that regularly crop up in early fiction. At the age of six, for example, 41 per cent of the children in Arthur Applebee's study had firmly developed expectations about the roles of typical early fictional characters like lions, wolves, rabbits, foxes, fairies and witches, but this figure rises to 86 per cent of children by the age of nine.[6] Clearly, any story is much easier to follow once the reader can predict the likely outcome of certain set situations. At the same time, children will best be able to appreciate myths and legends when they are intellectually ready to understand both the questions posed about the nature of man or his environment in such writings, as well as the answers given. Myth has always interpreted man and his world according to their essential purpose and meaning, as seen by various early myth-makers. This particular purposeful way of picturing things can be especially meaningful to children, but only when they have got past the early stages of simply reacting to experience, and are able to start reaching out for more complex patterns of explanation as one way of trying to understand what is going on around them both in life and in books.

Another argument for the age of seven as the best time for at least some fairy stories, is that it is at this age that children are beginning to detach themselves from a literal belief in fiction. Although they may still think that events in a particular story may actually have happened, they may now distance themselves from them in other ways: Arthur Applebee discovered, for example, that while children around six years or so tend to believe that Cinderella really existed, few thought that she could actually be visited, either because she lived too far away, or because it might all have happened rather long ago.[7] This increasing detachment is also found at this age in children's reactions to their dreams, which may now be thought of as things that happen in the child's head while asleep, rather than as actual dramas acted out in the child's very room. Like dreams, however, fairy stories too can be convincing and sometimes disturbing, concerned as they are with the most important issues facing any human being, such as childhood, maturity, marriage, wealth, death, success or failure, cowardice or bravery. Children still with a quite literal belief in the events of fiction may occasionally find some of these concerns, and the way in which they are expressed, too powerful or even frightening, especially when they are backed up by lurid illustrations. But once children begin to distance themselves from absolute belief in fairy-tales, then obviously the material they can cope with can afford to become more urgent in what it has to say and how it chooses to say it. The alternative, when children are not so ready for

70

this type of confrontation, is either to risk terrifying them by tales which may occasionally be much too horrifying, as in some of Grimms' or Andersen's stories, or else to provide them with watered-down versions that may be insults to the truth and force of the original works. But at the same time, there are other more gentle, simpler legends and fairy-tales that even very young readers can sometimes follow and enjoy; thus the impossibility of suggesting any ideal age-range for all the various stories that now go under the one umbrella heading of fairy-tales.

In fact, whatever these stories have in common with each other, it is certainly not the presence of fairies. As an early collector once wrote,

> We have called our stories fairy tales though few of them speak of fairies. The same remark applies to the collection of the brothers Grimm and to all the other European collections ... The words 'Fairy Tale' must accordingly be taken to include tales in which occurs something 'fairy', something extraordinary — fairies, giants, dwarfs, speaking animals. It must be taken also to cover tales in which what is extraordinary is the stupidity of some of the actors.[8]

It was probably the late seventeenth-century French author, Charles Perrault, who was primarily responsible for giving disproportionate importance to fairies as such, substituting them in his famous collection for the ghosts, demons, wonder-working beasts or whoever else made magic in the European folk-tale tradition. Another French writer from the same period, Madame D'Aulnoy, created the literary fairy story, with its miniature gauze-winged creatures fluttering around in the type of unreally pretty, pastel landscape which can still be found in films, pantomimes and books today, although rarely in any of the great collections.

The story forms that have enabled fairy-tales to survive for centuries, and sometimes to spread across seas and continents to the most distant cultures, are also particularly well adapted to the needs of younger readers. In the form in which collectors found them, prior to writing them down, these stories were sometimes confined to the barest essentials as far as plot is concerned (one reason why early folklorists tended to pad them out and generally give them better literary shape before publication). Those plots and details that have survived over long periods of time, however, must have a certain human significance and the form in which they were told has an economy that is unique — the final boiling-down of a story to a narrative pattern that has proved popular with generations of listeners.

Many fairy stories are not only quite short, they are also extremely direct. The classic opening, 'Once upon a time', serves to launch a story straight into flight, with little of the exposition common to other narrative forms. It does not matter in fairy stories which country they are set in. If a king is dishonest, a brother jealous or a family starving, then this is simply stated rather than explained or justified.

With this type of cast, the story itself will usually proceed very quickly; even the passage of a long period of time may only take up a sentence or two. Elsewhere, events may follow hard upon each other with no particular logic, rather as children tell a story, the narrative kept going by casual rather than causal explanations — a succession of 'and then . . . and then . . . ' rather than whys and wherefores. This is because at certain stages children will not generally be in a position to notice much pattern in what is happening around them, and events may simply be linked together in the young mind because they take place one after the other — a thought-process that Piaget once described as 'childish arbitrary syncreticism'. Stories, therefore, that do not involve much more than a clear catalogue of events may be particularly suitable at an early stage, especially if they also include regular chunks of repetition, which can help to give any story a stable and memorable shape, like the giant's 'Fe!Fi!Fo!Fum!' in *Jack and the Beanstalk*. No one knows what this ominous slogan stands for, but like 'Nimmy nimmy not, my name is Tom Tit Tot' and many other catch-phrases, it sounds right and is good for audience participation. In one fairy story, a particular slogan even goes against common sense. 'No, No, by the hair of my chinny-chin-chin', chant each of the three little pigs, to the wolf's suggestion that he be admitted into their houses. Pigs, of course, do not have hair upon their chins, and the phrase is probably a carry-over from a previous version involving young goats. But as it is a rhythmic, catchy chant that is fun to anticipate, it obviously proved too good to drop. In the early stages it is sometimes hard for a child to remember any plot; easily memorised phrases, however, can quickly be recognised, and a certain amount of repetition may soon give children the chance to feel at home in particular stories. Later on, a young reader may also start to recognise and anticipate some of the more repetitive plot structures from one favourite fairy story to another, such as the rule of three, with three brothers, perhaps, who may have three tasks to perform, each one harder than the last. A child can soon learn to anticipate that it will almost inevitably be the third brother who will be the hero, and that he will usually win the prize at the third attempt and then possibly get married and live happily ever after — another excellent device for tidying up a story in quick time. A child, therefore, may soon feel at ease in this romantic but in other ways often clear-cut and predictable environment, with 'its brevity, its severe restraints on description, its flexible traditionalism, its inflexible hostility to all analysis, digression, reflections'.[9]

The belief in magic in various forms that runs through so many fairy-tales may also be in accordance with how younger children themselves think about certain events in the outside world. Later on, children will start moving on to more logical thought, when they have attained a certain age and have more experience. Until then, fairy stories in particular may be essentially in tune with earlier modes of thought; far from confusing children, they may help to build the intellectual confidence that usually comes when young people are given material especially adapted to their current capabilities. An intellect encouraged in this sense, even though by a pre-scientific way of thought that will eventually be rejected, may do better than an intellect balked by forcible exposure to more complex ideas at too early an age. This is not to say that children should always be addressed in ways they can very quickly understand: within reason, a certain continuous clash with more complex, adult thought is also healthy. But if children are always out of sympathy with what they are reading or hearing, this usually only serves to drive their more typically childish tastes underground, rather than out of their heads altogether.

Where belief in forms of magic is concerned, for example, children at an early age appear to go through what Piaget calls an 'autistic' stage of thought, which originates from their uncertain ability to differentiate the self from the external world, and establish clear boundaries between the 'me' and the 'not me'. In this situation, where their own feelings and wishes may sometimes be as real to children as anything in the objective world, they sometimes blur the difference between internal, psychological processes and external reality itself, with thoughts occasionally becoming confused with action, and wishes with fact. Small children, therefore, can sometimes imagine that they, or their parents, have the power to control physical events by the force of their wishes alone: a rhyme like 'Rain, rain, go away, come again another day', is a typical example of this fantasy in action. Linked with this omnipotent belief is the idea that everything in the universe is made solely for the use and convenience of man; as Piaget puts it, 'Organic life is, for the child, a sort of story, well-regulated according to the wishes and intentions of its inventor.'[10] The inventor, of course, is man himself, upon whom — in this view — the sun shines for the express purpose of keeping him warm, and for whom night falls so that it can be dark enough for the purposes of sleep.

Within this sort of conceptual framework, it is easy to see how some of the conventions of myth and fairy-tales have become so acceptable to children. A number of stories, on topics like 'Why the sea is salt', for example, explain natural phenomena in terms of human intervention long ago — a mental process described by Piaget as 'artificialism' — which is certainly easier for the young to understand than any scientific explanation. In the same way, there are stories on how animals came to be shaped or coloured in their distinctive ways, again usually attributable to some particular action in the past. The same reasoning can also be found in local legends, for example those that seek to explain the shapes of certain mountains.

Ideas of magic both in life and in fairy stories also stem from a belief in the possibility of human omnipotence. As it is, almost anyone can perform magic in fairy-tales: Grimms' *Goose Girl*, for example, summons up a puff of wind at a moment's notice even for the trivial reason of blowing off her suitor's hat. It is true that on other occasions the same Goose Girl weeps and grieves with no magic to help her out, but neither fairy-tales nor children's early thought patterns are logically consistent. As Piaget has pointed out, a child's idea of magic is weak and discontinuous — and therefore different from the more organised magical beliefs that can be found in primitive adult thought systems.[11] As children get older, they will discover that their magical, omnipotent expectations of life will have to be modified to fit their growing understanding of reality, but this will be a piecemeal process of re-accommodation. Even small children can be quite objective in their outlook at times when they have had particular opportunity to test out fantasies against the demands of reality. But in other, untested areas, the same child may remain quite openly ignorant or superstitious. In this way, magic in fairy-tales and magical beliefs in children themselves can both be arbitrary processes, appealed to at one moment, and ignored in favour of a more recognisable reality in the next.

At the same time the child may continue to attribute human

thoughts and feelings to most things within this magical universe; something reflected in Grimms' fairy stories, where sausages, straws, coats and beans may all on occasions have the power of speech and movement. Later, though, children may confine these animistic beliefs to objects which have the power to move by their own volition; an intellectual stage which is again reflected in stories, fairy or otherwise, where humanised animals play such an important part, as we have already seen in the previous chapter. These animal characters may have their own kings, queens, heroes and villains, and meet together in debate, as in Chaucer's *Parlement of Foules*. When faced with injustice, either to themselves or towards others, they often show strong feelings and take steps to rectify things. In this way their motivation, speech and goals will be indistinguishable from those of humans and indeed, these characters sometimes *are* human, but suffering under the temporary embarrassment of an evil spell.

This whole idea of a pre-lapsarian paradise, where man and beast converse and live together in peace, is one that can be found in many myths and religions as well as in the Bible, and is obviously a vision that has strong appeal. In fairy stories, talking animals are popular because this is how young children imagine animals to be, and later on, perhaps when they know better, how they would still like animals to behave, at least in the imagination. Such humanised animals and magical human beings have a natural place in the personalised world of the fairy-tale, where all the elements work together. This idea of a morally coherent and humanly motivated universe is fundamental to a small child's outlook, and can be found, in essence, within most types of children's literature; acceptance of the possibility of a more fortuitously organised moral order of things, is one of the major steps between the thinking of a child and that of an educated adult. Piaget illustrates the first stages of this transition in an experiment where a group of children, between six and eleven years old, were told the following story:

Once there were two children who were stealing apples in an orchard. Suddenly a policeman comes along and the two children run away. One of them is caught. The other one, going home by a roundabout way, crosses a river on a rotten bridge and falls into the water. Now what do you think? If he had not stolen the apples and had crossed the river on that rotten bridge all the same, would he also have fallen into the water?[12]

When questioned afterwards, most of the six year olds seemed to believe that the bridge broke because it *knew* that the boy was a thief and deserved punishment. The same opinion was held by a majority of the seven and eight year olds, but with older children the results were mixed. For the younger child, though, this evident belief in what Piaget calls 'immanent justice' presupposes a universe where things are ordered and intentional. When children ask 'why' questions about the causes of particular happenings, therefore, they may in fact be looking for moral explanations rather than for anything involving impersonal causal factors. The idea of chance, for example, will be very hard for a small child to accept since, in Piaget's words, this whole concept is something only gradually 'forced upon us by our own powerlessness to explain'. But before this stage has been reached, Piaget continues, the child 'will always look for the whys and wherefores of all the fortuitous juxtapositions he meets with in experience'.[13] In the same way, young children find the idea of coincidence hard to understand, since for them everything must have a reason. Again, this is something that is often found in uneducated thought; it was only in the late seventeenth century that the word 'coincidence' first became current — a sign that semi-magical beliefs in a deterministic universe were beginning to give way. Up to this time the magical background to fairy-tales would have been accepted as true by the majority of both adults and children. With the growth of education, though, belief in fairy stories — at least in the Western world — gradually became relegated to the young or to the uneducated and in this century, simply to children on their own.

Even so, many adults in our own culture as well as elsewhere still preserve some vestiges of belief in a type of magical thinking, for example when it comes to popular superstition. Such magical beliefs, after all, can have the function of converting man from being a helpless bystander into thinking he is someone who is an active agent in forces normally beyond his control.[14] But while educated adults are also capable of accepting more rational, scientific explanations for many things, children find these difficult when they are still naturally disposed to believe in something more like a fairy-tale world, where dreams, omens or prophecies about the ultimate success of the good and the doom of the bad can sometimes come true.

This sort of morally-charged universe does not always make for a cosy life in fairyland for those who transgress in however minor a way, but it does ensure a comprehensible existence, at least in a child's own terms. Time and again, where hero or heroine have respected the scenery and cherished animal life, they duly receive their reward, unlike the villain, who may find every beast, stone and river ultimately ranged against him as a punishment for previous bad behaviour *en route*. Children can easily accept the possibility of this type of moral intervention from outside, not because it happens in real life, as they may even then be discovering, but because a child's world-view is subjective and moral, not objective, and constructed around what ought to be true, not what is. This does not mean that children are consciously deluding themselves, but anything like the 'agnosticism of everyday life' is altogether too sophisticated and demanding an outlook to suit young people still straining to make moral sense of things. So long as children at the egocentric stage believe that the world was created purely for man, with Fate or God as a type of super-parent, then they will look for the clear workings of human laws of morality in everything, both animate and inanimate.

Whilst this type of vision can be found in a great deal of children's literature, it is seen most clearly in fairy stories, where the endings, if not always happy, at least usually make firm moral sense; if a hero or heroine disobeys a prohibition, for example, he or she may have to expect stern retribution. Secure in this framework, the reader can more easily accept temporary disaster in fairy stories, since if an eye is lost, through unjust dealings by others, it will probably be restored via magic ointment by the end, and unwarranted death itself may be reversible.

But within this fairy-tale world organised along the acceptance of strict moral rules and general conventions that a child can soon understand, there can still be degrees of complexity and variety. Where animism is concerned, for example, while even pins and needles may have the power of speech in some stories, in others it may only be animals that can speak, and then horses, dogs or birds. Sometimes the human hero may be able to converse quite freely with these animals, but at other times may only be able to communicate with them after some special magical event, such as Siegfried's first tasting of dragon's blood. There will also be other stories where animals behave exactly like animals — dumb props for human actors, simply to be sold at market or ridden on a journey. The extent of this type of variation means that fairy-tales can cater for a considerable span of mental age. Fiction that reflects one consistently infantile level of thought and nothing else soon becomes boring to its young audience; fairy-tales, in their various collections, usually avoid this danger.

The same 'mixed-stage' pattern can also be found in the use of magic in fairy-tales. This can be very simple stuff, such as tables that lay themselves, or scissors that cut out clothes from the air. But fairy-tale magic is not restricted to this level of mere wish-fulfilment; characters cannot always call upon supernatural powers to get them out of difficulties, and like Hercules, may have to labour hard as well. Sometimes magic even turns out badly, as in the Grimm story, *The Fisherman's Wife*. From living in a broken chamber-pot, later euphemised by English translators into 'a little hut', a fisherman is forced by his shrewish wife into winning favours from a magic fish. Soon house, palace and the Vatican itself are substituted for their original modest dwelling place, but the wife finally wishes to be God, and instead is returned to her former state. This is hardly a happy ending, but certainly in children's eyes a just one. Other stories suggest different moral lessons, as in the Grimms' tale, *The Master Thief* which, like other tales about cunning rogues, can show bad behaviour actually prospering, though admittedly at the expense of other people's folly. *The Cat and the Mouse in Partnership*, on the other hand, suggests a very harsh natural order indeed. 'This happens every day in the world', concludes this story, which describes how the perfidious cat finally swallows up the mouse, despite all their plans for friendship.

Attitudes can thus vary throughout the great collections, from optimism to cynical worldliness, with something to offer readers in all sorts of moods. Similarly, the 'beauty is good' convention can sometimes be dropped; every now and again there are characters who are both beautiful and bad, eventually spurned by the hero in favour of honest toil and tattered clothes. Again, normally reliable practices, such as granting the prize after three successful exploits, are occasionally broken, just as Hercules was once short-changed over his labours.

I rather doubt, therefore, the following generalisation from the Opies, who are usually so wise in their judgements on all matters of child-lore and literature. 'Characters in fairy stories', they write, 'are stock figures. They are either altogether good or altogether bad, and there is no evolution of character.'[15] This may often be the case, but just as there is occasional variety in other fairy-tale conventions, so can there be variation in the presentation of hero and heroine. There may be brave figures, like Jack the Giant-killer, but there may also be coarse simpletons like Lazy Jack, not necessarily a bad character, but by no means an outstandingly good one, and little meriting the huge reward that comes his way through that fairy-tale equivalent to winning the pools: success in making a princess laugh. Even within a story, characters may change, sometimes through learning some painful lessons. The proud young bride of King Thrushbeard, for example, is forced to discover that looks and riches are not everything, and ends her story a nicer person, just as Beauty comes to realise that she owes her true loyalty to the Beast, not to her father and family.

Even so, it is still true that it is stock figures who are the most popular character-types in fairy-tales, such as Jack the Giant-killer and Simple Simon, who crop up over and over again in chap-book literature and other early, catch-penny stuff. Two such diverse characters, hero and anti-hero, offer a truly contrasting choice of model, yet both may find an echo within the same reader's personality. Not surprisingly, most children enjoy occasional fantasies of omnipotence, either in their own games and daydreams or else in their favourite stories. As it is, children often

Feel powerless compared with adults. In a battle of wills, parents often take care to make it seem that they have won, even though in fact the child has carried the day. Adults' ability to foresee consequences must sometimes seem like magical powers to the child: 'Careful, you'll hurt yourself! ... There, I *told* you you would', cries the mother — did she make it happen? Adults have a mental scheme of what is planned for the next few days; children, whose time sense is poor, are constantly astonished by the arrival of events, in a way which would seem intolerable to adults ... Playing at being powerful, even though one's power may only be over dolls, teddy-bears and peg-men, redresses the balance of powerlessness and makes the child's limitations tolerable to her.[16]

In the same way, therefore, it can also be satisfying for children to identify from time to time with the many characters in their fiction who tend to carry everything before them. For other moments, though, when children may be more conscious of their own real-life lack of muscle, there are also favourite characters in fairy stories who achieve their ends not through brute force but through skill or their ability to appeal favourably to others. Such characters will often be 'the youngest son, the weakest, the least clever, the one whom everybody would judge as least likely to succeed'. But this character, in fact, often

turns out to be the hero when his manifest betters have failed. He owes his success not to his own powers, but to the fairies, magicians and animals who help him, and he is able to enlist their help because, unlike his betters, he is humble enough to take advice, and kind enough to give assistance to strangers who, like himself, appear to be nobody in particular.[17]

In other moods, however, children can also be very conscious of their own comparative impotence in most fields, and consequently impatient or uneasy with any type of compensatory daydream. One can therefore also find in fairy-tales, and indeed in all children's literature, stories which generally make mock of typical omnipotent fantasies. In these, heroes are no longer in control of what is happening around them, and attempts at magic generally go askew. Another popular literary technique for this sort of mood exaggerates particular favourite fantasies to such an extent that they finally look absurd rather than heroic, as in the tall story.

This occasional urge towards satire even of the most treasured day-dreams can also be found in jokes as well as literature, and — it is often argued — may well be one of the ways in which human beings help preserve a good balance in the imagination between optimistic projections and stern reality. Like everyone else, children soon seem to develop a need to put particular daydreams into a more critical perspective from time to time, before reality itself pulls them up too sharply; it may only be the isolated, sometimes rather disturbed child who resists ever bringing their fantasy life down to earth in this way. For the rest, however, there are also other satisfactions available in stories where it is the anti-hero who tends to come out on top. In such stories, after all, the adult world is also frequently satirised, often pictured as a place run by capricious people who tend to disperse rewards and punishments accidentally and who themselves can easily be fooled. Younger readers, who may still want to work off resentment against adult authority in their imagination, can do so here by identifying this time with an anti-hero who although lacking in glamour still usually manages to do better than the equally ridiculous characters ranged against him. The same readers, though, may also appreciate other stories where inexperienced heroes are put right by altogether wiser, older authorities, for those moods when children are extra conscious of their own vulnerability and the consequent need for powerful, mature leaders in their lives.

This variety of approach, where the hero can range from Superman to buffoon, is especially evident in fairy-tales, and another reason, perhaps why they have lasted so long. There are many other ways, too, in which readers of these stories can find sometimes quite contrasting approaches within otherwise predictable conventions. When it comes to identifying with different levels of intellectual maturity, for example, the story of *The Three Little Pigs* mirrors the progress of a child's own thinking over a number of years, and readers will respond to it at whatever level of understanding they may have acquired. Smaller children may sympathise with the first two little pigs who, like them, live very much in the present, quickly building their inadequate houses and then getting on with their games. Older children, though, may immediately understand and approve of the more solemn third little pig, who shows that he is both able to learn from the past and to anticipate the future when he builds his safe house of brick.

The riddles and guessing games that crop up in fairy-tales can also act as introductions to more complex ways of thinking. This is illustrated in one of the Grimms' tales, *The Wolf and the Seven Kids*, where the wolf tries to trick his way into the house after the departure of the mother goat. The wolf wastes little time in getting down to the eternal business of the dishonest doorstep salesman, always very threatening to the young and inexperienced. ' "Open the door my dear children, your mother is here and has brought you each something". But the little goats perceived from the rough voice that it was the wolf.' This is excellent reasoning from the particular to the general, something that an adult will take for granted, but a skill that the young may still have to learn. The wolf's next trick — to soften his voice — also fails, as the logical kids can still see his black paws on the window sill, but when the wolf whitens these with dough, they are properly fooled and pay the penalty. Within the limitations of concrete reasoning, however, based on the logical analysis of evidence taken only from the here and now, the seven little goats put up a good initial resistance. It should certainly interest children who themselves have just arrived at that stage of inductive reasoning, as well as those who have not yet got there, but are beginning to see what it is all about.

Even so, the way that fairy tales can both echo a child's thought patterns and in some cases take them a step further along, is by no means unique; all stories for the young have something of this function. For example, while children can understand absolute judgements, such as 'biggest' and 'smallest', younger ones may find it harder to understand concepts like 'the middle one' or 'medium' which depend upon an ability to make comparisons between one object and at least two others. Fairy stories, among others, are full of examples of these concepts — think of Mother Bear in *Goldilocks*, with her determined preference for the middle way, even reflected in the pitch of her voice. This same story also abounds in various quantitative terms and graduations: 'The three bowls of porridge are of different sizes, the porridge itself is at different temperatures, the beds are of different size and degrees of hardness . . . Children like to hear fairy tales again and again, in part at least, because they provide nourishment for the child's growing quantitative abilities.'[18]

Possibilities for this type of intellectual practice and incidental learning occur in all manner of literature, but fairy-tales have so many ways of interesting young readers, and thereby holding their attention to a text which may contain more than merely a good story. Most children, for example, are fascinated by the exotic; when five year olds make up their own stories, they often prefer to set them in exciting locations such as foreign countries, the sea, sky, forests or mountains.[19] Sceptics may see this as owing to the influence of fairy-tales and their settings, but it is not certain that all children always hear these stories. Their responses could equally be one more example of how fairy-tales follow, rather than trigger off, particular patterns in a child's imaginative development. The appeal of the exotic, in a sense, is the appeal of the imagination itself: a glimpse of a world more vivid, exciting and unpredictable than that offered by the children's own environment, once they have got to know their way round it. In fairyland, by contrast, there may be a multiplication of the rare and unlikely, such as jewels, gold coins and precious clothes, perhaps guarded by a soldier with a nose that grows over a mile long. One of the Grimms' most popular tales, *The Six Servants*, is in fact populated by a cast of such nonpareils, who can drain an ocean dry, shatter a mountain with one look, or sit in the middle of a fire and still freeze.

This vivid detail is an imaginative challenge and extension to the normal conditions in which we live, and popular perhaps for that very reason. Mention of Cinderella's glass slipper, for example, can be found even in some cultures that never wear shoes. Baba-yaga's hut that travels on giant chicken legs, Rapunzel's wonderfully long hair, Jack's amazing magic beans — such things have an intrinsic interest, whatever they may also happen to symbolise, simply because they are bizarre and therefore fascinating, whether heard today in the safety of suburbia, or hundreds of years ago in a tiny village. More homely details can also be memorable, as in the Grimms' version of *Snow White*. Even without accompanying illustrations, it is not difficult to picture vivid details like the three drops of blood that fall in the snow, and the child who is later born white as snow, red as blood and with hair as black as ebony. With the addition of other striking detail, such as the speaking mirror, the huntsman who cuts out the heart of a young boar instead of killing Snow White herself, the dwarves' little house and the heroine's transparent coffin, the imaginative appeal of this one story, put across in simple but very effective language, is surely no mystery. But even so, the argument must be taken further: children often remember particular details of any fairy story, but they are just as likely to recall the main plot, too. What is there about these stories as *narratives* that has made them so popular over such a long period?

There have been many possible explanations. For some nineteenth-century folklorists, fairy-tales were remnants of a once world-wide mythology, there to explain certain natural phenomena. George William Cox, for example, adhered to the 'solar theory' to explain fairy-tales, 'The story of the sun starting in weakness and ending in victory, waging a long warfare against darkness, clouds and storms, and scattering them in the end, is the story of all patient self-sacrifice.'[20] By the same reasoning, *Cinderella* was seen as a fable about night and day, where Cinderella herself is Aurora, the Dawn — hence the references to the brilliance of her hair. She is hidden from the sun by envious clouds (the ugly sisters), and finally is nearly extinguished in the dark cinders by her evil stepmother (the night). But rescue comes from the Prince (the morning sun), and Cinderella is restored to her true radiance — dawn breaks once again. Viewed this way, *Sleeping Beauty* symbolises the long sleep of winter, to be awoken by the Prince, who is Spring, while *Little Red Riding Hood* is the glow of sunset before it is devoured by the wolf — night.

Other scholars, notably Andrew Lang and the Grimms, could not accept that fairy stories were simply there to explain to primitive man night and day or the seasons in terms of symbolic stories. For them, these tales were anthropological survivals from once-primitive cultures. Thus Cinderella sleeps on the hearth because, as the youngest child who in some cultures inherited everything, she quite literally chose to sit upon her inheritance. Other details from the tales, it was thought, like magical beliefs, animal-worship and hints at cannibalism, similarly date back to primitive religions, and even dwarves were held to originate from memories of a prehistoric Mongolian race that died out after being driven into the mountains and forests by the Celts.

These arguments, which were conducted fiercely during the nineteenth century and produced many more equally ingenious interpretations, were never interested in explaining the continuing contemporary popularity of fairy-tales. This however has become the concern of twentieth-century, post-Freudian commentators, who now take the line that 'Mythology is psychology, mis-read as cosmology, history and biography.'[21] As for fairy stories, 'It is now fairly agreed that the general continuity, and an occasional correspondence in the detail, can be referred to the psychological unity of the human species.'[22] Readers coming to these tales, therefore, are thought to find within them reflections of some of their own most vital personal fantasies, but disguised by fairy-tale imagery. In this way, as Freud once wrote, fairy stories can 'Enable us to enjoy our own day-dreams without shame or guilt.'

Those who still feel that psychoanalytic explanations of fairy stories are also exercises in imagination must admit, however, that such interpretations are occasionally endorsed by the stories themselves. In *Allerleirauh* from the Grimms' collection, for example, the father's incestuous design upon his daughter is openly stated, and the common psychoanalytic idea that animal characters often symbolise parents or siblings in the child's imagination is echoed in stories like *The Twelve Brothers* or *The Seven Ravens*, where whole human families are changed into animals during the process of the tale. Freudians would also claim, however, that there are many less overt references to vital areas of the unconscious in fairy-tales, particularly to the so-called Oedipus complex. This, for psychoanalysts, is the result of a stage when young children go through a period of possessive, erotic attachment to the parent of the opposite sex. They can also, at the time, become very jealous and resentful of their parental rival of the same sex. These 'Oedipal' feelings, Freud suggests, may later become too threatening for children to admit to, especially when they are developing a conscience which will make it more difficult for them to integrate such aggressive feelings along with the other, more positive emotions that they will also have for their would-be parental rivals. But when general anti-adult feelings are reflected in fairy stories, readers may then feel some measure of relief, as already seen in previous discussion of some of the rougher nursery rhymes also available to the young. The male and female adult characters who act as butts in these settings, it is argued, can often be made to stand in for the resented mother or father in the child's own imagination.

In orthodox psychoanalytic theory, therefore, fairy stories often portray a symbolic re-enactment and resolution of the reader's own

Oedipus complex, as in the common story where hero or heroine must overcome powerful enemies, very often witches or giants, in order to steal away the prize, usually a prince or princess. In this light, this story symbolises children's jealous attachment to the parent of the opposite sex, which they see as thwarted by the general family situation. By way of compensation, however, the child can go on to win his or her victory through the fantasy world of fairy-tales, by identifying with the hero or heroine who defeats the giant or witch — symbols of the resented side to parents in children's imagination — and wins the prince or princess, who stand for the idealised versions of the parent for whom the child may have strong erotic feelings.

Children's Oedipal feelings are only one aspect of a whole range of emotions, both positive and negative, which they can have towards their parents, but even so many adults find it hard to admit to the existence of any unconscious hostile fantasies in children. Freud's theory of inevitable Oedipal conflict, therefore, can still in itself cause considerable hostility — evidence, for psychoanalysts at least, of denial in the face of some unpalatable, personal truths. Expressed in stories, however, this type of charged Oedipal fantasy — it is claimed — can then become much more acceptable to everyone. Giants, for example, may not be taken seriously by adults, since they only occur in stories. But for a child, 'The conception of giants, with their clumsy stupidity and their alternations of kindliness and ogrish devouring of children, is a projection of various infantile thought about grownups, particularly the parents.'[23] In fact, giants are nearly always male; their wives tend to be normal size, so supporting the psychoanalytic interpretation that giants symbolise the fantasy father, who seems to wish to dominate all those around him, even his spouse. It is the witch or evil stepmother who stands in for negative fantasies about the mother, and witches have been found in stories from almost every culture, again suggesting that they must be serving some important need in the imagination.

As Ernest Jones has written elsewhere

We observe that children commonly listen to fairy tales with an air of fascinated horror, or even with gusto, and demand the reading to be repeated. Yet the gruesome figures of these tales, e.g. cannibalistic giants, enter into the frightful nightmares which so many children have to endure. It would therefore seem plain sense to avoid such horror-raising stimulation. But the matter turns out to be not so simple. We find that young children *spontaneously* create in their imagination, both consciously and still more unconsciously, the same images of horror

85

and terror, and that they suffer from nightmares without ever having listened to a fairy story.[24]

Today, these witches and giants are sometimes joined or replaced in children's imagination by vampires or various types of monster often drawn from film, comic or television, but their symbolic meaning to the child probably remains very similar to that of the more traditional frighteners found in fairy-tales.

Parents who read aloud a story which takes up, say, typically childish fantasies of omnipotence or anti-adult aggression, however, may be reassuring their children at the same time that there is nothing terribly wrong with having or enjoying hearing about these fantasies — otherwise why should they — the adults — be reading aloud and also taking pleasure in such stories themselves? Going even further, though, parents may themselves become a temporary witch or giant in any story-telling session, when reading out villainous dialogue with appropriate relish. Children who at times resent their father or mother can go through considerable guilt and anxiety if normally equable parents never really behave in ways that can justify such occasionally strong emotions. A mother suddenly transformed into a witch, however, can for that moment be as feared and hated as it is possible to be; when her voice returns to normal, so will the child's ordinary, positive emotions, but for that moment before it may be no bad thing to allow children opportunity to experience without guilt the latent hostility that can co-exist in all of us towards our nearest and dearest.

But even if it is allowed that literature has a special, symbolic meaning for its readers, there is little agreement over what various common fairy-tale symbols represent. Most orthodox Freudian approaches to fairy stories are concerned with their possible sexual symbolism; but not all psychoanalytic thinkers see them in this way, with the emphasis necessarily always upon children's fantasies about the primal, family situation. Followers of Jung, for example, explain fairy stories as having more to do with an individual's struggle with himself, rather than with those around him. Carrying off the bride, or marrying the prince at the end of the story does not, in this view, represent a child's fantasy of finally possessing the loved parent against the claims of more powerful rivals. Instead, this victory may stand for a child's desire to reach more general maturity, both sexual and economic, and very often fairy-tale marriages are, in fact, accompanied by golden handshakes, such as the addition of half a kingdom.

On the long journey towards this goal, the defeat of monsters and victory over physical obstacles like high mountains and thick forests, may represent a young person's victory over his own dark, animal side in favour of what Jung calls the upper world of light. In this sense, the fairy adventure story symbolises the ascent of consciousness, and the reader, identifying with the heroic figure in these stories,

can be liberated from his personal impotence and misery and endowed (at least temporarily) with an almost superhuman quality. Often enough such a conviction will sustain him for a long time and give a certain style to his life. It may even set the tone of a whole society.[25]

Jung and Freud became estranged over their differences about the significance of sexual repression in the growth of personality, with Jung increasingly giving greater importance to mystical and religious experience. This variation in approach, when it comes to interpreting fairy-tales, becomes more striking when critics from both camps try analysing the same story, as in the case of the Grimms' *The Frog Prince*. Here, a frog does a favour for a princess on condition that they live afterwards as man and wife. The princess rather casually agrees to this, and the frog later takes up her promise. He insists on sharing her table and bedroom, but when he tries to hop into bed, enough is enough and she dashes him against a wall, although in other versions this only happens after the frog has spent three nights with her. Gratifyingly, the frog then changes into a handsome prince, who has been under the spell of a witch, and under these more auspicious circumstances, the princess has no further objections to matrimony.

For a Freudian, the symbolic meaning to the story of *The Frog Prince* could lie in a young girl's mixture of fascination and horror over the sexual act. As in another fairy tale, *Beauty and the Beast*, sex is represented at a base, animal level: the frog, with its 'thick ugly head', who wants to sleep in the princess's 'beautiful, clean bed', is here a negative symbol for the male sexual organ. But when the princess finally dashes away her old disgust, she is then enabled to see sex in a new, positive light, possibly after the act of love itself.

Jungians, by contrast, tend to see this story in wider terms. The frog here represents not simply sex but the whole 'unconscious deep' of any individual, filled with hidden treasures but like serpents, dragons or other traditional animal frighteners, loathsome in its initial appearance. But if the heroine can accept these riches, and break through the taboos and fears that sometimes stop us from embracing unconscious fantasies, hitherto inaccessible because they deal with various 'forbidden' topics and feelings, then she may end by realising the richness of her total personality. With soul no longer split off from body, there will be no further need to continue living only at half strength.

But even within one particular psychoanalytic approach, there is no necessary uniformity of interpretation over details. In *Jack and the Beanstalk*, for example, one critic sees Jack as an 'oral dependent' type, immature and incapable of competing successfully with his contemporaries in the market place. The magic beanstalk represents the masturbation fantasy of this depressed, inferior being, and cutting it down symbolises self-castration as a way of escaping the pursuing Oedipal hostility of the father-giant, on his way to punish Jack for his sexual presumption. But another critic views chopping down the beanstalk as a symbolic castration of the father, with the active collusion of two mother-figures: the giant's wife, who hides Jack away and helps him in his thefts, and Jack's own mother, who hands him the hatchet at the crucial moment. In this context, it is Jack's Oedipal designs which are the main focus of interpretation, with the giant-father chanting words to the effect, 'Fe! Fi! Fo! Fum!, Here's Jack who wants to marry Mum!'[26] Like Aladdin's lamp, the beanstalk has proved too tempting a phallic symbol for psychoanalytic critics to pass over, just as Cinderella's slipper is nearly always interpreted in female sexual terms. But after this, agreement generally ends. 'The analysts do agree that the beanstalk is a penis. The question is whose?'[27]

Little Red Riding Hood is another story that has attracted much psychoanalytic speculation. For Erich Fromm, the heroine is a girl on the verge of puberty — her red hood symbolising the onset of menstruation — and so presented with the problems of her budding sexuality. Her mother forbids her to stray into the woods, which for Fromm is a veiled warning about not losing her virginity. The wolf, however, is male sexuality rampant; his desire to eat Red Riding Hood is symbolic of sexual intercourse. Little Red Riding Hood — for all her show of demure innocence — co-operates with the wolf, following his suggestions that she go 'deeper and deeper into the woods'. But, as Fromm concludes, 'This deviation from the straight path of virtue is punished severely.'[28] Ideas of devouring and loving here have often been linked, both in lovers' vocabulary and children's fantasy, and Red Riding Hood's unhappy end also symbolises the loss of her virginity.

Dr Bruno Bettelheim has brought a more Oedipal interpretation to this sexual symbolism. The wolf, for him, is the father's sexuality. Red Riding Hood, like all little girls in the family, is half-attracted by this, and therefore helps the wolf when he wants to know the way to the grandmother's house. Once the grandmother, who here stands for the child's own mother, is got out of the way, then everything is free for the wolf-father to attain his true desire: the sexual devouring of his own adolescent daughter. If the woodcutter intervenes before this, as he does in some later versions, then this represents the higher-conscience, superego of the father, anxious in his better moments to kill off his bestial 'id' forces that urge him on to such prohibited desires.[29]

Other fairy stories, it has been argued, also carry within them complementary characters of the same sex who can symbolise different aspects of the parent in the reader's imagination, but split into two contrasting personalities: the idealised hero and the wicked villain. This process, according to the psychoanalytic writings of Melanie Klein, particularly reflects the feelings of the child about the mother who, from the first few months, represents 'the whole of the external world; therefore both good and bad come in his mind from her, and this leads to a twofold attitude towards the mother even under the best possible circumstances'.[30] Eventually a child will learn to accept that the same parent — or person — can be both giving *and* denying, or in Melanie Klein's phraseology, both a good as well as a dangerous object, but before this stage has been reached, infantile moods may frequently swing from extreme affection to equally definite resentment. In children's imagination, however, the extremes of these mood-swings can be represented by the splitting of parent-figures into both good and bad fantasy objects. In this way, one such figure can then be loved and admired and the other detested and feared, without the child having to solve the emotional and intellectual problem posed by the fact that both figures symbolise aspects of the same person. Thus the habitual coupling of extremes in the imagination and in fairy-tales: the idealised princess and the fearful witch; the kind father and the savage ogre; the rampant wolf and the benign woodcutter. By this splitting, Melanie Klein argues, children's fantasy image of the 'good mother', necessary for their psychological security, is in no way threatened, since all really negative impressions of her can instead be projected on to a convenient, hateful villain, who may come back in nightmares, where dreams about witches still tend to be very common, especially at a young age. At the same time, children may sometimes be very conscious of their own capacity for more general, violent, aggression, which for Melanie Klein goes far beyond mere bad temper, and can involve what she terms 'infantile sadism', with its desire to bite, maim and generally 'mess up'. In this sense, fairy-tale characters, like cannibalistic ogres, or devouring wolves, can reflect a child's own sadistic anger against others, as may other rough characters in children's fiction discussed in previous chapters, but once again in a form where readers can deny to themselves the personal origin of such fantasies. Indeed, the appeal of violence in fairy stories can sometimes be very great, especially amongst deprived or frustrated children, as the American author Richard Wright describes in his autobiography. As an unhappy small boy, he writes that after hearing the story of Bluebeard, 'I hungered for the sharp, frightening, breathtaking, almost painful excitement that the story had given me, and I vowed that as soon as I was old enough I would buy all the novels there were and read them to feed that thirst for violence that was in me, for intrigue, for plotting, for secrecy, for bloody murders.'[31]

The same psychological process of splitting between the good and bad may also occur in the reader's possible identification with the hero and with the villain in fairy-tales. The two brothers or sisters common in such stories, where one has all the virtues and the other all the faults, may represent children's own alternating views — the idealised and the negative — of themselves as well as of others around them. Once again, it may be more comfortable and comprehensible to see these contrasts represented in two distinct figures rather than in one person. Most readers, for example, prefer to hate and condemn the wolf and to excuse Red Riding Hood from any responsibility for what happens, even going to the extent of idealising her. As Dickens himself once declared, 'Little Red Riding Hood was my first love. I felt that if I could have married Little Red Riding Hood, I should have known perfect bliss.'[32] Although tongue in cheek, this is a revealing statement from a great author who was apt to think in terms of over-idealised heroines, both in his fiction and in his own life, not always with the happiest results.

Kleinian theory would probably interpret *Little Red Riding Hood* again in Oedipal terms, where the wolf would represent children's fantasy of their own potential for destructiveness in the family situation, while Jungians would no doubt see the wolf as symbolic of our whole instinctive nature, which can threaten to devour us unless we can first recognise it and then draw upon its great animal strength. But by now the point will have become obvious: psychoanalytic interpretations of fairy-tales are often ingenious, but mutually inconsistent. All such interpretations — especially when they claim to be exclusive — should therefore be treated with caution, but to rule them out altogether would be to abandon the only type of explanation which has gone anywhere near accounting for the world-wide popularity of fairy-tales. As it is, these traditional stories *do* often seem to get near to particular, personal fantasy: themes like the slaying of monsters, sibling rivalry or Oedipal conflict, for example, where a child may be the subject of dispute between parents, are common to all folk stories, and to have lasted so long, they must have a significance at levels beyond mere entertainment. But because individual readers react to these stories according to their own particular needs, the various psychoanalytic interpretations already discussed may always seem much more valid in some cases than in others. A Freudian interpretation, for example, may be extremely pertinent when it comes to describing readers who react positively to certain stories because of strong Oedipal pressures in their own lives. As the most exhaustive survey so far conducted on individual responses to literature finally concludes, 'A reader responds to a literary work by using it to re-create his own psychological processes.'[33] Those who try to claim their own interpretations of literature as appropriate for every reader, therefore, simply risk reproducing personal reactions under the guise of a universal literary truth. But it is also likely that particular interpretations will be highly relevant in the case of some readers, whilst also applying at a less urgent level to other readers who only retain vestiges of the same type of response within themselves.

All psychoanalytic interpretations of fairy-tales, however, have sometimes spoilt their case, by their penchant for overstatement, either for the merits of their particular theory, or for the whole psychological approach to fairy stories, as if to exclude the possibility of any other alternative or complementary explanations for their popularity. C.S. Lewis, himself steeped in fairy literature, was perhaps justifiably irritated by a typical example of this from Freud himself who once wrote, 'Does it not begin to dawn upon us that the many fairy-tales which begin with the words, "Once upon a time there were a king and a queen" simply mean "Once upon a time there were a father and mother"?'[34] As C.S. Lewis himself went on to point out, of course kings and queens may sometimes symbolise parents to a child, but they may also stand for power and exoticism — the palaces they live in, in some ways an excuse for the description of opulent detail. Their princes and princesses are usually beautiful, and the rest of the population properly respectful. It would not be surprising, therefore, that at a simple level of daydreaming, kings and queens, princes and princesses, may also be fantasy objects in more material respects.

This particular type of appeal seems to have little to do with family dynamics, but this only qualifies Freud's previous interpretation; it does not rule it out altogether. The imagination does not necessarily work in any unitary fashion; different appeals may register at different levels. Returning to *Little Red Riding Hood*, the forest — for Dr Bettelheim — is really our unconscious, where we expect to find crude, sometimes disturbing fantasies dressed up in the form of wild animals. But a forest can also be something that is frightening in its own right, whether it stands for the unconscious or not, just as children may be scared of large animals for quite realistic reasons, whatever else they may also possibly symbolise for them. Red Riding Hood's coloured cloak may have associations with puberty for some readers, but it also creates a powerful visual image — the red cloak in the dark forest — that over the years has appealed to numerous illustrators as well as to children looking at such pictures. The wolf in the bed, whatever else he may mean, also provides listeners with the delicious suspense that goes with any nursery rhyme or fairy story that ends on a sudden note of shout and grab, producing its usual chorus of terrified squeals and requests for more of the same.

The genius of fairy stories lies in the combination of this type of vivid, imaginative detail with those immemorial plots and themes, handed down over the generations, which touch on matters of eternal interest. Many fairy stories deal with human aspirations that seem reasonably common in most societies, such as the desire to win the prize and defeat the enemy, to test oneself and learn some vital lesson, or to ward off danger and achieve final security. These plots are peopled by figures who are usually nameless, stateless and often without strong individual characteristics, so that identification — for all readers — can be an easy matter. Some of the individual or family tensions that fairy stories seem to resolve in the imagination may indeed be of universal application. At other times, however, fairy stories illustrate visions of the world, and an individual's hopes and fears for his own future within it, which reflect cultural norms that are more parochial. In Western society, emphasis in fairy stories is often, though not always, on worldly success, where 'The rewards sought after are wealth, comfortable living and an ideal partner.'[35] Other cultures, however, may produce folk-tales which reflect a more fatalistic view of an individual's hopes of happiness within a hostile, less malleable environment. Writing about Andrew Lang's nineteenth-century selection of fairy-tales, for example, Matthew Hodgart declared that 'You could even have predicted the future from these stories.'[36] Tales chosen from East Europe, for example, with its unsettled history and tradition of political tyranny, tended to contain plots where everything seemed to go wrong most of the time, with danger still threatening at the end of each story. Selections from Scandinavia, on the other hand, although full of solid terrors always managed to end on a note of cosiness, with trolls safely turned into stone and no other peril in sight.

But despite this evidence of cultural diversity, there are also other compensatory fantasies in fairy stories that seem to be more or less universal. *Cinderella*, for example, is the classic story of the sudden reversal of fortune, and one Victorian scholar collected 345 variations on this basic plot throughout the world. The attraction of such plots, both in fairy stories and in popular novels over the centuries, has been described by John Buchan as the appeal of 'The survival of the Unfittest, the victory against odds of the unlikeliest people', with a ubiquity which reflects 'the incurable optimism of human nature'.[37] This seems overstated, however; the vicarious satisfaction provided by an optimistic story may be very different from a belief that such things will one day actually happen. Indeed, readers sometimes turn to this type of literature because it offers more rewards than they have come to expect from their real existence. Even young children, with the rest of their lives in front of them, will soon realise that their more extreme infantile fantasies of omnipotence are never going to come true. They can still enjoy these daydreams when they are reflected in fairy stories, however, where

Fantasies of omnipotence are and remain the dominating ones. Just where we have most humbly to bow before the forces of Nature, the fairy-tale comes to our aid with its typical motives. In reality we are weak, hence the heroes of fairy-tales are strong and unconquerable; in our activities and our knowledge we are cramped and hindered by time and space, hence in fairy-tales one is immortal, is in a hundred places at the same time, sees into the future and knows the past. The ponderousness, the solidity, and the impenetrability of matter obstruct our way every moment; in the fairy-tale, however, man has wings, his eyes pierce the walls, his magic wand opens all doors. Reality is a hard fight for existence; in the fairy-tale the words 'little table, be spread' are sufficient. A man may live in per-petual fear of attacks from dangerous beasts and fierce foes; in the fairy-tale a magic cap enables every transformation and makes us inaccessible. How hard it is in reality to attain love that can fulfil all our wishes! In the fairy-tale, the hero is irresistible, or he bewitches with a magic gesture. Thus the fairy-tale, through which grown-ups are so fond of relating to their children their own unfulfilled and repressed wishes, really brings the forfeited situation of omnipotence to a last, artistic presentation.[38]

This is to stress the compensatory nature of fairy-tale fantasy; other stories, however, may stimulate more philosophical, sometimes fatalistic insights into the human condition. While the unconscious fantasies that Freud claimed to have found in children may seem un-relievedly crude and violent, other schools of psychology have suggested a more positive aspect to unconscious wishes, reflected in the optimistic, heroic side of fairy stories. A case could also be made for fairy stories sometimes setting goals and suggesting aspirations rather than forever taking on the function of imaginative consolation. Heroic fantasy for one reader may provide an escape from the prob-lems of living; for another it may act as a positive inspiration. Reactions will depend on personality, prevailing attitudes and situ-ations in life. A story that describes a hero who triumphs over various obstacles may principally appeal to one reader because it appears to illustrate the resolution of an Oedipal situation; for another reader, for whom family conflicts may not be such an individual pre-occupation, the same story may appeal in quite different terms.

In this way, fairy stories act as a mirror wherein different members of an audience can see a vivid reflection of some of their deepest and most important areas of the imagination. At the same time, this mirror can also become a crystal ball, reflecting images which may offer a good fit to a reader's own future aspirations. The fact that individuals within this audience react in different ways is only to be expected; if fairy-story imagery is particularly powerful, it will naturally tend to get through to the most personal, private areas of any reader's imagination. Evidence for this type of variety in response has always been there. Hitler, for example, was enthusiastic about the Grimms' tales, seeing them as part of a Teutonic heritage teaching valuable lessons about bravery and the necessity of cruelty, although fairy-tale editions brought out by Nazi educators deliberately exaggerated such aspects in the original versions, including their occasional anti-semitism.[39] Dr Bettelheim, on the other hand, who was at one period imprisoned in a Nazi concentration camp, views the Grimms' stories as 'a priceless source of aesthetic pleasure and emotional and moral sustenance'. It would seem unlikely on the surface that both could be right, but once again fairy stories get through to different individuals in quite different ways, and even where one reader is concerned, they may convey more than one single meaning at a time. The imagination, once stimulated, is quite vast and complex enough to find a whole range of identifications within these stories, though possibly at different levels of consciousness and personal significance.

When children look at their own contemporary books it may occasionally be hard for them to find any adequate reflection in them of the more aggressive parts of their fantasy life. Stories about a few, fairly innocuously 'naughty' children are not enough, and one reason for turning to the knockabout humour and violence of comics may be because they go some way towards representing the more primitive aspects of a child's personality and imagination. Nursery rhymes and fairy stories, however, depict for a child a world that is sometimes savage and cruel. There are fairy stories, for example, where parents who are themselves starving to death abandon their children to wild animals as in *Hansel and Gretel*, or where within families, the struggle for power or for the father's inheritance may be brutal or murderous, as in the Grimms' story *The Singing Bone*. Outside the family, sudden death may alternate with torture as punishment for misdeeds or bad judgement, as with all those suitors who doom themselves by unsuccessfully putting in a bid for the princess's hand.

Thus, more than most other literature, fairy stories provide the child with the 'knowledge that he is born into a world of death, violence, wounds, adventure, heroism and cowardice, good and evil'.[40] Children will probably not yet know this to be true from their own experience, but this knowledge may still strike a chord within them, possibly even from memories of their own more violent fantasies and nightmares. It may also start providing them with some sort of mental preparation for those more violent aspects of adult society which they will soon also notice, for example by watching television news bulletins. In much children's literature, we often

95

prefer to portray a world that is lacking in any serious problems or dangers; if this is overdone, however, there may then be a risk of presenting a picture which, however safe, may eventually seem a little dull. Fairy-tales, on the other hand, offer a universe of imaginative extremes, where the hero may and generally does get his heart's desire, but sometimes only after running fairly terrifying risks. All this may be put forward in quasi-magical terms, which reflect a type of wish-fulfilment, and may also keep close to a child's own intellectual formulations at this stage. In many senses, therefore, the fairy-tale world is one of unique meaning to young readers, and as such, something always to be treasured.

4 · Early fiction (ages 7 – 11)

By now, children with experience of books may have learned to recognise the typical conventions of early fiction so that, for example, they will normally expect certain stereotyped characters to act in certain stock ways, and will feel cheated if popular heroes or heroines are not finally rewarded with happy conclusions to their various adventures.[1] This firm preference for the predictable is not really surprising for children still feeling their way through stories, and even so readers aged between six and eight years often continue to find it hard to have any idea how a stereotyped story will end, even when they have heard the first half of it.[2] This is a reminder that however predictable early, simple patterns and conventions in fiction may seem to adults, they may still come across to children as something new, to be learned about gradually through repetition of the same story or of other similar stories.

This early need for the safe and predictable can explain why small children sometimes disappoint ambitious parents by appearing to prefer writing that is full of clichés. Where fantasy is concerned, for example, Enid Blyton's stories about Noddy, an animated wooden doll living in a cosily suburban version of Toyland, are often as popular with infants as they are detested by adults. Here again, nothing very surprising happens in these stories, where the Golliwog is always naughty and Noddy regularly behaves like a perpetual innocent, but this is the type of trouble-free, fictional world where small children, never quite sure what may happen once a page has been turned, can soon relax and enjoy. There are also other attractions for children in these mini-adventures: for Enid Blyton herself, Noddy 'is like the children themselves, but more naive and stupid. Children like that — it makes them feel superior.'[3] What she did not point out, though, is that Noddy also generally receives far more praise than blame from other characters, and it is not at all unusual for a story to end with a virtual paean in favour of this 'clever little chap'. To this sort of praise, Noddy will often respond with one of his impromptu songs, again to general admiration, and then motor away to his own diminutive, cosy house. This other, more independent and competent side to Noddy can in turn act as fuel for children's lingering fantasies about the possibility of a similar type of existence for themselves, even though they may continue to laugh at him in other ways.

There are, however, other stories for the lower ranges of this age-group that remain within children's intellectual reach without descending to the same level of banality. A.A. Milne's Pooh stories, for example, continue the pleasant fantasy of an independent life in an animated toyland, punctuated by various enjoyable adventures and regular meals on demand, but again also show children — through the character of Pooh — how easy it sometimes is for an immature mind to misconstrue things. As Enid Blyton discovered, this is always a popular form of humour with readers, who often feel they are only just past that type of misapprehension themselves. As it is, Pooh's thought-processes, with their laborious step by step logic, their concentration upon food and creature comforts, their confusion between surface meanings and abstract ideas, as in the search for the *real* North Pole, and their frequent misunderstandings of adult phrases ('Crustimoney Proseedcake' for 'Customary Procedure') all recall the muddled, egocentric world of small children's thinking. Slightly older children, therefore, may understand the nature of this confusion quite well, even though they will miss a great deal of the more subtle adult humour in these stories. They may also, however, warm to the whole idea of a private, magical world, without any real danger and where Christopher Robin is a truly omnipotent, omniscient hero, always able to sort things out with maximum competence, and as such, another satisfying, flattering image of the child at this age.

The most famous fantasies ostensibly composed for children are of course Lewis Carroll's Alice books, which can sometimes rather frighten as well as amuse or intrigue younger readers. The loud weeping, tantrums and instant aggression in these stories, for example, may echo children's own infantile emotions, but more disturbingly here, since it is the adult characters like the Queen of Hearts or the Duchess, who are behaving in this generally out of control way. The more frightening experiences, too, such as falling down a deep hole, or growing too large for the space within which one is enclosed, also resemble personal nightmares or worrying fantasies. In his book *Some Versions of Pastoral*,[4] William Empson interprets the origin of these fears in terms of memories of the birth trauma, but whatever their possible source, their realisation in the Alice books makes a powerful impression.

Yet amidst the adult humour in these books, which young readers will not understand, Lewis Carroll also gets close to more childish aspects of thinking. Once again, his objects and animals have powers of thought and speech, and the puns over phrases like 'flower-beds' play with language at the literal level of a small child. Alice stands up to all the various would-be authoritarian figures in her adventures with a spirit that makes her a natural heroine for the young; her decision to abolish them at the end has the satisfying finality of a fairy-tale. Above all, her progress through the story, surrounded by adults asking impossible questions and answering her own objections with a bewildering absence of logic, parallels in part every child's experience of the long process of growing up. In this way, Alice herself is a spokesman for her young readers, battling her way through a story where the adult world often appears ridiculous and at the same time arbitrary and threatening, and so both comic and potentially disturbing.

Popular fiction for this age also often takes up children's common fantasy of an imaginary land existing parallel with the real one. Many children's writers have explored this idea, from Mrs Molesworth in *The Cuckoo Clock* and *The Tapestry Room* to Mary Norton's series about the Borrowers, a family of tiny people who live beneath the floorboards. Children, who may already have their own imaginary lands to escape into, usually enjoy the confirmation of this type of fantasy in print, themselves amused and sometimes relieved to discover that they are not the only ones to have had such notions. At the same time, these fictional models may help enrich and further populate some of the children's own personal, fantasy creations.

One of the most successful children's series incorporating an imaginary world was written by C.S. Lewis about the land of Narnia, first discovered when his child characters explore a wardrobe and find that the back of it gives on to an entirely new country. Here, the children meet talking trees, animals and fabulous beasts, all involved in an epic battle between good and evil — the sort of obvious, under-lined morality that young readers can readily understand. The author's own heavy-handed humour and prejudices may also be well within a child's grasp, such as all the fun had at the expense of 'very up to date' parents, who are 'vegetarians, non-smokers and tee-totallers and wore a special kind of under-clothes'. But the Christian doctrines of atonement and resurrection that Lewis also incorporated into these stories sometimes push the plot into directions that seem cruel and illogical. Even so, this has not affected the popularity with the young of these powerfully-realised books and it is only later, when the same readers are ready to start trying more complex epic writing, like the novels of Tolkien, that they may then begin to notice some of the flaws in Lewis's fiction.

Another appealing type of fantasy for this age-group is found in the animal story. Although children will generally be beyond the stage now of imagining that animals possess essentially human emotions and needs, this idea often persists at fantasy level in the same way as it does amongst many adult pet-owners. There are other ways, too, in which animal life in reality as well as in fiction appeals to the young; like children themselves, animals can also be small, vulnerable and inarticulate, as well as open and quite artless in their appetites and needs. For children, gradually learning to hold back some of their spontaneous emotions and generally coming to accept the mantle of socialisation, animals in real life — whether affection-ate, greedy, cowardly, aggressive or sensual — still offer a fascinating, even enviable picture of what may sometimes appear as a basically shameless and lusty instinctive life.

In fiction, therefore, readers can enjoy identifying with animal characters, just as children become fond of their own domestic pets. Animals in fiction may not behave in any particularly instinctive way, it is true, but their general mode of life provides an ever-interesting amalgam of the ways of both man and beast, as shown in the earlier section on Beatrix Potter's stories. Some fictional animals, for example, live in families alongside wives and children, but others are blissfully free from domestic responsibilities. Economically, ani-mal characters usually live casually off the land, leaving them with ample time for gossip, adventure and visiting each other in their neat little dwelling-places. Indeed, the gang life in animal stories is one of their most striking characteristics: within species, readers are often given the impression of the common purpose and sympathy that can make life so much easier and more attractive, and across species as well there may sometimes be friendships, courtship and marriage.

With so much on its side, therefore, it is not surprising that children have always been attracted by the animal story, even when its real point may have been quite above their heads. Young children, for example, taken up merely with the surface meaning of words, are not good at working out the particular significance of Aesop's fables, the Brer Rabbit stories or even much later, *Animal Farm*. But the idea of a mouse talking to a lion has its own fascination for children, whatever else it may be supposed to signify, especially if later on such a small insignificant animal is then able to help the traditional king of the beasts (in itself another example of how animals have so often been thought about and categorised in terms of purely human hierarchies).

Many older stories, therefore, have been popular with children simply because of their animal theme alone. Former favourites like Dorothy Kilner's *The Life and Perambulations of a Mouse*, for example, or A.L.O.E.'s *Rambles of a Rat*, written over a hundred years later in 1887, are not very entertaining in any other way, although even they were more lively than another one-time best-seller for children, Mrs Trimmer's *The History of the Robins*, published in 1786. Here, Pecksy, the young bird hero, is little more than a prig with wings. On offering his mother 'a fine fat spider', for example, he adds, 'Accept, my dear parent, the first tribute of gratitude which I have ever been able to offer you.' Even when this model son comes to a sticky end, shot by a small boy, he is still able to contribute one more moral exhortation, 'Oh, my dear father! Why did I not listen to your admonitions which I now find, too late, were the dictates of tenderness.' Many adults were later to remember this book as part of their favourite childhood reading, possibly because at the time there was such little competition, and also perhaps because of the fascination with the idea of talking, humanised robins, however pompous they turned out to be.

A far more approachable animal world was created by Kenneth Grahame in *The Wind in the Willows*, with characters like Toad who boast, lie, rage and weep with the emotional lability of a spoilt child. Mr Badger, on the other hand, is very much the gruff old bachelor, and between these two extremes Mole and Rat vary their behaviour, and even their physical shape, in accordance with the happenings of the moment. Toad does this too, of course; he is sometimes small enough to be tossed from a barge, but also quite able to make an albeit ineffectual attempt at washing the fat bargewoman's clothes. *The Times* originally dismissed this classic story with the memorable words, 'As a contribution to natural history, the work is negligible.' In fact, it describes a safe little bachelor world, in Kenneth Grahame's own phrase elsewhere, 'clean of the clash of sex',[5] where a serene leisured existence is threatened both from within and without. It is a world also governed by certain rules: animal etiquette, for example, demands that no one ever disturbs hibernation, except in a major crisis, or comments upon another animal's sudden disappearance in pursuit of its prey. Other fundamental rules are the more familiar ones about maintaining the social *status quo*; Toad, who challenges it by his wild behaviour, eventually pays the price — arrested and imprisoned by grotesque human forces and losing his property to the lower-order stoats and weasels of the Wild Wood, the other menace to this Edwardian, land-owning animal society. Readers can of course both identify with the spoilt, vainglorious Toad, revelling in his magnificently irresponsible behaviour, and also sympathise with his more sober, long-suffering friends. Both sets of characters represent the opposite poles of a child's imagination, from still surviving, infantile, egocentric fantasies of wilfulness to their more recent ideas of responsible, socialised behaviour. This double-edged appeal to the imagination has always been a familiar one: irresponsible rascals, who have finally to be put in their place, have made excellent characters ever since the advent of Mr Punch.

As Kenneth Grahame once wrote about his book to Teddy Roosevelt (nineteenth-century political leaders have a remarkable record for taking an interest in children's literature!), 'Its qualities, if any, are mostly negative — i.e. no problems, no sex, no second meanings — it is only an expression of the very simplest joys of life as lived by the simplest beings of a class that you are specially familiar with and will not misunderstand.'[6] In fact, that assessment — though understated — is quite a good summing up of this novel's appeal. *The Wind in the Willows* does indeed provide an excellent, beautifully-written rural escape both from the pressures of an industrial society and also, as Grahame hints, from some domestic realities as well. Himself a lonely, badger-like figure, unhappily married and disliking his London job in contrast to the pleasures of the countryside or solitary, 'messing about in boats', he offers in his book a back to nature, anti-contemporary idyll, rejecting both modern technology — the dreaded motorcar — and the pompous spokesmen for such a society, summed up in his caricatures of judges and barristers. The appearance of the great God Pan is unconvincing in this context, and can easily be skipped altogether, as generations of child readers have discovered. In fact, there is little that is at all instinctive or pagan in this story, whose author seemed to prefer a safer, more tranquil kind of alternative to modern living — a return to a traditional rural society where everyone knew their place in the best of possible worlds.

This sense of settled, social harmony may have its attractions for many readers, but particularly so for children, who find it easier to make sense of their environment by seeing it in terms of firm rules and hierarchies. At the same time, they may have a half-admiring, half-admonitory attitude towards anyone who dares to threaten this order, by way of naughty rather than wicked behaviour. Mischievous, good-hearted characters like Toad can always be brought back into line after they have had their fling, however, though the same audience may also feel that the really evil should be more firmly punished. But while there are some tough battles in this novel, there are no deaths, though the moments of fear and panic are real enough, with the Wild Wood a genuinely terrifying place — simply traversing it in the imagination will be test enough for many children. In other, more gentle ways, the attraction of this book for children is probably not so different from its continual appeal to adults, with its pleasant, Arcadian picture of a life made up of river-trips, picnics, unlimited money and leisure, no boring domestic responsibilities, charming little houses, and delightful moments when pompous authority is put to flight, with Toad a worthy successor and at times a conscious imitation of Shakespeare's Falstaff.[7]

Few animal fairy-tales since have had this success with all ages, though Hugh Lofting, in his *Dr Dolittle* series, always denied writing down to his audience, just as he disputed divisions between adult and children's literature, suggesting 'senile' as the true alternative to 'juvenile' stories. But although his vision of talking animals and a cosy, all-together domesticity has retained some of its former popularity with children, his books have dated in other ways. The insensitive humour wrung from Prince Bumpo's desire to change his colour from black to white in *The Story of Dr Dolittle*, for example, now seems most offensive.

Other critics, however, have always protested from time to time against all animal fairy tales on the grounds that since well-dressed animals who exchange human conversation do not exist, this mendacious picture should not therefore be suggested to still impressionable minds. Deborah Shields Tully, for example, writing in an

American teachers' magazine with a lack of humour not unknown in the critical discussion of children's literature, complains that in an otherwise well-written book, *The Sea Pair*,[8] the author states that a female otter 'knows' that she is about to have her very last pup. But of course, 'Mammals cannot remember how many pups they have had in the past or know that they could or could not have more in the future. Their off-spring are not the result of a conscious act of procreation.' Again, a novel called *Forest Folk*,[9] about a colony of deer, includes another heretical sentence, 'He is now king of the forest, as he had always hoped he might be, one day.' But

Deer do not feel hope or remember past events in their lives or search out specific rivals ... Some writers even go so far as to refer to the pair as Mr and Mrs, denoting a lasting relationship between animals where pair bonds last only one season, if that long ... children are also led to believe that domestic dogs and cats (the most promiscuous species around) mate for life ... Parent animals do not attempt to divide the food evenly in fairness to all their young ... So the reader finds ... an enormity of misinformation and over-characterisation.[10]

This sort of criticism, however, surely misses the point. Children at a certain stage will imagine animal life in humanised terms, whether ethologically-minded critics approve of their so doing or not. Stories that take up this fantasy simply reflect rather than inculcate this way of thinking. It would be different, perhaps, if humanised animal stories were the only source of information children could turn to about wild life, but this is not so.

Perhaps the most typical sort of reading for this age-group, how-ever, is the heady world of domestic adventure, usually set in an ostensibly recognisable world of reality, but otherwise fuelled by unreal fantasies. These adventures often involve heroic children who act effectively without any real adult help or supervision at all, and such daydreams of independence have obvious attractions. As it is, children will now have got past the stage when they think that their parents are themselves more or less omnipotent and at the centre of the universe. Instead, in Piaget's words, 'As the child grows older, his respect for the superiority of the adult diminishes or at least alters in character. The adult ceases to represent unquestioned or even un-questionable Truth and interrogation becomes discussion.'[11] Corres-pondingly the parental attitude towards a three year old and later a nine year old often shows some decrease in warmth and understand-ing, as lovable infant is replaced by occasionally argumentative pre-teenager.

One result of all this is that children may often develop a particular attitude, described by the American psychologist David Elkind as 'cognitive conceit', which is both an extension and also a refinement of earlier infantile fantasies of omnipotence. At this stage, children who are discovering that they too can sometimes argue things out for themselves may also get the idea that this makes them the equal or even the superior of adults when it comes to tackling most problems and situations. But however intelligent children may be, they will usually lack the experience that will also help inform an adult's judgement. If children at this age are sometimes disappointed by the results of their independent actions in real life, they can always turn to child heroes or heroines in favourite stories who are regularly shown overcoming the most formidable obstacles with very little trouble. For David Elkind, once again, 'Children's literature abounds in evidence of the cognitive conceit of children. Whether it is *Emil and the Detectives*, or *Tom Sawyer* ... or *Alice in Wonderland* in each story adults are outwitted and made to look like fools by children.'[12]

The same type of appeal can also be found in many of the children's books written by Enid Blyton, a perennial best-seller for this age-group, and as such worth considering in some detail. Although her Noddy books are popular with younger children, her particular strength has always been with readers aged seven to eleven, at the first stages of starting to read simple novels right through for themselves. Books for these children should normally possess simple vocabularies, short sentences and clear, concrete plots, since children's concentration span and powers of abstract reasoning will still be limited. Many authors have written for this younger readership, but Enid Blyton stands out because of her truly massive appeal during her own lifetime, which still shows few signs of diminishing, given the large sales her books continue to enjoy, and the fact that some of her stories have been made into a popular adventure series for children's television. At her peak she was writing one novel each week, so giving rise to the baseless rumour that she employed other writers to share some of her work. Taken together, her books offer a good illustration of what children at this stage easily understand and enjoy, but also what they must eventually grow away from, and older readers often find themselves looking back upon their one-time pleasure in her works with mixed feelings. But for those earlier ages the author identified so closely with the needs and outlook of her

105

young readers that it was sometimes said that if children were capable of writing novels, they would write like Enid Blyton.

Certainly, everything is always made gratifyingly easy in her books. The vocabulary tends to be as repetitive as the plots, and even simple notions may be buttressed to convey their meaning twice over, as in ' "Good", said Anne, pleased', or ' "Really?" said Dick, interested.' Settings for these stories are almost always placed in the countryside — quickly suggested in a few clichés, peopled by main characters who are shallow and stereotyped. Each may have one clearly distinguishing characteristic, though, such as an uncanny power to tame animals, a liking for crude practical jokes, or excessive nervousness in the face of danger. Once established, however, they sail through their adventure stories, untroubled by introspection, moral dilemma — and perhaps most importantly, by any reasonable sense of reality.

One result of this simplification is that Blyton stories can move at a truly spanking pace. As a young fan once wrote for a student's project on this topic, 'She makes books that you have to read all the way through because some people would skip a chapter and the story would still make sense but with her books if you miss a page or a chapter you cannot follow them.' Once started a Blyton story usually takes a child by the hand — an image she often liked to use herself, when asked to explain her popularity — and then leads the young reader without faltering from one stock situation to another, described in an equally stock vocabulary.

In many ways, her books never move far from children's own, egocentric, quasi-magical views about life. In *The Folk of the Faraway Tree*, or *The Magic Walking Stick*, for example, where a pixie is chased and punished by a stick whenever he tells tales, there is as much magic as in any fairy story. In later adventure stories for older readers magic is still present, though hidden under the surface appearance of reality. This often makes her books seem extremely childish, but it may account for some of her continuing appeal. For example, however tough the country, there will be no real obstacles to the physical feats her adventurous young heroes decide to perform: boats are rowed effortlessly across choppy seas, mountains climbed, and underground passages explored without the difficulties of everyday life, just as crooks are regularly rounded up and handed over to the police, however improbably. As one critic wrote, reviewing *The Sea of Adventure*, 'What hope has a band of desperate men against four children?'

106

The coincidences, strokes of luck and unlikely adult behaviour that help sustain these impossible stories are also reminiscent of typically childish daydreams; and Enid Blyton's fictional pets, too, tend to be fantasy objects, usually with the most extraordinary intelligence. Unless they are parrots, who always manage to say the appropriate thing at exactly the right time, the Blyton menagerie while not actually talking, still shares its young masters' or mistresses' lives in the fullest sense. Monkeys, dogs and ponies are often quite capable of taking messages, identifying villains, and — like their young owners — ultimately proving too much for any threatening adult who comes their way.

Even when children become more sceptical about such possibilities in real life, this benign, malleable, ever-adventurous universe can still remain a popular setting for fantasy, perhaps to be indulged in during those 'continued stories' that the majority of children make up for themselves in bed before drifting off to sleep.[13] At whatever level of literal belief or romantic daydream, however, Enid Blyton always gave children a world they could both understand and sympathise with. Her views on morals, for example, were strict. In her autobiography she describes some swans nesting in her pond who were stoned by boys. 'I think both those boys should have been well and truly whipped, don't you? There are just a few things that I think whipping should be the punishment for, and cruelty to animals or birds is one of them. I know you will agree with me in that.'[14]

Almost certainly, most young children will. They believe in a strict moral code, as yet untroubled by those irritating complexities that can sometimes make both simple black and white judgements, and a belief in the efficacy of harsh punishment as an answer to all bad behaviour, increasingly hard to maintain. For children, and apparently Enid Blyton, even the possibility of extenuating circumstances or of a more subtle approach, would seem irrelevant: bad children are bad, and must be treated as such. As she wrote elsewhere:

Children's writers have definite responsibilities towards their young public. For this reason they should be certain always that their stories have sound morals — children *like* them. Right should always be right, and wrong should be wrong, the hero should be rewarded, the villain punished.[15]

This view undoubtedly makes it much simpler to write melodramatic adventure stories. The bad make no demands upon the reader's sympathy, and obligingly behave and dress according to their moral labels, which in Enid Blyton's case usually meant conforming to a particular stereotype of evil, viewed through middle-class eyes, such as the 'rough gypsy' or cockney crook. The good, on the other hand, are equally self-evidently all right, protected by a moral and social order that always ensures their surviving to a happy ending. This could be said of much romantic fiction, but in Enid Blyton's work, this excessively simple world picture is carried to extremes.

She also provides numerous examples in her fiction of the type of 'cognitive conceit' already discussed that helps fuel children's fantasies of super-competence at this age. In her *Famous Five* adventure stories, for example, parents are usually more than willing to give their children a free hand, and a typical story will end with a chorus of trusting adults returning to express wonder and gratitude at the skill of their offspring in solving mysteries that have baffled everyone else. Those adults who stay around to get in the way, however, are portrayed as beings hardly more competent or threatening than rather unpleasant overgrown children. One such adult, a villain characteristically named Ebenezer (soon shortened by the Five to 'Ebby') at one time becomes irritated with these superior children, and tries to frighten them off. Accordingly, 'He determined to follow the little company, and made rude remarks all the time. So he tailed them, and shouted at them from a safe distance.'[16] But it is not always villains who are infantilised. One particular enemy of the Famous Five is Mr Goon, the frog-eyed policeman, who is continually foiled by the superior intelligence and forensic skill of his young rivals. As he is shown to be stupid and pompous, no one — least of all the author — questions the cruelty with which he is teased, or ever displays any compassion for him during the final humiliation he is always made to suffer when dressed down by his Detective Inspector — in this case a particular friend and social equal of the Famous Five.

Children from another Blyton gang also have a habit of doing everything for themselves, in this case the Secret Seven, a group sensitively abbreviated by Miss Blyton to the initials SS, and whose first adventures appeared only four years after the end of the Second World War. Indeed, at school, 'All the Secret Seven wore their little badges with SS embroidered on the button. It was fun to see the other children looking enviously at them wishing they could have one too.'[17] These children are even younger than the Famous Five, but this does not discourage them from indulging themselves in the same type of fantasy of super-competence. For example:

It suddenly dawned on the Seven that there must be quite a big gang engaged in this particular robbery. 'I think we ought to tell somebody,' said Pam. Peter shook his head. 'No. Let's find out more if we can.'[18]

Later, they get into trouble with the local constable, with whom they as usual refuse to cooperate, but this is taken very lightly by all except one of them: ' "Look at Barbara crying over a policeman taking her name and address! What use would *she* be on an evening with dangerous things going on?" '[19]

It is interesting how an author as establishment-minded as Enid Blyton could also have gone along so easily with this intermittent contempt for various representatives of law and order. Her own snobbery, however, was always very evident in her writing, and comes out strongly in the way her well-heeled child heroes are made to behave patronisingly towards certain working-class characters, including policemen. In the same way, properly humble working folk are often made to address the young adventurers as 'Young master' or 'Young sir', and a Welsh guide, with monotonously comic English is written off by the public-school Jack as 'A poor stick . . . not much brain.'[20] This type of snobbery may appeal to all children who enjoy reversing roles in fantasy, when they themselves, or those with whom they identify in fiction, can feel superior to certain adult characters who would normally be daunting in real life. It is not only middle-class children who recognise something of themselves in typical Blyton child heroes, as is sometimes argued. What she describes in her books is not a twentieth-century social reality, but a type of general and occasionally anti-adult fantasy world, which still appeals to child readers from all social classes.

Nearer home, Enid Blyton also provided readers with fictional parents who must sometimes be successfully defied. A continual sub-plot in the 'Famous Five' stories is the rivalry between Georgina, the girl who always wants to be taken for a boy, and her father, known to the others as Uncle Quentin, a scientist unwise enough to try working in a house full of children. And so, ' "What's all this noise? Can't we have a moment's peace?" ',[21] and Uncle Quentin is on the rampage again, providing me at least, when I first read these books as a child, with a far more fearsome object than any of the stop-at-nothing crooks who appear later. Georgina usually answers back, and on this occasion, her pet monkey gratifyingly showers her father with handfuls of raisins. Nice parents, on the other hand, tend to depart early on, as otherwise they would be bound to interfere, even in stories as unlikely as these, thus challenging the freedom of the child characters to do everything their own way so successfully. In *Six Cousins Again*, however, there is a different type of parental conflict when the children of the marriage are required to choose between their pretty, spoilt mother and her long-suffering, farmer husband. But in the end, with a few tears and promises to behave better in the future, especially over the matter of new dresses, the mother agrees to stay. Once again, Enid Blyton portrays a very childish adult who can therefore easily be patronised, both by the children in the book and by young readers enjoying all this and perhaps paying off a few family scores in their own imagination.

Blyton children also often have some surprisingly impressive possessions. Georgina, for example, owns her own island, while Tinker, a friend of the gang, goes even better: 'How very, very proud he was of his light-house!'[22] Somewhat unsportingly, this same character at one stage says to the androgynous Georgina ('George' for short),

'I bet *you* wish you had a light-house of your own, George.'

'Well, yes I do', said George, gazing up at the towering light-house, now so near to them.'[23]

Psychoanalysts have yet to analyse the treasure-trove of Enid Blyton's fantasy world, but when they do it will be hard to resist interpreting symbolism like this, where Tinker's most treasured possession even puts Jack's bean-stalk into the shade.

This basic theme of children having everything their own way, however unlikely, is developed in every area of the plot. As well as having super-intelligent pets, for example, Enid Blyton's characters also have ways of communicating with them denied to other mortals:

He made a curious little bleating noise, and all the goats looked round and stopped eating. The kid pricked up its little white ears, and stood quivering on its slender legs. It was very young and new. Philip made the noise again. The kid left its mother and came leaping to him. It sprang into his arms and nestled there, butting its soft white head against Philip's chin ... It was amazing the attraction that Philip had for creatures of any kind. Even a moth would rest contentedly on his finger.[24]

Although the Famous Five range in age from twelve to seventeen years old, there is never any sexual attraction between them to slow down the action and bore pre-adolescent readers. But children may still have a very sensual side to them, and this too finds its expression in Blyton books. There is, for example, a great deal of animal cuddling and affection in her stories; in one, for example, Snowy (the kid) sleeps on top of Philip, and Timmy (the dog) shares a space with 'George', 'occasionally licking her ear with his big tongue'.

' "*Dear* Timmy!" said George, sleepily, " I love you — but do please keep your tongue to yourself!" '[25]

Again, most of her stories include lavish descriptions of food, and once more Enid Blyton shows how close she could get to childish ideas of pleasure. Apart from the cakes and cream-buns that also appear in children's comics, there may be hurriedly put-together dishes for exciting picnics, with sausages, fried eggs, honey and jam eaten all at once. Such a meal may be nauseating to adult taste, but just the sort of thing a smaller child might like, and comparable, perhaps, to Lewis Carroll's description of a 'very nice' drink in *Alice in Wonderland*: 'A sort of mixed flavour of cherry-tart, custard, pineapple, roast turkey, toffy and hot buttered toast.' In fact, an orgy of eating occurs at some stage in most of Enid Blyton's books — one more pleasant fantasy to add to the effortless adventures of this idealised group of children. The closeness of typical Blyton gangs is another popular daydream put into print for young readers, who may sometimes turn to books as a substitute for play with real children. Even if readers have plenty of friends, their own gangs will never form such friendly, positive and cohesive groups as in a Blyton story. Because her child characters tend to be so faceless, a reader can easily identify with any one of them or indeed with the whole group. There is a general longing for social inclusion during this age, whether as one of a pair of twins — another popular fantasy that Enid Blyton also takes up on occasions — or else as a member of an idealised gang, without any of the tensions or difficulties of peer-group relationships in real life.

In response to such appealing, fictional fantasies, children have made Enid Blyton into one of the most popular authors in the world, where she is third in the list of Britain's most translated writers, beaten only by Shakespeare and Agatha Christie. Although she was a teacher, and wrote successful books on natural history for primary-school pupils as well as many articles on infant education, she seldom preaches at children in her stories, which are almost all plot, conveyed largely through dialogue. Other authors have tried such a formula, but none have succeeded to the same extent. As a child, Enid Blyton had often consoled herself by her habit of making up imaginary, romantic stories, and as an adult writer she still seemed able to recapture the essence of these childish daydreams with ease and a rare accuracy. When questioned, she would insist, quite sincerely, that she never knew quite what she was going to write; it was just a matter of sitting down at the typewriter and letting it all come pouring out, unchecked by second thoughts or literary finesse. As she always had complete confidence in what she was doing, she never felt the necessity for self-criticism, and rejected it from other quarters with scorn. In her own words, she wrote for children because 'I love them and understand them, and know exactly what they want.'[26] In later life, writing became something of an addiction; without it, she once complained, her thoughts kept 'closing in' on her.[27] Elsewhere, she sometimes insisted upon preserving a type of fantasy world for outward appearances, denying, for example, that a favourite dog had died until long after the event, and continuing to idealise her first marriage in print when the relationship had become very strained.

No writer's appeal can ever be explained totally in terms of their own personal psychology, however, and as well as being a compulsive chronicler of infantile fantasies, Enid Blyton was an extraordinarily hard worker and also, in her way, a skilled literary craftswoman who knew how to get through to children. This she learned not simply by writing prodigious amounts for them, but also through being concerned with infant education over many years.

In this sense, Enid Blyton remains a very positive person for the young. In her prose, she offers them a pleasant, easily comprehensible world, where children are always heroes, occupying themselves with the sort of things they would like to do if they had the chance and ability. In all her stories, too, there is a belief in the goodness and competence of children, whether as characters in her fiction or as members of her huge audience. This was not just a matter of writing pleasant, flattering books for young readers; in her lifetime she was also constantly putting real children to work, whether getting them to organise blanket collections for charity or write letters to town children telling them about life in the country. The various clubs she formed — Busy Bee (Enid Blyton the Queen Bee, of course); Pug Pup (Pick up Glass, Pick up Paper Society); or Sunbeam Society — were highly successful: children *did* cheerfully set to work, money *did* flow in, and good results *did* materialise. Children could also join the 'Famous Five' club, complete with badge, newsletter and secret sign, and so feel even closer to that charmed, sociable group of adventurers. The accompanying letter from the author would be warm and direct, assuring a new member of her friendship, and she would be equally assured of her young fan's positive response. 'Everyone loves Enid Blyton', one slogan used to go, and for certain ages this was largely true, both for the good images she offered children of themselves in her books and in real life as well.

Some of her ideas about education, too, were strikingly child-centred for her times. For example, she constantly used to advise teachers to encourage pupils to find things out for themselves, well before this became the general fashion, and her own handbooks for children, also written in this spirit, still read well, especially on her favourite topic of the countryside. She was, in all, someone who got on very well with children, at least in the abstract, giving them what they appeared to want in her books, warmly answering most of their letters with her incredible industry, narrating her own stories on various public occasions with marked success, and sometimes putting all these gifts of communication to practical effect in her clubs and various occasional schemes. Whether as competent book-readers, potential heroes by identification, club-members or active students of nature, the image of childhood she presented to her readers was in many ways both purposive and optimistic. Those who so often criticise her without recognising this do her an injustice.

Her final positive achievement was to offer children long stories they could actually read and understand for themselves. As it is, a novel is in many ways a daunting prospect for the very young reader. This is not just a question of vocabulary and sentence length; the ability to piece together cause and effect, or remember which character is which and who has already done what, can all be real problems for limited concentration and reading skills, as we have already seen. But a Blyton book, apart from dealing with very popular action put into practice by heroic child characters, is also an exercise in professional writing skill, forging ahead in an ecstasy of action, with frequent exclamation marks, italics, capital letters and asides from the author herself, all making obvious points even clearer, and nudging the reader into an appropriate response. The clichés, stereotyped plots and stock, unimaginative characters in her stories, although sometimes boring for older children, may be just those short-cuts towards immediate comprehension that immature, unpractised readers are grateful for. When one book was finished, there would always be more in the familiar mould for children to choose from. Blyton fans, therefore, could feel doubly competent, both by identifying with the ever-successful child detectives in her novels, and also

113

because of their own accomplishment as readers in getting through the books in the first place. At the same time, children would also be able to derive the emotional and intellectual satisfaction from Blyton mystery stories that adults later receive from detective novels, with red herrings cast aside, clues followed back to true culprits, and a final dénouement that tidies up every loose end — all at a level of deduction easy enough for a younger child to understand.

Enid Blyton is, then, sometimes a far more skilful writer for children than she has been given credit for. She had a good sense of literary suspense; although the excitement and happy endings of her novels are always predictable, the details in between are not, and for a time can keep even an older reader guessing. While her characters are mostly very dull, Georgina — with whom she identified — is rather different, a really tough individual, and a good representative of the unsocialised, egocentric child that most readers will admire without daring to emulate in their own lives. Her presence usually introduced a certain tension into the blandest of plots, and her implicit protest against the fluttering femininity of the other girl characters was as valid then as it is now at a time of heightened awareness about sexual stereotyping. This is something to remember when Enid Blyton is criticised for her excessive conservatism; members of the Women's Movement today have sometimes spoken of the effect Georgina had upon them as child readers, far outweighing the feeble example set by the other female members of the various gangs. *Five go to Mystery Moor*, in fact, goes even further with two androgynous heroines: 'George' and 'Henry', short for Henrietta. Blanket condemnation of Enid Blyton often overlooks such points; even her so-called 'limited vocabulary' has been exaggerated by her critics. In the last ten pages of *The Mystery of the Spiteful Letters*, for example, one can find 'righteous', 'mystification', 'reprimanded', 'courteous', 'anonymous' and 'deduction' — hardly an over-adventurous vocabulary, but certainly not the baby-talk that critics have sometimes suggested.

When it comes to action, her writing can still take on the hectic pace and suggestion of pleasurable fear also found in popular adult best-sellers. When 'George' was caught by the usual gypsy-villains, 'She kicked and fought and wriggled and struggled. She was held in a grip like iron. She heard Anne scream once, and knew that she was caught too.'[28] Encounters with evil scientists out for world domination again anticipate adult thrillers when — for example, the children discover a hidden laboratory in the middle of a mountain, manned by Japanese in the business of extracting uranium. The laboratory had

A vast network of gleaming wires, great glass jars standing together, crystal boxes in which sparks and flames shot up and down, and rows upon rows of silently spinning wheels that shone queerly as they spun. The wires ran from there all over the place ... The great lamp in the middle suddenly grew bright, so bright that the children crouched back afraid. It grew crimson, the brightest crimson they had ever seen in their lives. It began to belch out tiny puffs of crimson smoke.[29]

It is interesting that adults who dislike children reading this sort of thing usually complain less about grown-up taste for similar material in novels like Ian Fleming's *Dr No*. But then, there has always been a type of Puritan objection to the idea of too much undemanding enjoyment in the lives of the young, whether in literature or elsewhere. Children, it is sometimes argued, must learn that life is not all pleasure. Any situation, therefore, that allows them to luxuriate in unthinking, infantile enjoyment for lengthy periods, with no accompanying hint of self-improvement or education, can make some critics very uneasy. For one thing, they themselves as adults may long since have suppressed their own unbridled infantile fantasies. The spectacle of children still enjoying the same things, therefore, unchecked or actually encouraged by other, possibly renegade adults, may cause not only uneasiness but even perhaps a type of unconscious envy. There may also be another reason for this sort of adult anxiety. 'The world-wide fraternity of children', it has been said, 'is the greatest of savage tribes, and the only one which shows no sign of dying out.'[30] Some adults find this potentially primitive side to childhood very alarming, seeing children as beings constantly about to revert to barbarism unless they are firmly controlled. Nursery rhymes in the past, and comics or best-selling authors like Enid Blyton today who may seem to side with children instead of always setting them good, mature examples, may again appear positively dangerous to such critics, to be discouraged or even banned whenever possible.

This is not to say that all adult criticism of Enid Blyton is based on fear or envy; yet some extra explanation seems needed to account for the degree of hostility she has always provoked. In fact, children can be their own best judges of when this type of writing begins to pall, and literature that caters only for the immaturity of its audience can ultimately seem as embarrassing or irritating to the young as

115

those family friends who never want them to grow up, and are forever trying to fob them off with soft answers to important questions.
Most children's writers offer their audience unreal fantasy at some
stage, of course, but in Blyton books the separation from reality is at
its most extreme. Elsewhere, she often sides with children against
even the possibility of their ever taking on more adult attitudes;
something that may seem comfortably reassuring to younger readers,
but which later can look crude and philistine. From *Six Cousins
Again*, for example: 'Cyril had been rather silly, lately, Roddy considered — spouting poetry again, and going on about the wonderful
music on the Third Programme. Roddy didn't care about the Third
Programme. There was never anything funny or exciting on it.'

Children will eventually revolt against being addressed in these
patronising tones, just as one day they may no longer be able to
believe in other aspects of Enid Blyton's fantasy world. A teacher
once told me that only after an experience of real camping, including
water leaking through the bottom of the tent, did her pupils finally
reject the serene, trouble-free world of a typical Blyton out-of-doors
holiday. In future, such pupils may only enjoy a Blyton book for
odd, regressive moments rather than for habitual reading; as a fifteen-
year-old schoolgirl once said, 'I enjoy reading Enid Blyton before
exams, because you don't have to think much.' But others may turn
against her almost as extremely as they once relished her books; in a
reading survey I was concerned with, it was common to find Enid
Blyton as both favourite and least favourite author, according to
age.[31] For most older children, her books will come to be seen as
literature that treats them as if they were infants, sharing and
encouraging immature fantasies and misconceptions, but with none
of the energy of a nursery rhyme, the irony of a Beatrix Potter, or
the variety, aesthetic balance and potent symbolism of a fairy-tale.

Other literature for children can sometimes reveal new perspectives
when read again in later years; Enid Blyton, however, creates an
encapsulated world for young readers that simply dissolves with age,
leaving behind only memories of excitement and strong identification.
Her novels may still sometimes be found side by side with 'O' level
literature texts by a child's bedside, but like fizzy drinks and sticky
food, they are a taste that older children may increasingly only feel
like satisfying at odd moments of stress or boredom.

A different and more lively best-selling literature for this age was
provided by Richmal Crompton, like Enid Blyton another ex-teacher.

Her famous character William Brown began life in stories addressed
to adults, rather in the manner of Saki, another contemporary writer
who occasionally took advantage of the public's reaction against
previous over-sentimental views of children in fiction. This more
caustic approach can also be found in Kenneth Grahame's *Dream
Days*, where child characters scorn adults' distant, generally uninformed ideas about them, as in Kipling's *Stalky & Co*. It was later
sustained by the gallows humour of Belloc's *Cautionary Tales*, Harry
Graham's popular *Ruthless Rhymes*, which read very like today's
sick jokes, and finally by Miss Crompton herself. One of the favourite
techniques in this sort of humour is to exaggerate the untamed,
potentially destructive nature of childhood; in William books this
leads to numerous comic set-pieces, but it also provided child readers
with a picture of themselves which was again in some ways pleasantly
flattering. There is something awesome about a child character who
can pose such a threat to normally domineering adults, and William
— according to his creator — was indeed 'a little savage'; someone she
would never herself want around the house. In the stories, he is the
enemy of all authority, from parents to policemen, school teachers,
vicars and organising ladies. According to one William fan, this makes
him into 'a natural anarchist. He believed in no rule but the rule of
dirt. Unlike Arthur Ransome's books, which are careful adult propaganda, encouraging Gordonstoun initiative and well-planned explorers'
diets, Richmal Crompton's William stories are pure revolutionary
documents, preaching sedition and gob-stoppers.'[32]

It is certainly true that in many ways William is very much like a
personification of the unsocialised, individual within all readers, but
much nearer the surface in a child. In this way, he exhibits behaviour
no normal child could expect to get away with, but which is fun to
read about. As a small child 'he had invariably answered "Villum"
when asked whom he loved best in the world', but despite never
losing this egocentricity, much of the trouble he causes is in fact
through trying to help, rather than hinder. In this sense, the joke is
often as much on him as anyone else — hardly the treatment usually
accorded to a revolutionary leader.

In fact, William is quite a complex individual. He scorns some girls,
but falls heavily in love with others. He is a natural focus for social
activity and a permanent gang leader, but also enjoys long periods of
solitude and an active fantasy life, whether poring over books or
simply daydreaming. Sometimes he ends a story in disgrace, but at

other times — having unwittingly caught a burglar, perhaps, or forced an unwelcome aunt or uncle to cut short their stay — he then becomes the family hero. He adores his pet dog, but is not beyond tormenting stray cats, poisoning one with a sleeping draught, and accidentally killing another with his air-gun, recalling some of the similarly offhand callous behaviour towards animals found in Kipling's schoolboys in *Stalky & Co*.

Whether he is acting out of mischief or misplaced altruism, however, William's ideas of grandeur, his constant greed, open stealing and rivalry with every other member of his family, apart perhaps from his mother, are very reminiscent of the unsocialised behaviour of a spoilt infant. This type of personality may especially appeal to slightly older readers who are growing out of this lawless stage themselves, but are still fascinated by and perhaps slightly nostalgic for it. When William gives presents to others — for example one Christmas he offers his father 'a bottle of highly-coloured sweets', and his nineteen-year-old sister a box of chalks — these are often things that he really wants for himself, something usually found at earlier stages of development where children, disarmingly oblivious to the possibility that another person may have quite different tastes to their own, sometimes offer them toys or a half-sucked sweet as gifts.

This celebration of the untamed, instinctive child is accompanied by a comic and destructive view of adults in authority. Children who increasingly have to accept adult control in their own lives often enjoy this type of social iconoclasm in their fiction. Mr Brown, William's father, is adult authority incarnate: confiscating favourite toys, prohibiting noise and grimly watchful over his domestic empire. He and William have no illusions about each other, and although William never plots against him directly, his father's periodic collapses of dignity, whether slipping over on a rice-pudding or finding himself locked in a coal-cellar, are always due to the activities of his younger son. Such basic conflict in the father—son relationship offers readers a good chance to pay off any lingering Oedipal grudges of their own, but through the safety-valve of fantasy, and Mr Brown is only one of a long line of father or father-figures in children's fiction who are regularly cut down in their pride. A similar kind of warfare is maintained against any other adult who offends William, or even worse, tries to improve him, from pompous uncles and religious-minded aunts to pacifists, Fabians, or any other would-be promoters of higher thought. Typically, the men with whom William does get on well are slightly broken-down characters who pose no threat to his own rampant individuality, such as out-of-luck Punch and Judy men or inefficient sweet-shop managers. His older brother and sister, Robert and Ethel, also suffer from deliberately engineered mischief, as victims of the sibling rivalry that again often finds expression in popular children's fiction. The same aggressive treatment is accorded to children whom William sees as having defected to the enemy camp of the adult world, as far as 'good' behaviour and 'correct' social attitudes are concerned, and who receive all the loathing so often reserved for any traditional goody-goody or teacher's pet, although William does have a soft spot for certain very beautiful, well-mannered little girls. But rough, lively children, whether from William's own gang, well-named 'The Outlaws', or drawn from the whole, socially outcast world of travelling circus or gypsy camp, win his full approval.

William becomes entangled in some fairly routine plots, revolving around mistaken identities, good deeds that turn sour, and social functions that culminate in disaster. As well as planning the obvious downfall of adult authority, however, William is often involved in something more subtle. His very egocentricity, and accompanying lack of social awareness, can result in the exposure of adult hypocrisy, very much as in Hans Andersen's *The Emperor's New Clothes*. Take William and Christmas presents, for example:

'It's very kind of you,' said Aunt Emma still struggling with the string. 'It's not kind,' said William still treading doggedly the path of truth. 'Mother said I'd got to bring you something.' Mrs Brown coughed suddenly and loudly but not in time to drown the fatal words of truth.

'But still — er — very kind,' said Aunt Emma though with less enthusiasm. At last she brought out a small pincushion.

'Thank you very much, William,' she said. 'You really oughtn't to have spent your money on me like this.'

'I din't,' said William stonily. 'I hadn't any money, but I'm very glad you like it. It was left over from Mother's stall at the Sale of Work, an' Mother said it was no use keepin' it for nex' year because it had got so faded.'

Again Mrs Brown coughed loudly but too late. Aunt Emma said coldly: 'I see. Yes. Your mother was quite right. But thank you all the same, William.'

Uncle Frederick had now taken the wrappings from his present and held up a leather purse.

'Ah, this is a really useful present,' he said jovially.

'I'm 'fraid it's not very useful,' said William. 'Uncle Jim sent it to father for his birthday, but father said it was no use 'cause the catch wouldn' catch so he gave it to me to give to you.'[33]

In fact, William is not normally as truthful as this, but having just attended a sermon that advocated complete candour, he decided to apply its lesson wholesale, but with the typical insensitivity of a half-socialised child. Sometimes his appalling tactlessness, a compound itself of lack of awareness and general aggression, can be utilised by the adults around him in order to unmask frauds or get rid of obtrusive visitors, but on the whole those who tangle with it lose heavily.

On the surface, William has many attributes that children find attractive or amusing. His leadership qualities, unrestrained fantasy-life and determined rejection of adult standards of dress, etiquette and modes of speech, do give him some of the traditional appeal of the anti-establishment rebel already mentioned by Penelope Gilliat, and the adults he makes look silly are just those grown-ups that sometimes sit rather heavily upon young people. But William is also a victim of his own obvious immaturity: things rarely happen as he wishes them to — often very much the reverse. This is in marked contrast to Enid Blyton adventure stories, where everything always works out well. With William, plans are usually bungled, and his audience is encouraged to see why and to laugh at the results. William's romanticism, for example, makes him the softest of touches for crooks with a good line in sob-stories, and his strong feelings for the opposite sex are made to seem ridiculous, especially when aimed at the mature young ladies that the much older Robert fancies. While physical difficulties disappear and child-heroes emerge unscathed in a Blyton novel, with William reality undermines most of his grandiose intentions, and his reception at the end of each adventure is usually not a flattering one. He will always defend his actions though, and fail to understand or learn from his mistakes — another aspect of that same egocentricity which better-behaved readers may admire for its audacity however immature it may also appear.

In this way, William can sometimes be a butt for others, as he has some of the innocence as well as the egotistic assertiveness of a much younger child. Take this passage, where he is trying to make positive overtures towards his otherwise rejecting father (although once again, the strong possibility of William's underlying aggression in all this must also be considered):

William, standing at the dining-room window and surveying the world at large, could not for the moment think of anything to do. From the window he saw the figure of his father, who sat peacefully on the lawn reading a newspaper. William was not fond of his own society. He liked company of any sort. He went out to the lawn and stood by his father's chair.

'You've not got much hair on the top of your head, father,' he said pleasantly and conversationally.

120

There was no answer.

'I said you'd not got much hair on the top of your head,' repeated William in a louder tone.

'I heard you,' said his father coldly.

'Oh,' said William, sitting down on the ground. There was silence for a minute, then William said in friendly tones:

'I only said it again 'cause I thought you didn't hear the first time. I thought you'd have said, "Oh", or "Yes", or "No", or something if you'd heard.'

There was no answer, and again after a long silence, William spoke.

'I didn't mind you not sayin' "Oh", or "Yes", or "No",' he said, 'only that was what made me say it again, 'cause with you not sayin' it I thought you'd not heard.'

Mr Brown arose and moved his chair several feet away. William, on whom hints were wasted, followed.

'I was readin' a tale yesterday,' he said, 'about a man wot's legs got bit off by sharks — '

Mr Brown groaned.

'William', he said politely, 'pray don't let me keep you from your friends.'

'Oh, no, that's quite all right,' said William. 'Well — p'raps Ginger is lookin' for me. Well, I'll finish about the man an' the sharks after tea. You'll be here then, won't you?'

'Please, don't trouble,' said Mr Brown with sarcasm that was entirely lost on his son.

'Oh, it's not a trouble,' said William as he strolled off. 'I like talkin' to people.'[34]

Most of his readers, however, will understand Mr Brown's sarcasm, even if William cannot, just as they will see the obvious flaws in his schemes and general perception of events. So although William's fans can revel in the things he does, they are not at the same time encouraged to accept him as an idealised fantasy about themselves. In this sense, Enid Blyton colludes with the immaturity of her audience's response, by taking up children's most infantile fantasies at face value, while Richmal Crompton suggests that such immature daydreams never prove very effective when put into practice, however funny they may be to read about. There may not be the same quality of adventurous abandon in reading a William book, therefore, but far more opportunity for humour, something always likely when there are large gaps between a character's hopes and performance. William thus belongs to a long line of comic anti-heroes in literature who never understand quite how incompetent they are, and a young audience can feel pleasantly superior when confronted by such examples of misadventure.

As we have already seen in the chapter on fairy stories, one important theme for readers in the mid-years of childhood is the constant tension between their still surviving infantile fantasies, and their increasingly accurate perceptions of the demands of reality. Both Enid Blyton and Richmal Crompton offer their readers the chance to indulge various of these immature fantasies in their fiction, though with Richmal Crompton these are often qualified by an ironic humour. The popularity of their books, and the hostility they have sometimes provoked amongst adults, is perhaps indicative both of their success in getting close to a child, and — particularly in the case of Enid Blyton — of an unwillingness to qualify or criticise their own fictional characters' openly expressed immaturity.

These books, therefore, remain suitable for children or not according to different adult views on the nature of childhood itself, and the type of balance that needs to be struck in literature, between undemanding entertainment and an acknowledgement of reality. Some adults try to discourage such reading altogether, and others may be quite happy to see children reading only this type of material. A more reasonable line, however, would allow for the importance of both types of fiction, the escapist and the more demanding, just as individual fantasy itself can work as a regressive retreat from reality, but elsewhere act as a valuable preparatory stage for later action or decisions in the actual world.

This argument has sometimes been complicated, however, by those who fear that if children once start on popular fiction, and particularly the works of Enid Blyton, then they will somehow become quite addicted and read nothing else. Children do indeed go through phases where this seems to be true, but research into reading habits suggests that children who read a lot of any type of literature, whether it is comics, Enid Blyton or whatever else, will in the long run read other types of literature too. This is of course more likely to happen when readers have a wide selection of books to choose from, and at one time, before there was a greater choice of popular children's literature available, Blyton books did sometimes seem to monopolise shelf-space in some shops. Because she wrote for a comparatively wide age-range, it was therefore perhaps more possible than it would be now for some children almost to be reared on Blyton books, and this fact may help explain the extra hostility or even fear that her name used once to conjure up amongst teachers and librarians, eager for their charges to read as many authors as possible, but always anxious lest they be lured away into exclusive patronage of such an addictive and alarmingly productive author.

There are, of course, other popular writers and literary genres that also appeal to many children at this age. Ghost stories, for example, have always fascinated readers, but especially the young, anxious to test themselves out against some of their own most basic fears. Accordingly, every year various best-selling collections appear aimed at children, all promising to be as terrifying as humanly, or super-naturally possible, with Alfred Hitchcock — who lends his name to one such anthology — occasionally emerging as one of the year's best-selling children's authors. Young readers may also have more interest now in starting to extend their concepts of time and space, either by reading historical novels or else books about other people in other countries, like the outdated but once enormously popular series about sets of twins of different nationalities, written by the American author, Lucy Fitch Perkins. Simple mystery and detective novels may also be popular, once children start developing their deductive powers of intelligence, and can understand more easily how certain clues can be pieced together to make up a reasonable hypothesis.

One of the most pressing needs for this age, however, will be children's desire to develop a sense of their own sexual identity. It is not surprising, therefore, that between the ages of seven and eleven there is sometimes a split between books concerned with conventional masculine characters and attitudes, and others which instead centre around a feminine cast involved in an equally sexually-stereotyped set of interests. Where boy readers are concerned, stories of hectic adventure become popular at this stage, while girl readers often turn instead to the more domestic type of story written especially for them. In each case, such writing will suggest various models of behaviour which readers may or may not accept for themselves, but which will still be of interest to them when it comes to testing out their own self-concepts in relation to those suggested from other sources.

Single-sex school stories, for example, tend to provide very clear models for what is supposed to be 'typical' masculine or feminine behaviour. Where boys' stories are concerned, these still often take their bearings from the type of fantasy once provided by the pseud-onymous Frank Richards in *The Magnet*, where the heroics of the Famous Five, led by Harry Wharton, contrasted with the gross, knockabout humour of Billy Bunter. Frank Richards himself had little time for subtlety either in his writing or his own leisure time reading, where he once confessed to finding Shaw, Ibsen and Chekhov 'duds', and Shakespeare long-winded and a 'beastly snob'. He depicts an utterly unreal world in his stories, cut down to the most narrow stereotypes and repetitive, ever-predictable situations. Taxed on this by George Orwell in his famous essay *Boys' Weeklies*, Richards' reply still stands as a coherent defence of all purely escapist, undemanding literature:

> Let youth be happy, or as happy as possible . . . Every day of happiness, illusory or otherwise — and most happiness is illusory — is so much to the good. It will help to give the boy confidence and hope. Frank Richards tells him that there are some splendid fellows in a world that is, after all, a decent sort of place. He likes to think himself like one of these fellows, and is happy in his day-dreams. Mr Orwell would have him told that he is a shabby little blighter, his father an ill-used serf, his world a dirty, muddled, rotten sort of show. I don't think it would be fair play to take his twopence for telling him that![35]

Of course, it is not only children who enjoy this optimistic, wish-fulfilling stuff; in 1927 *The Magnet*, where many of Mr Richards' stories were first published, was carrying advertisements for curing baldness. Even so, despite the activities of comic collectors and a few adult fan-clubs, Frank Richards in the main wrote directly for the needs and limited understanding of children. Something like this tradition is kept up today by another best-selling author for children, Anthony Buckeridge, whose chief character Jennings is neither hero nor buffoon, but always good at bungling things in a way that brings maximum danger to himself from his irascible teachers. Once again, these novels allow readers to work off aggression against adults in the imagination, but without ever having to face up to what they are doing, since — like William — most of the disasters that Jennings causes happen because he is trying to help; a type of unconscious aggression, perhaps, but one that children still seem to find very entertaining in print.

Girls' school stories also contain their share of mischief, along with rich possibilities for humour or drama, for example when it comes to outwitting crooks, spies, unpopular pupils or nasty teachers. There are, too, some altogether quieter but still very popular stories in this genre, such as the fifty-eight Chalet School books written by the late Elinor Brent-Dyer, who provided readers with a sustained fantasy of idealised group living, even to the extent of producing a regular newsletter for her many fans about the extra-literary lives and habits of some of her fictional heroines right up to their marriages and families. The image of the Chalet School itself, with its international population of pupils, provides readers with a pleasant fantasy of social togetherness and independence from parents. The special, schoolgirl slang invented by the author — including the expression 'fab', later to pass into genuine teenage *argot* — emphasised the exclusive nature of this cosy assembly of pupils, set in an exciting part of the Swiss Alps. The teachers are fun, too, 'gurgling' with mirth in the privacy of their own rooms, and equal to coping, along with the girls, with the melodramas that come their way. The fantasy that is offered here seems mainly to do with living a more interesting life in glamorous surroundings, which are systematically built up in the imagination through the massive accumulation of minute detail — from the whereabouts of the school showers ('Splasheries') to a more or less complete timetable of the day's doings. Characters are again easy to identify with, as they tend to be flat stereotypes based on various supposedly national traits.

It is all, however, a much tamer world than that provided by Enid Blyton, with little of her bravura heroics and riot of action; and the style of writing, too, is far more turgid. The fact that these stories were also popular suggests that fantasy does not always have to cater for wish-fulfilment on a grand scale. There is apparently a need for safer, even sometimes rather dull daydreams, where every detail of various, unreal surroundings soon becomes familiar, so providing readers with an instant and secure imaginative haven. This type of retreat into an imaginary, self-contained world is another example of how literature for this age-group can take up and then embroider upon a very common fantasy. A further example of catering for these dreams is found in some of Enid Blyton's stories set in idealised and closely described farms, circuses or again boarding-schools, though these settings are seldom developed quite as obsessively as is the case in Miss Brent-Dyer's books.

There are, of course, many other books, catering for both sexes, which stress the idea of special friendships between children, now that readers themselves will be ceasing to be quite so dependent on and therefore preoccupied with their relationships with their parents. Instead, their earlier egocentricity will gradually be replaced by a point of view that takes more account of what other children may be expecting of them. In games, for example, children should now be able to play cooperatively with others, and outside the home, group influences will become increasingly important in determining their opinions and conduct. In literature, whether in the school stories already discussed or else in more domestic settings, children will now particularly enjoy stories about twins, perhaps, or gangs that may concern a large family of cousins or simply a group of friends. Such characters often pursue some adventure or mystery together, with the individual hero of former stories giving way to a more collective leadership. The inevitably successful conclusions to these stories, when adult characters are finally outwitted and caught, also usually depend upon the help of other children, as in Erich Kästner's story *Emil and the Detectives*.

Although children are often quite engrossed in these gang stories, or indeed in any of the other favourite genres of literature discussed so far in this chapter, it is still not at all easy for them to explain what exactly they are getting out of their reading, should the question ever be put to them. In this sense, stories are something to be entered into and enjoyed, but rarely to be thought about in any more detached way — that must generally wait until children are over the age of eleven, and better able to stand back from their immediate experience in order to assess it in more abstract terms. This is not to say that the reading of books has no effect upon younger children, but individual reactions tend to be a personal matter, and the manner in which literature can extend the understanding of thought or feelings will always affect some children more than others. This can be seen, for example, where change and growth in children's moral judgements is concerned, and any possible contributions literature can make towards this process.

To begin with, most small children have very simple moral beliefs, often based on crude concepts of fairness, conformity, equal shares and obedience to authority. While this type of conventional morality may be adequate on many occasions, it usually does not — at around the age of eight, or so — have the flexibility necessary to deal with more subtle situations, where it might also be important to look at the motivation for certain behaviour, as well as that behaviour's end results. One researcher, for example, questioned some five-year-old children who watched the television series *Colditz*, which featured heroic British prisoners of war trying to escape from their German captors. She discovered that these young viewers still believed that the prisoners deserved to be shot by the Germans if caught, because it was thought that anyone who tried to escape from any prison must be a bad person.[36] Or to quote an example from the work of Piaget, small children commonly think it is much more naughty for a child to break ten glasses when he or she is doing their best to help, than for a child to break one glass on purpose in a fit of rage. Once again, it is the act itself that is being judged here, rather than any of the possible good or bad motivations leading up to it.

Childish ideas of natural justice are often similarly crude. Small children begin by believing in an expiatory form of justice, where the wrong-doer should be made to suffer a punishment painful in proportion to the offence committed, and this leads to the harsh moral judgements which sometimes puzzle adults looking for something rather more sweet and innocent in the young. But this stage will usually be succeeded by the idea of reciprocity, where punishment is seen in terms of its logical relationship to the offence, and finally young people may move to a stage where they start to look at punishment in more relative terms, with greater emphasis — for example, upon restitution for the victim and the possibility of reform for the culprit.

These different notions of justice never entirely supplant each other, and elements from all of them can be found in most of us. But as a general rule, individuals who are stimulated to think about such things will in time move from simple stages of moral reasoning to slightly more complex levels, although always with the inevitable inconsistencies. An American psychologist, Lawrence Kohlberg, however, has done some experiments where children are told stories which involve genuine and sometimes difficult moral conflicts, rather than what he terms as those 'Pat little stories in school readers in which virtue always triumphs or in which everyone is really nice'.[37] In discussion afterwards, children often seemed stimulated to think and talk in terms appropriate to the moral stage just *above* the level previously displayed by them in other tests of moral judgement. As another psychologist has put it, children tend to 'prefer reasoning at a higher stage of judgements before they understand it, understand it before they fully assimilate it, and assimilate it before they use it'.[38]

These gains in understanding are also possible when children simply read to themselves a book which stimulates them to think in more complex ways about some moral issues. Kohlberg and his associates, however, produced changes in children's moral thinking by linking the experience of certain stories with discussion or role-playing exercises afterwards, and without this extra help it is probable that many children, reading similar stories quietly to themselves, will not notice anything in particular and afterwards go on exactly as before with their normal attitudes. But when readers become really

127

caught up in a story, and find themselves perhaps acting out in their own minds some of a novel's most crucial moments of insight or discussion, there may also be the sensation of a much greater understanding at the end of the day. Quite which children react in this way, however, and which others remain unmoved and unchanged, will always be another matter.

A similar growth of skills also occurs within this age-group in the development of what is variously described as accurate empathy, social cognition, person perception or even people-reading. As we saw, small children begin by going through a very egocentric stage of understanding; something evident in the 'many touching accounts of childhood experience' collected from adults by Francis Galton, one of the first British psychologists. All Galton's respondents reported that as children they had apparently 'Imagined at first that everyone else had the same way of regarding things as themselves. Then they betrayed their peculiarities by some chance remark that called forth a stare of surprise, or a sharp scolding for their silliness.'[39]

This apparent inability at one stage to take on a different point of view received what looked like endorsement from Piaget's well-known experiment where children were shown a particular three-dimensional scene, made up of models of houses, animals and mountains. They were then asked to select from appropriate photographs a picture reflecting what the same model would look like if viewed by someone else from another angle. Children under seven tended to choose photographs of the view as it still appeared to them from where they were standing; older children, however, more often chose photographs which showed alternative perspectives from the one directly in front of them.

This whole idea, however, that children below and around the age of seven have no idea that other people may view things differently from themselves has now been modified. As other psychologists have pointed out, even children of four years old will sometimes adjust their speech according to the needs, as they see them, of the person they are talking to. Another psychologist, meanwhile, who put on an experiment similar to Piaget's three-dimensional mountain experiment, but with tasks more age-appropriate to small children, found that even three year olds can accurately reflect a different perspective from their own at least 80 per cent of the time.[40] In other words, small children do sometimes seem capable of showing some empathy 'so long as they are dealing with "real-life" meaningful situations'.[41]

In this sense, 'taking the role of another person as he stands on the opposite of Piaget's three papier-mâché mountains might not be characterised as a task of particular high empathic relevance, whereas seriously attempting to adopt the perspective of a starving Asian child almost certainly would be.'[42]

But while small children may find it difficult to take on another point of view in more abstract situations, 'real-life, meaningful' stories, especially perhaps when related by a parent, offer them an excellent chance to develop some understanding of others, even from quite an early age. As it is, children listening to stories very often interrupt the parent–reader with spontaneous questions and interjections, sometimes showing 'a rich harvest of evidence of reasoning' even under the age of six.[43] After a story has finished, it is usually too difficult for children to repeat such spontaneous questions and observations, but at the time, faced by the stimulus of an engrossing story, and prompted by the reactions of a narrator already familiar to them, then children may well become able to enter into the feelings of characters quite different from themselves, and even at times begin to understand how some things can be viewed from less familiar vantage points.

While pre-school children are just beginning to acquire an ability to understand other people's possible intentions, therefore, the years between seven and eleven are an important time for learning basic role-taking skills. In fact, children up to the age of six seldom talk about other people's likely intentions, and statements about motivation are also uncommon. Instead, children at this age tend to see others not as unique beings but more as vague types, describing individuals, when asked, in terms of general physical characteristics, with little to say about particular personality traits. In this way, it is the 'size, colouring, name, age, clothes, home or possessions' that may seem the most important factors about anyone.[44] Even so, younger children at this six-year-old level can still draw reasonable inferences about characters in simple stories who are of roughly the same age, and conduct themselves in ways that their audience can fairly easily recognise from their own behaviour.[45] So although unfamiliar behaviour or apparent ambiguity in adult characters may generally be too hard for this age-group to understand, realistic stories about endearingly good–bad children, like Dorothy Edwards's *My Naughty Little Sister* series,[46] will probably not present many problems to a young audience.

129

On the whole, however, favourite fiction around this lower age concentrates on action rather than analysis, with an emphasis upon surface behaviour and its immediate appearance, rather than upon less obvious reasons for such actions. Where adventure stories are concerned, adult characters may be seen as either good or bad but rarely both. There may also be a similar inability to mix categories in other areas where it is necessary to yoke together two superficially contradictory ideas into one concept. When children are asked, for example, whether a man could be a doctor and also a drunkard, most younger ones tend to answer in the negative. This recalls Piaget's findings about children's general difficulties over relational concepts, where again it may be hard for them to realise that a father, for example, can also be a son, brother, cousin, or nephew all at the same time.

This intellectual difficulty was attributed by Piaget to an inability to *conserve* in thinking — in other words, to appreciate that something can change its name and sometimes its outward appearance too, and yet in essence still remain the same. Learning to understand such 'conservation' is a universal stage in intellectual growth; before it has been reached, Piaget suggests, children necessarily see things very much as they appear immediately at the time and on the surface. This living very much in the here and now also means that children often have difficulty in testing out ideas by thinking them through in an orderly way, or in attempting to work back from the conclusion of a thought sequence to its initial premise. Again, Piaget sees the acquiring of this ability to reverse thought processes as another essential step forward towards intellectual maturity. Otherwise, children will always have problems in learning from the past and in predicting what should happen in the near future.

Piaget was always careful not to suggest any specific chronological age when children should start moving towards more mature thinking, but this gradual changeover tends to begin at around the age of seven, so that by the time he or she is aged eleven or more, a child should be ready to start adopting more logical, analytic attitudes. Where fiction is concerned, for example, these older children tend to get better at accepting less obvious wish-fulfilment and often prefer something closer to realism.[47] They can also, at this age, begin to differentiate people or fictional characters more clearly from one another, not simply through crude differences in age or physical appearance, just as they can now start accepting the notion that both desirable and undesirable characteristics can at times co-exist within the same person.[48] With younger children, however, novelists must always take some inevitable immaturity of understanding into account, although as we have seen, this can be overestimated, where children's ability to recognise behaviour that is already familiar to them from their own lives in various child or childlike characters is concerned. More adult, less egocentric behaviour, whether in life or in novels, can sometimes present greater problems in understanding, however; children even up to the age of seven, for example, can still sometimes confuse the concept of disinterested kindness with ideas of basic self-interest.[49]

It would seem, therefore, that novels for younger children in this age-group must on the whole stay with their readers at a fairly narrow, immediately recognisable grasp of human psychology if they are going to be fully understood. Many books for children at this age, therefore, stick to largely stereotyped, unadventurous ways of seeing things, but even so, there will still be opportunity here to start broadening concepts and introducing more subtle ways of thinking at the same time. Literature at any age can always both confirm immature patterns of thought and feeling and also suggest that these patterns may not always be sufficient in themselves. Young readers, faced by this choice, often choose stories that more or less confirm them in what they think or feel, but there is always the possibility that more subtle forms of writing may also be read or listened to from time to time. An involvement in a good, convincing story at an appropriate intellectual and emotional level can help children, without their necessarily recognising it, towards understanding why people act in the more puzzling ways that they sometimes do, where comparison with the reader's own likely behaviour in similar situations seems to throw even less light on the subject than usual. Naturally, people in real life may not always behave with the same obliging clarity of purpose and obvious motivation that so often seems to characterise them in children's fiction, but this merely provides another reason for the popularity of clear-cut stories with the young.

It is not only others who sometimes seem more explicable in fiction; while small children may often believe that everyone is bound to think and feel about most things in the same way that they do, there may also be another, more private range of feelings where children are convinced that they are the only ones ever to have experienced such strong, and occasionally disturbing emotions. For young children, these may be anger, jealousy, aggression or any other of the deadly sins of the nursery which teachers and parents will be doing their best to discourage — sometimes even to the extent of expecting children to disown these emotions altogether. What a relief, therefore, to find similar behaviour described in favourite books or comics, and to discover that other — albeit fictitious — beings feel the same sort of thing on occasions, without necessarily being condemned as sinful beyond hope!

For readers towards the end of this age-group, it may also be a question of finding a reflection in literature of their increasing introspection and consciousness of mixed, sometimes confused feelings towards others or themselves. Literature is well suited to portray and to some extent explain such mixed feelings, just as it can suggest, in describing the moods of various characters, the first intimations of future adolescent depression, which can otherwise seem so inexplicable when it first arrives. At the same time, by no means all personal daydreams are concerned with optimistic projections of the self in the imagination; individuals may also have other morbid or anxious fantasies, and finding these mirrored in print can again be both reassuring and sometimes fascinating, particularly for child readers, with so much less experience — both of themselves or of other people — to draw upon.

This is not to say, of course, that young or old readers necessarily turn to novels in order to increase their psychological understanding. The chief lure of any story is always the initial interest that the plot gives rise to, and the way in which the reader's curiosity, once aroused, is then satisfied in the pages to come. But the opportunity for incidental learning, in addition to the basic satisfaction of hearing a good story, is always there, and perhaps particularly so at this pre-adolescent time in a child's life, where infantile ideas are gradually shed and the basis is laid for a more adult understanding in the future.

5 · Juvenile comics (ages 7 – 11)

Books written about children's literature often omit any reference to comics, but for anyone interested in children's reactions to literature, the continuing popularity of juvenile comics is highly relevant, and certainly worth discussing. Despite the arrival of almost universal television ownership, which some thought might kill off comics altogether, they are still doing well today, with over forty different titles, read in varied quantities by nine out of ten children between the ages of five and fifteen. The same children spend roughly 5½ per cent of their total annual income on magazines and comics — the second highest accountable source of expenditure, after sweets and ice-creams (books, incidentally, account for only 1.8 per cent of children's annual expenditure).[1] A more recent survey has confirmed the continuing popularity of comics with the young; after hosts of statistical tables summarising research into all types of reading, Frank Whitehead and his team were compelled to state that 'Comics are the most potent form of periodical reading for the majority of the age groups we are concerned with.'[2] In fact, the particular age-span under investigation in their study ranged from ten to fifteen, but there is plenty of other evidence for the popularity of comics before this time.

Roughly between the ages of six and eleven, although with the usual variation that applies to any generalisation about children's behaviour, one particular favourite type of comic — referred to in the trade as the 'thick-ear market' — is chiefly concerned with crude, knockabout humour. For those who have recently mastered reading, this humour is easy to follow, having less plot and fewer verbal explanations than more complex adventure stories might require. The clichés for this type of slapstick are soon established and then remorselessly exercised, especially since a good proportion of comic material is regularly recycled from back-numbers. Crack-pot

133

inventors, short-sighted professors, wet paint, dramatically potent hair-restorer, newly put-down cement and other old favourites all serve as comic-strip shorthand for instant, predictable humour.

As well as being easy to follow, this graphic humour can also be a mirror for primitive, violent emotions at this age. Other favourite literature for children may also have this function, but rarely with such lack of inhibition as in these comics, where children can still find vivid examples of the messy play and temper tantrums that they are otherwise learning to leave behind in real life. In comics, however, paint, mud or ink regularly manages to spurt up into people's faces, leaving visible only a pair of outraged eyes. Violence is equally pervasive, often directed against authority figures like Dad, teachers or policemen. Characters may literally flatten themselves when they trip over, or else have enormous, egg-shaped lumps on their heads, so that violence is not only done, but seen to be done, far more clearly than is possible in real life. In return, culprits are beaten on the bottom with a slipper or a thick cane — another occasion for laughter, often led by a chorus of onlookers. Although readers enjoy the mischief, the more socialised part of their personality will also approve the harsh punishment reserved for the culprits at the end of the day, when order is restored.

This instant retribution also means that there need be no lingering guilt for the damage caused: since both crime and punishment in comics exist at an easy, concrete level, awkward questions or more complex emotions simply do not arise. The violence in them can be enjoyed without any worries, since it never really seems to hurt. In fact, no one ever bleeds or even weeps in these comics; instead characters may rage, fume or howl after one of their frequent reverses, but this is more bad temper than genuine anguish. Of course the child has to learn one day that life is not so simple, but this is not the job of the comics; rather, they act as a refuge from any such complexities.

It is difficult for any book to rival entertainment at this primitive level because this sort of slapstick lends itself better to pictorial than to verbal humour. At the same time, few adult novelists would ever wish to become involved with the more scabrous side of children's popular humour, like its endless fascination with excretory functions. But while comics also never descend to the level of genuine playground scatology, they can still get fairly close to it through the crude symbolism of favourite topics like stink-bombs, sudden

134

explosions and endless messy soiling. 'Way down upon um smellee river' sing some of the standard *Beano* Red Indians (feather in head-dress, wigwam in the background) and the jokes children are encouraged to send in are often just as crude. All this offers readers a good opportunity for harmless and temporary regression to infantile modes of thought — a useful safety-valve for children who may be making a good job of growing up, but cannot deny to themselves the reality of some of their persistent primitive preoccupations. Children who read these comics as well as more demanding books, as many do, will be feeding both sides of their personality: the more and the less mature.

In the comic-strip world, however, almost every young person is their own Bash Street Kid — the monstrous, zany, anarchic class of schoolchildren first invented for the *Beano* by Leo Baxendale, one of the really original post-war British comic-strip artists. This coarse, rougher image may quite well express children's perception of their own ugly emotions and fantasies — in Freudian terms, the unsocialised 'id' itself — but any guilt that could also be aroused by the portrayal of this overt aggression is purged by laughter and by comic-strip conventions that portray both children and adults as a new breed of grotesque, misshapen little people, living in their own comic universe. In this sense, children will not necessarily recognise themselves or their parents in these strips, at least at a conscious level, but the basic anti-authority theme of this humour, dressed up in comic-strip disguise, will still enable them to vent their own more suppressed aggression or resentment against parents and teachers without experiencing any anxiety. Indeed, children at all anxious about their own violent fantasies could find these strips very relieving, since the brutality within them is so pervasive that it soon becomes repetitive and very much the norm, so that readers can eventually become habituated both to the violence on the page, and also to the admission of some interest in violence within themselves.

At another level, however, the comic's view of other children, and indeed of the whole child universe, may not always be very different from how a child is experiencing the real thing. Slapstick comic-strip characters, for example, tend to be lazy, badly-dressed, dirty, greedy, cowardly, opportunist and thieving young thugs, living in gritty, unromanticised urban surroundings. The 'pranks' they play upon each other and on older authority figures are often excuses for aggression for its own sake. But life in the street or playground can

135

sometimes be fairly rough, crude and cynical, and a child's own friends or enemies may occasionally behave in ways that are ugly, sloppy and dirty, whether in the school dining hall or the playground lavatories. Cowardice, theft, laziness, greed and all the other vices regularly portrayed or guyed in these comics are not unknown to young children, if not in their own behaviour, then certainly in that of others. This darker picture is not the whole truth about children and childhood, of course, but still an aspect that other literature for this age often chooses to ignore or play down until the child is old enough to tackle adult novels that deal with this side of being young. It could be argued, for example, that the final, savage behaviour of the school boys in William Golding's novel, *Lord of the Flies*, has more in common with, say the Bash Street kids than with the characters in more respectable children's literature.

As it is, certain characters and situations regularly crop up in these comics. The David and Goliath plot is a favourite one, for example, represented by animals like a cat and mouse or spider and fly, with an obvious relevance to small children, surrounded as they are by domineering adults or much bigger children who can sometimes seem so threatening in the school playground or on the way home. Another popular character is that genial, ugly, strong-man, Desperate Dan, still taking up his place in the *Dandy* which remains, with the *Beano*, the most widely read British comic. His enormous strength often gets him into trouble, however inadvertently, but things are always sorted out in the end; he is no real threat to law and order. As with all the violence in these comics, Desperate Dan reflects the aggressive fantasies of his audience, but neutralises them of any accompanying anxiety by his own pervasive slapstick humour.

Perhaps it is not surprising that adults sometimes take an unfavourable view of these comics (although children commonly report that their fathers in particular may 'just happen' to pick one up if they are left around at home). In them, after all, authority is regularly made to look absurd, violence is supreme and life made to seem nasty and brutish as well as funny. All the positive attitudes parents and teachers are at pains to build up — towards school, older people and personal control — here seem to be undermined. Old and sometimes fairly savage stereotypes still persist in their pages, like convicts with cropped heads and uniforms covered with short, broad arrows, dentists with names like 'I. Pullem', whose most prominent dental implement is still a large pair of pliers, and of course mortar-boarded teachers with their omnipresent stout canes, to be used at a moment's notice with every appearance of enjoyment. But much of this humour, as in fairy-tales, once again, is that of the tall story, complete with obvious anachronisms and ludicrous hyperbole, which both takes up certain childish fantasies, particularly those to do with individual power and independence from social control, and then makes fun of them. Although in this sense children may be encouraged to laugh at themselves, they will also have the chance to mock those who finally restore order, whether in comics or in real life — the adult figures who are made to appear equally grotesque. Mum and Dad, for example, are nearly always ugly, bad-tempered, and rejecting characters, but as easy to dupe as the procession of vain, ineffective, disagreeable teachers also found in these pages. Authority may ultimately be triumphant, but it has no dignity and is in continual danger. These comics offer readers, in fact, a Saturnalia in miniature, where authority is flouted and made ridiculous by characters who are themselves absurd and unreal. The topsy-turvy world of the Feast of Fools has always had an attraction for human beings of all ages, as long as everyone understands that order will be safely restored at the end of the day. Knockabout comics, then, although only appearing comparatively recently in our history, belong to a much older tradition of humour, where the organised, sensible world of reality can be safely suspended for the temporary disorder of comic relief. It is significant, though, that certain extra sensitive areas of childhood are usually avoided in these comics, for example when it comes to anything touching on the child's basic security within the family, such as divorce or death. So although Mum and Dad may be very quick to reach for the admonitory slipper, this is not the sort of violence that leads to any more final break-up of the family than may be involved perhaps in something like a few smashed windows. One rare example where the theme of emotional rejection does crop up in these comics, however, is in the more realistic adventures of Black Bob, a sheepdog who for the last thirty years has suffered kidnapping, emotional rejection and various other traumatic events in the pages of the *Dandy*. Once again, this is another example where younger children seem to find it more acceptable to read about certain potentially worrying issues when they involve animal rather than human characters.

As children begin to approach puberty, however, comics of this type begin to lose their appeal, with knockabout humour coming to

137

be seen as 'stupid' or 'impossible'. Instead, children may prefer single jokes to funny strips, with the focus of interest passing from humour to excitement and action in comic strips. Older children around the ages of ten or eleven should now have the concentration and reading ability to take on more complex plots, or even catch up on a serial adventure story when they may have missed some intervening episodes. They may also be anxious to put some of their more clearly infantile tastes behind them: a child's dependence on and domination by adults, so regularly guyed in slapstick comics, may no longer be such an important issue. They may now feel instead that they have won sufficient independence to be able to imagine themselves in more heroic, possibly adult roles, in settings closer to real life. It is at this stage, too, that separate publications begin for boys and girls, now that readers are becoming more interested in the whole issue of establishing their sexual identity.

There is still a strong, regressive element in these adventure comics, but this now appears in a rather different way. Whereas books for children at this age sometimes offer heroes and heroines who are frequently highly and flatteringly competent in what they set out to achieve in the natural world, adventure comics tend to go much further where this sort of wish-fulfilment fantasy is concerned. Their main characters are often omnipotent beings able to fly or perform other impossible feats, sometimes with the supernatural aid of x-ray eyes, plastic arms or invisible cloaks. Faced by this type of imaginative excess, readers can indulge themselves in compensatory power fantasies where they are blissfully free from the social and physical restrictions that they will be becoming increasingly aware of in real life. In this way, adventure comics both cater for the lingering, omnipotent infantile fantasies that children may still keep locked away in the privacy of their imagination, while also providing the excitement of fast-moving stories where good regularly defeats bad in the most conclusive and satisfying way.

The British comic, aimed more exclusively at children than its American counterpart, usually chooses to concentrate on less fantastic settings, however, like school, the football side and, increasingly, the last war, where the Germans are still receiving their weekly defeats, whatever the odds. These stories are never in the least subtle; villains are easily distinguishable, if not by their Nazi uniform, then by the standard narrow face and black hair. The problems they set the hero, however, can usually be solved by a good sock on the jaw.

Within these repetitive settings, melodrama rides again, often in Cinderella-type plots, where the main character — sometimes in disguise — continues to suffer unappreciated for his or her true worth.

This is particularly evident in girls' adventure comics, where action lies more in the world of feeling and relationships. But there will also be those familiar, tangible obstacles and objectives of traditional romance, where the heroine has to struggle for success, whether in ballet, riding or boarding school. Popular stories may centre around pets, themselves sometimes fighting for similar personal justice, as in *Tammy*'s 'Glen — a dog on a lonely Quest'. In such stories, everything is still seen largely in terms of black and white, with useful coincidences and near escapes galore, and little overall contact with reality, despite the semblance of a recognisable world. At the same time, readers' imaginations are still allowed to feed on other obviously infantile notions, such as talking animals, magical gadgets or extraordinary metamorphoses. In this way, young readers are always assured of an outlook that is romantic, and where certain daydreams seem to come true week after week.

The illustrations for these girls' stories are as stereotyped as the plots, which themselves continue to use well-worn melodramatic devices ranging from the heroine's loss of memory to the immemorial plight of orphans deprived of their rightful heritage. But the social or geographical settings to these stories are at least more varied than the fixation upon the last war found in boys' comics, and in the same way there is usually an assortment of sports to win in the last frame, rather than the everlasting football match. At their most banal, plots may suggest Angela Brazil, but elsewhere there is some of the romantic melodrama of a Mary Stewart or Daphne du Maurier novel. Girls' comics thus give the impression of looking forward to other forms of light fiction. Boys' comics, on the other hand, seem a dead-end; nothing really follows on from them except more comics — few novels could get anywhere near rivalling such simplicity of observation and presentation. In fact, surveys of children's reading habits suggest that when boys eventually give up comics, many of them never willingly look at another work of fiction again, instead preferring newspapers and hobby magazines.

Even so, there is no discounting the popularity of comics at the time, nor the very real nostalgia they can arouse later in adults, when they join extinct types of sweets, smells and noises in golden memories of childhood. This sort of nostalgia is not confined to

139

those with a romantic, conservative view of the past: George Orwell (*The Magnet*) and Aneurin Bevan (*The Gem*) both referred with unmistakeable affection to this part of their early reading, and even a fierce critic of contemporary comics like David Holbrook writes warmly about the former pleasures he once found in *The Wizard*.

In some moods and contexts, children may be fascinated by the complexity of the world around them, and will do their best to cope with it, whether in real life or in print. This is only half the story, however; few human beings, of whatever age, wish to live at a constant peak of mental stimulation. For other moods, it is equally natural to want to turn towards something undemanding, and there is nothing in literature to rival the picture-strip comic for sheer ease of communication. As one distinguished author for children has written, 'Nobody who has not spent a whole sunny afternoon under his bed rereading a pile of comics left over from the previous holidays has any real idea of the meaning of intellectual freedom.'[3] 'Freedom', in this sense, implies a lack of intellectual obstacle or fantasy inhibition, almost as if readers were indulging in their own daydreams. Even the normal physical constraints of poor reading ability may not apply here; the picture-strip format is easy to follow and has been used throughout history as an effective technique for communicating with large, barely literate audiences, whether in murals on cathedral walls, Trajan's Column, or in early advertising. The pictures in comics offer an instant comment and interpretation on every passage of dialogue; comedy is underlined by explicit, exaggerated effects, and various familiar props will always announce themselves through larger-than-life illustrations. (In the all-important world of food, for example, Christmas puddings have remained globular, jellies invariably castellated, and cakes, dripping with icing, are always crowned by the inevitable cherry.) Adventure stories also communicate with readers by using various well-worn tricks of narrative device and dramatic colouring, such as heavy shadows, figures isolated dramatically against backgrounds, and character-revealing costumes, cloaks and hats. With the whole of a story often visible on a two-page spread, it is not hard to follow a logical sequence of events, illustrated by those 'before and after' pictures that tell their own simple story of what is happening. A final, explicit frame also usually provides the key to the whole of the plot, just in case readers half-way through are beginning to lose their way, and may want to take a quick look to see how everything is going to work out. The self-proclaiming speech styles of the main characters, and their periodic 'thinks' bubbles also offer an obvious commentary on events for anyone who is still confused. As the Swiss educationalist Rudolphe Töpffer, an early propagandist for 'picture stories' once said over a hundred years ago, 'He who uses such a direct method will have the advantage over those who talk in chapters.'[4]

The cliché situations that critics sometimes complain about in comics, therefore, where Chinese may still sometimes wear pig-tails and trail rick-shaws, and evil gypsies plot against benighted orphans, are also part of this same facile appeal. This is not a justification for these stereotypes, but simply an explanation for their continued use. Private boarding-schools, threatened circuses, one-eyed crooks, coroneted Dukes, top-hatted millionaires, heroic British Tommies and slit-eyed, fiendish Japanese — whether one approves of them or not — such emblematic figures still get through very quickly to the popular imagination. Readers can therefore soon identify the hero and the villain, locked in the basic combat of good against bad. Other literature also revolves around this conflict, of course, but never so simply as in the comic-strip, which, in the words of Jules Feiffer, himself a former comic-book artist, 'Finds the lowest fantasmal common denominator and proceeds from there'.[5]

For a child, fantasies of this type may still come across with a freshness and immediacy as yet unstaled by custom or experience. The very presentation of a comic conveys what looks like spontaneous enthusiasm and friendliness — a commercial ploy which requires a certain amount of experience and maturity to assess for what it really is. Almost every week, the reader will be regaled with 'sensational free offers', and self-styled 'thrilling' or 'fabulous' yarns. There is no danger of false modesty here, nor any let-up from the effusive chumminess of 'your pal' the editor. Gone are the days when nineteenth-century publishers like Samuel Orchard Beeton could criticise young readers' letters so magisterially for their 'slipshod grammar and orthography, prolixity, juvenility, priggishness and plagiarism'.[6] Any form of self-education in today's comics for the mid-years of childhood will either be in picture-form, under headings like 'Our amazing universe', or will consist of a few simple, unrelated factual statements — the size of the Atlantic Ocean, perhaps, or the origin of the yo-yo — squeezed into any space left at the bottom of a page, along with riddles, jokes, rhymed couplets or any other traditional 'fillers'.

Occasionally the undemanding daydream element in comics can develop into something more interesting, rather as Desperate Dan grew from a stereotyped aggressive strong-man to his own individual character today.[7] Story editors may be pushed fairly hard to think of new material for very familiar plots and characters in those weeks when it is not simply a matter of rehashing old stuff. Accordingly, comic-strips can occasionally approach almost surreal levels of fantasy; given, for example, that the usual football story is always going to centre around the big match, gimmicks for varying this classic formula have included the presence of haunted football boots, or an ace player who has been reared by kangaroos. A format that accepts a certain amount of magic within its conventions can use these possibilities quite creatively, inventing something like a twentieth-century fairy-tale, and various comic-strip heroes are in some ways today's descendants of those once equally popular magical heroes of myth and legend. Superman, for example, is firmly in the tradition of any supernaturally-aided giant-killer, regularly purging society of the monsters that prey upon it, and a former hero of British comics, Wilson the Wonder, was very like those apparently poorly-endowed third sons of fairy-tales who go on to master everyone else through unexpected strength or skill. Various comic-strip heroes, in fact, often begin with some minor or even major handicap in their own lives, thereby attracting a type of easy, self-pitying sympathy from readers, who may identify what they feel to be their own weaknesses with these more dramatic personal disadvantages. Typically, however, these heroes or heroines effectively shed their handicaps at the crucial moment, either through magical transformations into a variant of Superman, or else by overcoming them in a way that can still enable them to outstrip all their normally endowed competitors. As we have already seen, such overt power fantasies also particularly appeal to children who, because of their lowly position in an adult-oriented society, easily identify with daydreams of this type. Those who continue to buy comics in great quantity, however, and spend significantly more time reading or re-reading them, very often turn out to be under-privileged or socially isolated individuals, and therefore people for whom the transparently omnipotent fantasies of these comics have extra special attractions. Some American research once suggested that the really avid readers of the 'invincible hero' type of comic strip were more than three times as likely to be small rather than tall for their age.[8]

In most respects, American adventure comics are more inventive than their British counterparts. Since many comics in the USA can count on an adult following, too, they have developed in terms of style, political awareness and satire. Their stories include more original variations upon familiar themes of omnipotence, destructiveness and retaliatory humour, while their illustrations have an occasional creative inventiveness that has had an influence upon the whole course of modern art. British comics, on the other hand, have always been traditionally aimed at a young audience; this means they have to be cheap, easy to understand and none too sophisticated.

Such comics, however, sometimes get extremely close to some, although by no means all, of the important aspects of a child's imagination. As Sartre wrote of his own vivid, youthful fantasies (so similar to typical comic-book material):

Every evening, I would . . . rush to my bed, gabble my prayers and slip between my sheets; I could not wait to get back to my mad audacity. I would age in the darkness and become a lonely adult, with neither father nor mother, hearth nor home, almost without a name. I would walk across a blazing roof, carrying a fainting woman in my arms; below me, the crowd would be shouting: it was obvious the building was about to crumble. At this point, I would say aloud the prophetic words: 'To be continued.' 'What do you say?' my mother would ask. I would reply, prudently, 'I'm holding myself in suspense.'[9]

For the seven-year-old Sartre, these fantasies were a compensation for sensations of inadequacy, where 'deep down I remained cold and unjustified'. Accordingly, 'Everything took place in my head; an imaginary child, I protected myself through the imagination.'[10] For all young people, who are beginning to grow away from their previous, infantile delusions of omnipotence, but who still want to preserve some of their former sensation of power in the imagination, comics can be a very useful fall-back.

From the age of eleven, children normally enter into what Piaget has described as the stage of 'formal operations' in their intellectual development, when it becomes possible for them to think in abstract as well as in more concrete terms. They may, therefore, start passing from acquiring and storing up knowledge to thinking about the nature of such knowledge in the first place; where moral judgements are concerned, for example, a child may now begin to question some conventional morality in favour of 'the morality of individual principles of conscience'.[1] Not surprisingly, therefore, books for this age-group often echo these more complex intellectual and emotional processes, with fictional characters also sometimes standing back from their immediate reactions in order to take a more analytic look at what is really happening.

This greater mental sophistication has other important implications for children's literature. Fiction for younger children, as we saw in the previous chapter, often accommodates itself to the immaturity of its audience by describing most behaviour, including that of adults, in child-centred terms. At the same time, characters are usually judged according to simplified, surface explanations or characteristics, and these judgements may be harsh and rigid. But once a child is better equipped to understand some of the more obvious contradictions between surface appearances and inner reality, and can have greater insight into the possible reasons for other people's behaviour, the novelist can afford to be more subtle in approach. Stories no longer have to be concerned largely with action; there will be more chance to explore the complexities of personality. As it is, children may now begin to understand people more in terms of their particular, differing personalities and also in relationship to other, more abstract influences in their lives, such as various aims and ambitions. Successfully integrating all these contributing, sometimes

144

apparently contradictory factors together into a unified impression of someone will involve use of the more abstract concepts now available to the young adolescent. This new type of understanding can be helped by various hints and explanations put forward by authors in the course of telling their story; one reason why novels about feelings and general relationships can start becoming popular at this age, when readers may first become fully conscious of the need to make greater sense of their own and other people's personalities.

At the same time, older children's firmer understanding of physical causation and worldly logic may lead them to become impatient with their previous thinking, once so faithfully reflected in books for the younger child. In the infant-centred world, for example, builders simply 'look for a place to build something' after they leave home each morning, and teachers are thought to own the schools they work in and teach pupils all for nothing, because that is what they like doing best.[2] But most remnants of these fundamentally playful images of persons in society have generally disappeared by the age of eleven, to be replaced by the idea that adults have to fulfil economic as well as social roles, which may sometimes incur unavoidable and irksome obligations. In terms of personality, too, characters may now be understood as occasionally having problems that do not disappear even after the arrival of an unforeseen stroke of luck, or any other instant solution. If they happen to be nasty, unattractive individuals, it may not be quite such fun now to see them as the butt for everyone else's humour or dislike. Children may even start wondering how individuals got to be like that in the first place, and perhaps sometimes feel a little sorry for them.

A skilful author, therefore, should now find it easier to help readers realise that their previous ways of explaining human beings to themselves were not very adequate. But other writers will also be at hand with fiction that helps confirm readers in their more stereotyped ways of thinking, for example in those moods when all that is desired is a nice, undemanding story. As George Eliot once wrote, 'It is so much easier to make up your mind that your neighbour is good for nothing, than to enter into all the circumstances that would oblige you to modify that opinion.'[3] Although she was writing about adults, her statement could equally apply to children, and especially to younger ones.

At whatever level of complexity, however, stories for the eleven to fourteen age-group usually reflect their audience's increasing pre-

145

occupation with the need to acquire a consistent sense of identity. Favourite novels, therefore, may now feature adults as principal characters, on hand in the pages of fiction to illustrate different models for the reader intent on establishing his or her own mature personality, and curious to see some of the examples set by other, older people. It is during this period that the school story drops out of popularity, perhaps because readers are now chiefly interested in more adult-seeming behaviour.

Other books for younger readers in this age-range, however, still concentrate on children's need for imaginary friends or gang-life, but now sometimes contained in novels that are rather more subtle. E. Nesbit, for example, produced a blend of fact and fantasy in which children could both recognise themselves and also, at other moments, revel in some of their favourite daydreams, such as the idea of travelling in time or having the power to make any wish. On the other hand, E. Nesbit's child characters usually end up by mis-handling or misunderstanding things in the way that children so often do — mistaking chance remarks for positive requests, for example, or allowing themselves to become carried away by their imagination. A magical wish in an E. Nesbit book, therefore, usually creates more trouble than it is worth; one good way of both indulging children in one of their favourite fantasies, and then revealing to them the essential unreality of such facile wish-fulfilment.

The portrayal of an extremely simplified adult world in these novels, however, also co-exists with more subtle descriptions, where readers are invited to question various conventional assumptions. In *The Story of the Amulet*, for example, the Queen of Babylon — transported in time to the slums of Edwardian London — pities the English 'slaves' that she sees toiling away in the East End. Artlessly, she enquires what good 'the vote', which the proudly democratic children had just been trying to explain to her, had ever done these pitiful specimens. Faced by such a direct question, young readers may also pause to think about this awkward matter, before passing on to the next jolly adventure.

This technique, whereby children's habitual attitudes are period-ically shown to be both hasty and immature, can also be found in other distinguished children's writers, like E. Nesbit's great pre-decessor, Mrs Molesworth. In *The Ruby Ring*, for example, the spoilt heroine Sybil is given three chances to explore existences which she imagines to be preferable to her own. Inevitably, given the choices she made, she is disillusioned – her picture of gypsy life, for example, quite shattered once she is exposed to the realities of begging and general tough living. As she says herself, things were much better 'When we *pretended* to be gypsies, and took our dinner to the wood, how different it was . . . The spoons and forks were silver, and the plates china.'[4] The same author was also adept at qualifying various character stereotypes, like the wicked giant who is then described as being 'very unkind, but still I think you would have been rather sorry for him too. He was old and all alone, and of course nobody loved him.'[5]

Various modern writers for children continue with this particular approach, with its obvious importance for children still trying to sort out truth from romance. As it is not possible to consider all of them here, I shall instead concentrate chiefly upon one particularly popular and successful contemporary writer, Nina Bawden, who regularly has the misconstruing of certain situations by child characters as a central issue in her novels, and who is a good representative of the way that modern writers can tackle this perennially interesting theme for a young audience. The various misapprehensions of her main child characters are always due to the romantic, sometimes superficial perception of things typical of younger children's thinking – just the sort of misunderstanding a slightly older audience should be growing away from. Immediately, therefore, Miss Bawden's stories have elements within them which most children can recognise from their own past or even present.

In her first book, *The Secret Passage*, for example, a lonely, fostered child spins a false story about a cruel grandfather to the children next door, who compound this with their fantasy that she may be their aunt's long-lost daughter (encouraged by finding the standard romantic locket containing its sprig of hair). This theme of self-delusion is also taken up in another book, *The White Horse Gang*, about children who plot to kidnap an obnoxious little boy in order to raise money for one of them to rejoin her parents abroad. Their badly thought-out plan is a miserable failure, however, ending with the little kidnapped boy more or less in charge, and the original gang feeling stupid and guilty. Again, in *The Runaway Summer*, Mary – an unhappy, angry child staying with her kindly grandparents – makes up a self-pitying fantasy where she announces herself as an orphan staying with an aunt who starves her. Maintaining this fantasy becomes increasingly awkward for Mary when other children take it quite literally, until there is a final show-down, bringing with it inevitable remorse.

Squib is the most harrowing of Miss Bawden's books for children, partly because within it such fantasies become most obtrusive and, in this case, dangerous. Kate, the heroine, believes she has rediscovered her dead brother in the shape of a battered, deprived little boy who lives with a psychopathic foster mother on a caravan site. At the same time, she invests the rest of her affection in an unreal relationship with a glamorous young mum and her baby boy down the road, only to find they have left one day without even saying good-bye. When her other fantasy collapses, too, she withdraws into herself altogether, but is saved by a sort of happy ending, where at least some things are partially resolved.

Plot summaries alone, however, give no idea of the charm and appeal of Miss Bawden's writing, and although she exposes unreal fantasies in her novels, this does not mean that her audience is always confronted by stark realism. All her books, for example, end with a more or less satisfying round-up, where obvious villains are despatched and the good re-group their forces, free now from danger. These are not necessarily the pat endings of romantic novels — characters may be rewarded by a change of attitude rather than by a stroke of fortune — but even so Miss Bawden ultimately always chooses to stay within a conventional fictional framework. This type of happy ending may indeed be another fantasy — life is seldom so obliging — but there are still hints that not everything is going to be easily resolved. In *The Peppermint Pig*, for example, although the family is re-united after the father has been cleared of a false charge, the beloved pet pig still finds his way to the butcher, despite the heroine's tears. Although it would be nice for pets always to survive, however, as in sentimental films, for this to happen here would be a falsification quite out of keeping with the general tone of Miss Bawden's novels. Again, in *Squib*, Kate's unworldly mother has to disappoint her daughter's appealing fantasy that she should adopt the little boy, once freed from his horrible captor. 'Her mother bent over her and stroked her hair. She said, "Darling, I really am sorry. I can see it would be nice; like a story. But in real life there aren't any right true happy endings. You have to get used to things as they are." '[6]

If some daydreams are knocked on the head, therefore, others — perhaps less exotic ones — are on hand to give heart to the reader. This may seem confused logic, but most younger children in this eleven to fourteen age-group, who make up the bulk of Miss Bawden's readership, will still not be ready for the depiction of a truly amoral universe, where natural justice may on occasions hardly figure at all. Younger readers need sustaining myths as well as glimpses of a sterner reality, and Miss Bawden balances both views in her novels with great skill. In *The Secret Passage*, for instance, although the child characters have to abandon their favourite daydreams, there is also by way of redress a bad-tempered old man who turns unexpectedly benevolent, so saving one of them from returning to her unhappy foster-home. In *The Runaway Summer* another bungled escapade also ends better than expected, and in *Squib* the little boy does finally get adopted — not by Kate's mother, but by someone almost as accessible.

Happy endings apart, there is otherwise little tolerance of unreal thinking in Miss Bawden's novels. Physical difficulties do not simply disappear when they threaten to get in the way of the plot. Instead, her characters are constantly made to recognise that most things do not work out as easily as 'something in a book' — a comment the author can get away with because her novels have that quality of the real. When Algy, in *A Handful of Thieves*, tries to shin up a drainpipe in the approved, adventurous manner, it simply comes away from the wall with a clang. In *The White Horse Gang*, the practical difficulties of organising a kidnap become clear even at the stage of composing an anonymous letter from newspaper cuttings: the inept results are far from threatening. If Miss Bawden's characters get into trouble with the police, however noble their motives, there is no twinkle-eyed Inspector to bail them out and promise to come to tea next day. Instead, it is more like the real thing, with police station, worried parents and cruel embarrassment. Again, when a crook is caught, it is a messy rather than heroic business, leaving characters feeling sick instead of excited. At the end of *The Witch's Daughter*, the young boy hero is addressed by an approving policeman in those familiar, flattering tones common to an Enid Blyton adventure story: 'You know, young man, if it should ever take your fancy, you'd make a very useful detective, some day.' Yet 'though this was something Tim had always longed to hear, for some reason it gave him no particular pleasure now. He said, rather coldly, "I think I'd rather be a botanist, like my father. Not so many people get hurt." ' Rather in the same way, unpopular characters do not necessarily bluster and make themselves seem more ridiculous when caught out or fooled in some way. Instead, they may disarm their young critics by looking vulnerable or even pathetic, turning a potential triumph into something that no longer feels quite so good.

Telling the truth to children, or at least some of it, sounds a severe brief for any writer, yet Miss Bawden's books could never be described as finger-wagging morality tales. Her characters are rumbustious, romantic, coarse, funny, bad-tempered and long-suffering: too real to fit into any tidy parable. Their mutual insults really sting, and when they are naughty, they can be very objectionable. In *The Runaway Summer*, for example, Mary taunts old-age pensioners sitting quietly on the beach, pinches sweets from a kiosk and makes two small children cry. Not a pleasant child, in fact; but readers are not encouraged to get away with any snap moral judgements about her, since she is also shown to be miserable in herself, reacting — however savagely — in ways readers may be forced into understanding. In their own lives, children also experience confused feelings, when they do not always say what they really mean, or do what is obviously best for them. One of Miss Bawden's achievements is to chart these areas of confusion and uncertainty, so that readers might get a better idea of why a certain child is still sulky with people who are always kind to her, why an old lady cannot bear to go to the police when she is robbed, or why members of a family still care for each other even though they quarrel most of the time. Things are not always as simple as they appear; nor are people. Miss Bawden is particularly good at getting this across about the semi-outcasts of our own society: the rough adolescent, the isolated and elderly, the difficult, ungracious child whom other children are quick to condemn but slow to recognise in some of their own behaviour.

In Nina Bawden's writing, it is quite possible for children to recognise some of their own typical, ambiguous attitudes, but always along with other aspects of being young that have nothing to do with psychology at all. A little insight can go a long way with a child audience, always wary of being preached at in their literature. Miss Bawden's skilful character studies in her novels, therefore, are balanced by descriptions of other uncomplicated behaviour, such as children's joy on first producing their own artificial belches, their irritation with adults who put on bright, insincere voices or their occasional boredom with school, or indeed with much of childhood.

'We could be a gang,' she said eagerly. 'I've never been in a gang.'

'I've been in thousands, just about,' Sam said, feeling superior. 'You get bored with gangs, after a bit.'[7]

Perhaps *A Handful of Thieves*, one of Miss Bawden's happiest, most endearing books, gets closest to a child's-eye-view of things, narrated as it is by its thirteen year old hero:

My name is Peter Henry McAlpine but I'm always called Fred, I'll explain why later . . . My Gran's name is Edwina Blackadder. She is 'as old as her tongue and a little older than her teeth'. I don't think this is a particularly funny joke — though I did when I was young — but it's what she always says when you ask her how old she is . . . I think she is probably pretty old as she's going bald and her legs are thin as sticks though the rest of her is quite fat.[8]

However authentic her child characters appear, though, and whatever the realities they are forced to acknowledge, they still manage to have a more exciting life than most of their readers will ever experience, and the friendships, family and gang life in her books have a similarly warm, attractive nature. Physical and practical difficulties, although often stressed, may not be quite so forbidding as in real life, and moral dilemmas also eventually resolve themselves with an enviable finality. But most stories by any author give life a clearer and often more attractive shape than readers can commonly hope to find in their own experience. In Miss Bawden's case, however, this appeal is more specifically child-centred, in that she deals with childish fantasies and explores them through plots that concentrate on action rather than introspection. As Piaget has always stressed, it is through action that children learn about the nature of the world around them, and the limitations of their own potential within it. Reading a novel, of course, is not the same as actually doing the things that the novel may be describing, but even so young readers of Miss Bawden's books can still learn something about themselves by following through the mistaken notions and misconceived fantasies of her fictional characters to their particular moment of truth. The success of her books suggests that this theme of personal growth is popular with many young readers, so long as it is also embedded in a good story.

Other distinguished contemporary writers for children whom I can only very briefly touch on here, also combine their own distinctive mixture of adult and more childlike perceptions in their works. Leon Garfield, for example, usually sets his novels in the eighteenth century, and in *Smith* — one of his most exciting stories — there is plenty that an immature imagination can immediately understand and sympathise with, such as a melodramatic villain and at the other extreme, a saintly philanthropist. In between these two, Smith — a

151

likeable pickpocket — almost perishes, but eventually fully deserves his happy ending. There are also in this seemingly black and white morality tale, several massive coincidences, sympathetic weather that darkens in accordance with the threat of evil, and even scenery that sometimes provides its own commentary on things — the pathetic fallacy so often used by Dickens, and a technique especially meaningful to children whose own imagination may also, not so long ago, have been quite willing to encompass the idea that clocks could sometimes frown, and buildings pull hideous faces.

This seems so far to be the kind of explicit, undemanding melodrama that children can appreciate without ever having to stretch their imagination, but this would be to underrate Mr Garfield's considerable subtlety. The blind, philanthropic magistrate who befriends the young hero also shares a type of moral blindness that Smith eventually is forced to expose. Minor characters who seem one thing, sometimes change on better acquaintance. In Mr Garfield's later books, this 'role-drift' becomes more pronounced. Readers who are ready to move on from the oversimplified parcelling up of characters into neat packages labelled either 'good' or 'bad' will respond to this type of subtlety, where even the appalling highwayman in *Black Jack* ends by appearing as a pathetic victim. In another fine novel, *Drummer Boy*, an allegory of innocence and corruption is followed through in a way that will bypass any reader happy simply to follow a good adventure story. Once again, it describes a situation where shabby, compromised characters at the start of the story eventually prove more worthwhile than superficially attractive but more sinister figures.

An author like William Mayne, however, often gets completely away from the easy stereotypes and good–bad morality that can be so meaningful to young readers (as Tolkien once wrote, children are more likely to ask of a particular character, 'Was he good? Was he wicked?' rather than simply, 'Is it true?').[9] William Mayne, though, portrays characters in his fiction who reveal themselves only fleetingly and piecemeal. His plots are also very unpredictable, revolving around seemingly real children and their authentic-sounding conversation, but described in such a way that readers often have to work hard, holding together all the elliptical snatches of dialogue and elusive, understated action in their own minds in order to make a coherent story out of it all. This has led critics to question whether these novels are for young readers at all; but for bright children, looking for books to tax their growing intellectual competence and emotional understanding, more complex fiction of this sort can be very stimulating.

Other popular genres in children's literature for this age also illustrate a gradual progression from the simple to the more complex. Historical fiction at its most melodramatic level, for example, still shares the former unquestioned chauvinism and black and white morality of nineteenth-century writers like Charles Kingsley. Even as a somewhat unlikely Professor of Modern History at Cambridge, supposedly dealing with fact rather than fiction, Kingsley still saw complex issues in essentially simple terms. As one of his enthusiastic undergraduate followers recorded at the time, 'Often and often as he told a story of heroism, of evil conquered by good, or uttered one of his noble sayings that rang through us all like trumpet calls, loud and sudden cheers would break out irresistibly — spontaneously.'[10] These gratifyingly simple and self-righteous views were also popular with the more limited understanding of an even younger audience reading Kingsley's historical novels. Here, English Protestant characters were always better than everyone else, and so were allowed full licence to put monks and foreigners to the sword in their determination to spread the British way of life. Thus Amyas Leigh in *Westward Ho!*, 'a symbol, though he knows it not, of brave young England longing to wing its way out of its island prison, to discover and to traffic, to colonise and civilise until no wind can sweep the earth which does not bear the echoes of an English voice'. This was heady stuff for young readers at the time, feeding a type of egocentric, omnipotent fantasy under the guise of a flattering patriotism, while also offering opportunities for private, sadistic reverie made respectable by being in the British cause. 'What a slayer was Hereward the Wake!' wrote Andrew Lang, one of Kingsley's many fans as a child. 'When the romance first came out in *Good Words*, we boys, on a Sunday, would reckon up Hereward's bag for the month. In one chapter he did not kill anyone, he only "thought of killing" an old woman! This was a disappointment to his backers.'[11]

Simplified historical fiction of this type has always been well-suited to the limited skills of younger readers, who normally prefer action to analysis, and who anyhow often have little idea of history up to the age of eleven or so, tending to lump everything that has happened together, from their own grandparents to Robin Hood, into one undifferentiated period of time in the past.[12] This lack of expertise in turn enables writers of historical fiction for children to get away with massive anachronisms in how certain characters think and speak, as well as with those extra, exciting incidents, such as secret passages, impervious disguises and extraordinary escapes, that only a professional historian or a sceptical adult would be in a position to question. Distance in time, again, also assists in the stereotyping of character; appalling villains and super-chivalrous heroes are often difficult to describe in terms of a recognisable contemporary reality, but are less open to disbelief once set more vaguely in the past. This means that historical writers can develop their stories at a good pace, using characters free to get away with the most unlikely behaviour.

Children today, then, have the choice between historical fiction where everything still stays at a traditional, simplified level of black and white morality, and the more sophisticated type of historical writing first hinted at perhaps in Kipling's *Puck of Pook's Hill* and *Rewards and Fairies*. Here, despite Kipling's obvious belief in the genius of the British race, there are also persistent undertones of melancholy, for example, in the way that the great men and innovators of history are often portrayed as lonely figures, who have had to sacrifice much of their own personal happiness. Some modern writers of historical fiction for children also take a more individual stance towards their material, no longer producing the sort of pre-war stuff derided by Geoffrey Trease, which 'still implied that war was glorious, that the British were superior to foreigners, that coloured "natives" were "loyal" if they sided with the invading white man and "treacherous" if they used their wits to counter-balance his overwhelming armaments.'[13] In fact, today even the most traditional historical clichés are sometimes challenged by children's writers: the last few novels dealing with Guy Fawkes, for example, have all portrayed him as sincere, idealistic and misguided — not the sort of person anyone would wish to see burnt on a bonfire. Geoffrey Trease himself has done something in his historical novels to reverse the former facile moral shifts he has criticised in the work of others, and another contemporary writer, Rosemary Sutcliff, shows in her books that even famous men like King Arthur may also possess some human failings. For children no longer so willing to be fobbed off with clichés, historical or otherwise, this greater complexity in stories about the past can be most appropriate. For those still uninterested in these approaches, however, there are always comic-strips and popular writing harking back to a more simple-minded, chauvinistic way of writing about history.

A growing interest in the past may also be linked to a greater understanding of time itself, and this too is a preoccupation catered for in books aimed at this age-group. As it is, children around the age of five live entirely in the present, with little sense of time passing, so that it may be hard for them to understand, say, the difference between morning and afternoon, or to know what particular day it might be. By the age of seven, however, most children have some conception of clock time, and by eight years old they generally know what year it is and the order of the months.[14] A nine year old may start getting some real idea of what the duration of time over many years actually implies, but even so, it may take children up to thirteen years before they realise that time is something essentially independent from the functioning of clocks. Before that, many children still believe, say, that they really are 'losing an hour' when all the clocks happen to be put forward.[15]

It is not surprising, then, that children can be truly fascinated by the whole topic of time as they gradually find out more about it, along with its other intimations of mortality and change. Philippa Pearce's superb novel *Tom's Midnight Garden*, for example, explores the obvious but still hard to grasp idea that the very old were once children too, and Penelope Farmer's brilliant *Charlotte Sometimes* takes up the ever-appealing fantasy of being able to meet children from the past. Other novels, like Alan Garner's *The Owl Service*, explore time in different ways, showing how the past can intrude upon the present, both psychologically and also in more unexplained, eerie ways. Science fiction too may start to interest children at this stage, with its own particular way of playing with time spans and the future.

In general, however, older readers often seem to prefer fantasy writing which is less taken up with immediate wish-fulfilment, and more involved instead with exploring aspects of the imagination which do not lend themselves so easily to more realistic types of fiction. Hans Andersen, for example, wrote some fairy stories that almost all children find immediately appealing, but his haunting, melancholy parables like *The Little Mermaid* may be liked and understood more by older children. At the same time, mature readers may also now be better equipped to take on and perhaps even enjoy the incidental horror in his stories. Elisa in *Eleven Wild Swans*, for example, sees witches digging their long fingers into new graves, pulling out the corpses and then eating the flesh — a different world from the Andersen stories which younger children particularly like and understand, where Don Juan shirt collars have love affairs with garters, and princesses, emperors, and palaces provide exotic images of beauty and wealth.

One of the most popular literary genres for children involving overt fantasy, however, is the adventure allegory, which combines the epic form with the supernatural. The most famous examples, such as the *Iliad* or *The Pilgrim's Progress*, have always been popular — at least in terms of their bare plots — with children as well as adults, and today the most successful writer in this vein, J.R.R. Tolkien, still has the power to satisfy an all-age audience. For those older readers perhaps a little embarrassed by the presence of wizards, talking trees and magic staffs, Tolkien provides such a framework of authenticity that disbelief is generally soon banished. In his foreword to *The Lord of the Rings*, he describes 'Glimpses that had arisen unbidden' of his later work while he was writing *The Hobbit*, which eventually 'revealed the Third Age and its culmination in the War of the Ring'. Tolkien is not being merely whimsical here; in private conversation he would discuss his characters as if they really had existed, and as a writer his manner is that of a faithful chronicler rather than an inventor. Hence the presence in his books of learned footnotes on hobbit lore, long appendices on the different languages of the Third Age, and maps, songs, pictures and runic inscriptions. The quality of this belief in what he was writing anticipated the hobbit-mania still to come. Certainly, if the eye of the author is ever turned upon the reader in these books, it is sternly, as if to challenge disbelief, rather than to exchange the wink of adult complicity in any cosy game of 'let's pretend'.

For his story, Tolkien chose the epic form that he knew so well from his own studies and translations of works like *Beowulf*. In these stories the hero sets out, usually accompanied by a band of devoted followers, to overcome obstacles on his journey and finally defeat his main adversary who is laying waste the land. As a literary formula this epic form — at least at its most basic level — has always been easily comprehensible for children since the emphasis is on physical, not psychological progress, with barriers outside rather than inside to be overcome, and with particular emphasis on the more obvious virtues, such as bravery and loyalty. Evil, too, is conveniently externalised in villains, eventually to be beaten by good and trustworthy heroes. Finally, everything returns to normal under surviving leaders who go on to impose the rule of the just.

The adventures described in *The Lord of the Rings* conform closely to this formula. Frodo, the bachelor hero, leaves domesticity behind on his travels, and through moving on from one situation to another avoids any romantic entanglements that could tie him down and turn his face away from adventure. In fact, everyone is noticeably celibate in these books, and the only events that could possibly be compared to orgies centre around either eating or killing. Again, Frodo has few economic worries; wherever he goes he is hospitably received and seen off with lavish gifts. When it comes to action, the right course — however arduous — is usually clear. If it involves a conflict, as it so often does, then the enemy must be killed without mercy, and Lenolas the Elf and Gimli the Dwarf sometimes vie with one another over who has bagged the most Orcs that day. There is no difficulty here separating good from evil: the bad obligingly look the part, with their misshapen bodies and nasty smells.

Despite the impressively elaborate sub-histories and philologies in *The Lord of the Rings*, its basic plot of the heroic quest has always been a popular one when it is set in a form which concentrates mainly on action and adventure. Freed from most conventional constraints — and sometimes even from physical reality through the use of magic, spells and miraculous animals — the epic hero can walk tall and act big, without risk of satire to cut him down (there is little humour in Tolkien's later work). Nor is there any limit to the memorable, exciting adventures a hero can encounter on his travels, and readers can come out from reading about such things not only stimulated to new heights in their own imaginations, but also perhaps themselves feeling more noble, magnanimous and brave through their sympathetic involvement with the main action.

Another reason for Tolkien's popularity, though, lies in his use of plots and characters that have always appealed to the imagination all over the world. Archetypal ideas such as the company of heroes, the quest, the numinous object, the old and wise helper, the sacredness of hierarchy and the importance of a just order, all play important parts in *The Lord of the Rings*. Not surprisingly, critics have reached different conclusions when attempting to interpret this great story. The desolated and ominous landscape of Mordor, for example, where Frodo finally defeats his adversary, has been explained in terms of scenes of trench warfare in the First World War, where Tolkien himself lost all but one of his closest friends. But others have seen it as the disastrous end-result of a polluted environment, the culmination of a nuclear war, or the final stages of an evil industrial—military dictatorship. One characteristic of so-called mythopoeic writing such as this, however, is its power to suggest different personal meanings to different people, through its use of certain, vital imagery and symbolism. Children, like adults, need literature in which they can find the expression of some of their hopes and fears. The sense of involvement that Tolkien's writings produce suggests that for many readers *The Lord of the Rings* has this function of myth, giving meaning to individual fantasies of achievement over adversity interpreted according to different personal needs and goals.

A different fantasy that is also popular with a wide age-group is the animal story, where main characters still realise the universal daydream that animals think and talk very like humans, but now usually in settings that approximate more closely to reality. Fictional wild animals, in particular, can now start giving older readers glimpses in their behaviour of the iron rules that govern all the natural world. Birth, securing a food supply, protecting one's immediate habitat, youth, mating, rivalry within a family, ageing and death are common both to the animal world and to human society. A writer like Jack London conveys a stark view of existence in his animal books by concentrating on the struggle of his animal heroes to survive at all, and on both the contrasts and the continuities this has with human behaviour in the same conditions.

Stories about domestic animals, on the other hand, view human society from the sometimes unflattering eye-view of a pet or a beast of burden. The most famous of these stories, *Black Beauty*, was not written originally for children at all, but aimed instead at suggesting more humane ways of behaviour to adults working with horses, and was sometimes given away free for that purpose to drivers and stablemen (in 1924 a Texas cowpuncher arraigned for ill-treating a pony was sentenced to jail for one month and ordered to read *Black Beauty* at least three times!).[16]

It is not, however, its campaigning against cruelty to animals that has made this novel a success; more fundamentally, it is yet another variation on the Cinderella theme, where nobility and virtue go unrecognised, to be rescued at the last moment from dishonourable oblivion. It is easy for readers to identify with the interests of the main, sympathetic characters in such an eternally appealing plot, especially since Black Beauty is in no true sense an animal. He and Ginger, for example, exchange very conventional human sentiments; one of their phrases, 'Good Heavens!' was later objected to by a critic since it referred to 'A place not dreamt of in Equine philosophy'.[17] It is not certain whether Anna Sewell would have accepted this comment, since in most other ways, except in his taste for oats and hay, Black Beauty's behaviour is what one might expect from a refined, sensitive young man who has suddenly had a saddle placed on his back and a crupper tied round his nether regions. As he says himself, 'Those who have never had a bit in their mouths cannot think how bad it feels'; readers, addressed so directly and perhaps fingering their own mouths, have little choice but to agree. He also has other typically human worries of a more class-conscious nature; from the earliest days, his mother had told him that he was 'well-bred and well-born', and for that reason should avoid the company of the young cart-horses who 'have not learned manners'. Later, he suffers the agony of social disgrace when he becomes a cab-horse, where he meets 'a good many like myself, handsome and high-bred, but fallen into the middle-calss through some accident or blemish.'

This particular underdog view of life can be one that has particularly strong, natural attractions for child readers of whatever social class, living as they all do in an adult-dominated world where other people usually have the last word over their conduct and destiny. Used to being patronised in their own lives, it must be a pleasant change for children to be able to feel more socially competent and therefore protective about some animal characters who are inevitably confused about many of the ways of man. Any child, for example, could do better than Jack London's otherwise ferocious, wolfish White Fang on his first encounter with fire:

Suddenly he saw a strange thing like mist beginning to arise from the sticks and moss . . . Then, amongst the sticks themselves, appeared a live thing, twisting and turning, of a colour like the colour of the sun and the sky . . . Then his nose touched the flame, and at the same instant his little tongue went out to it. For a moment he was paralysed. The unknown, lurking in the midst of the sticks and moss, was savagely clutching him by the nose.

Domestic animals in fiction are also constantly liable to be bossed around in an arbitrary way with no court of appeal, beyond their sometimes uncaring masters, to protect them except in the most extreme cases. Child readers, in their turn also very dependent upon the adult world, can easily be spurred on by such stories to wonder

159

how they might manage if they were similarly quite on their own — a fantasy that has always been very meaningful for children, and one reason for their general fascination with stories about orphans. A book like *Black Beauty*, therefore, about an ill-used, inarticulate animal who is also an orphan, has several obvious points of appeal. In addition to this, Black Beauty himself is a very sympathetic hero to children; his own enforced lack of sexuality makes him childlike in other ways, and many of his chief preoccupations are to do with his physical state — an easy dimension for children to understand, whether it concerns hunger, exhaustion, pain or illness. He is, also, a loving, friendly animal, again quite like a child in his ready affections and general anxiety to be accepted and to please. There is something childish, too, in his vanity, where he is so artlessly proud of his good looks and high quality.

There are more subtle themes in this book as well, giving it an extra interest for readers in this age-group. Anna Sewell, for example, could have blamed all cruelty to animals simply upon human wickedness, but instead she tries to guide readers towards a more complex view. Seedy Sam, for example, is a cab-driver who fearfully misuses his horses, but when criticised, he shows how his large family would certainly starve unless he worked his animals so hard. It is the social system that is wrong here — quite a stimulating jump in understanding for children to make, if they can, used as they once were to personifying evil simply as the individual responsibility of a few, unpleasant people.

Since Anna Sewell's time, the humanised animal story has become less generally didactic in tone, with Kipling, for example, using animal life in *The Jungle Book* to symbolise a type of order, rather than to make any particular social points. His Law of the jungle stands for a universal acceptance of certain moral standards, binding upon all animals except the degraded monkey society, the Bandar-Log. This vision of the perfect, logical balance of animal societies, where inhabitants follow the Law, also has its attractions for children who still like to see their own universe in similarly moral terms, where rules should be obeyed in a somehow pre-ordained, natural order of things. If they can manage Kipling's rather stately and over-ornate prose style, they may also warm to the loving relationship between Mowgli and his animal protectors, and appreciate the lively adventures and ever-present sense of danger in these tales.

In our own time, Richard Adams's best-selling saga about rabbits,

Watership Down, has also been a success with older children as well as adult readers. Once again, the animals talk like humans: 'You're just a silly show-off', snaps one rabbit at a crucial moment; 'You poor old chap', commiserates another, rescuing two comrades from an earthfall. Children will have little difficulty with this sort of dialogue and sentiment, and as in Jack London's animal stories, sex is something that is only very briefly referred to, rather in the style of a military despatch: 'There was some mating and a scuffle or two, but no-one was hurt.' Carry on, sergeant, indeed; but this type of brevity, shorn of more complicated emotional overtones, is an important aspect of a plot that moves at a good pace, concentrating on action rather than feeling, and once again proving the perennial appeal of the epic story of success over adversity.

As more is discovered by ethologists about the real social life and behaviour of animals, however, so does it sometimes become difficult for authors to re-create them as convincing and sympathetic human-ised characters in fiction. A robin, for example, may no longer seem quite the picture of Christmas-card innocence now that some of the realities of his tough, aggressive social life are better known and publicised on various schools' broadcasts or television documentaries. Again, even traditional animal villains, like Kipling's Shere Khan — the outcast tiger of *The Jungle Book* — would today more likely be pictured as a species in need of special protection, and as such a poor symbol for a once-terrifying marauder. In fact, some of the former popularity of the animal story for this age-group now seems to have switched to best-selling and often extremely romantic non-fiction about animals. Books like Joy Adamson's *Born Free*, or Gavin Maxwell's *A Ring of Bright Water*, still suggest an essentially unreal and very selective picture of some supposed natural affinity between man and wild beast, however shaky the evidence.

On the other hand, for young readers who want to move on from the humanised animal story to more realistic fiction about pets and animal companions, there are always those pony books where, if the animals do not actually speak, they may still act on occasions with an 'almost human' understanding. The animals within these stories are sometimes seen as sharing the problems and social disadvantages common to childhood, but in other ways they can be fierce, proud spirits, quite able — once their young mistresses have brought them under control — to run away with victories and snatch the prize. In this sense, stories of horse and rider still cater for those typical

161

fantasies of perfect friendship with a loving, idealised companion which can survive from infancy well into this particular age-group.

These books are extremely popular with pre-adolescent girl readers, but it would be wrong to imagine that their appeal is always of the same type. One particular brand of pony book, for example, represented by titles like Ruby Ferguson's *Jill Enjoys her Ponies*,[18] is mostly concerned with describing a mythical British countryside as an idealised setting for the mini-adventures of the fifteen-year-old heroine. In this rural Arcadia, 'Practically every child for miles around now rode', and the society of retired colonels and titled ladies who keep a benevolent eye on things is as static as it is traditional. For the climax of the book, Jill — the heroine — manages with her usual 'colossal nerve' to persuade the famous Captain Cholly-Sawcutt to ride in the local show. Meanwhile, Mrs Mains, the general help at home, prepares a lavish tea for the victors, including Jill, of course; all 'a beautiful golden dream' indeed.

For readers who want to escape into a different fantasy world, however, novels like Diana Pullein-Thompson's *Ponies on the Trail*[19] fulfil another popular daydream, where young girl readers are offered the chance to revolt, at least in the imagination, against the passive femininity they may feel they are expected to start acquiring at this age. In this particular novel, the heroine helps organise quite a rough, cross-country pony trek, and she herself is always happiest in jeans and wellington boots, busy with jobs like mucking out the stables. Her impressive knowledge of horses, too, helps fuel another fantasy of super-competence and independence among handsome but silent four-legged friends, who cause none of the awkwardness often experienced at this time by young adolescents in their real social lives.

The French writer René Guillot caters for a more omnipotent fantasy in his novel *The Wild White Stallion*.[20] This is about the stallions of the Camargue, who have little in common with the geldings that normally inhabit the stables of pony books. In this story, Folco — the boy hero — is the only one able to tame the magnificent, fearsome stallion White Crest, through the quality of his devoted love. Young readers, in reality usually rather frightened by large, untamed animals, may find this idea both appealing and, to an extent, consoling. Within the story, they can identify with the super-competent child hero, and also with the wild animal; like various untamed human characters in children's fiction, always a sympathetic symbol for the young who themselves have now been more or less broken in by the adult world, but who sometimes regret the loss of personal freedom as they approach the responsibilities and cares of adulthood.

Finally, novels like Monica Dickens's *The Horses of Follyfoot*[21] provide perhaps the most stirring fantasy found in pony books, where the most important factor is the physical relationship with the animal. Here, horses can play roles that vary between faithful servant to ideal companion or even something in the nature of a demon lover, with much emphasis on details like large, liquid eyes and quivering nostrils. Descriptions of riding with such partners often have unmistakeable sexual overtones, well suited to the emotional needs of female readers not yet at full sexual maturity themselves, but still curious to experiment, in the safety and privacy of the imagination, with related feelings in this area. In *The Horses of Follyfoot*, for example, during one particularly 'creamy' canter on her horse Robin, the young heroine Dora felt 'glued to the saddle, her torso moving rhythmically as he moved'. After such an intimate experience, she finds 'she is in love' with her horse, and there are many readers of the same sex fully able to sympathise with these strong feelings.

It would be a mistake, however, to see children's literary needs at this age only in terms of pleasurable fantasy. A chance to escape into an easier, more comprehensible and immediately satisfying imaginary world has always appealed to all ages, but there is also the need to grow away from some early, idealised notions in favour of discovering a more accurate picture of how things really are. Children's early ideas on politics, for example, tend to be very simple, and even by the age of twelve, 'The great majority of children of average ability still view the Queen as more important than the Prime Minister in the running of Britain.'[22] This view is quite understandable, where at first glance a monarch, complete with jewels, throne and a crown, obviously conveys a more impressive image than a mere prime minister dressed in ordinary clothes. Older children, however, will eventually have to see that simple ideas of society and its government no longer work, and that what happens cannot be explained in terms of the wishes of one absolute ruler, benevolent or otherwise. A book like *Anne Frank's Diary*, for example, gets across the idea that whole societies can act in lawless, brutal ways without anyone ever necessarily being able to call them to order, however 'silly' and pointless such behaviour may seem to a child reader today. If after reading Anne Frank, however, children are then inclined to believe that only Germans can behave in vile ways, there are, of course, many other stories about human cruelty and irrationality to put them right. The image of human beings suggested by such stories and other novels that begin to portray the more dangerous complexities of adult behaviour, may often be upsetting to children who still hanker after an idealistic view of things. But no child can or should remain indefinitely blinkered from all unpalatable truths, and novels for older children which touch on these things may still usually hold out some hope as well, to counter the possibility of total despair.

While many children's books at this age will be aimed at both sexes, there will also be novels directed more specifically at boys or girls, so continuing the split that first appeared in literature aimed at younger readers. As before, boys are still very often presented with stories that involve hectic adventure, whilst girls tend to be offered more domestic situations in their fiction, written with the emphasis on feeling rather than violent action. This division of interest, however, can be somewhat artificial, in that boys often read their sisters' comics, just as girls frequently have a taste for spirited adventure in their fiction. Quite how 'natural' these reading tastes may be at this age, therefore, so far as boys and girls are concerned, is a matter for controversy.

One basic, ever-popular adventure plot aimed mostly at boys, however, has always been some variant on the *Robinson Crusoe* story, although the same idea has been described from a girl's point of view in Scott O'Dell's fine novel, *Island of the Blue Dolphins*. These 'robinsonnades' have always been concerned with the idea of individuals left almost entirely to their own devices, lacking the normal props of civilisation, and confronted by doubts about their ability to cope regularly during such a severe test of human endurance. Since man is fundamentally a social animal, it might be more relevant to generalise about human beings by observing their behaviour in less extreme settings, but there is a pleasing simplicity in the idea of a single person, or group, up against it in this way, and thus supposedly revealing their true mettle, and by implication, something of a reader's own potentialities as well. The results of this confrontation, however unreal, will at least have the virtue of clarity — either the human characters will survive or perish, and if they survive, the manner of it will be crucial.

One of the many functions of literature has always been to personalise and so simplify certain perennial human concerns and curiosities; its answers, whether or not they make intellectual or psychological sense, may still be emotionally satisfying if they suggest definite conclusions to normally complex, abstract questions. Variants on the *Robinson Crusoe* plot usually convey a positive image of man — master of himself and everything else around him. If adult readers are interested in this story and its implications for themselves, how much more so will child readers be, who know even less about themselves and their contemporaries, and therefore have a correspondingly greater need to establish a coherent image of their own species. It is not surprising that the desert-island plot has particular appeal then; as J.M. Barrie once wrote in an introduction to another such story, *The Coral Island*, 'To be born is to be wrecked on an island,' and the same point has been made by the French critic Paul Hazard, discussing *Robinson Crusoe*. For him, children

also start out in life rather fearful. Like their great shipwrecked friend, they find themselves tossed onto an unknown land whose limits they will never know except by slow exploration. Like him, they are afraid of the darkness that falls . . . Little by little, they gain poise and are reassured, and begin to live on their own account. Just as Robinson does when he starts out to reconstruct his life.[23]

It is common in many popular children's adventure stories, as we have seen, to get rid of parents early on, so that child characters themselves have to make decisions, take on adversaries and of course receive all the credit for their success at the end of the day. Characters like Robinson Crusoe lend themselves well to fantasies where children imagine that they too could be supreme in their own independence. 'There is hardly an elf so devoid of imagination as not to have supposed for himself a solitary island in which he could act *Robinson Crusoe*, were it but in a corner of the nursery.' Thus Sir Walter Scott, and many other famous men have endorsed this book, or at least some cut-down version of it, as especially suitable for children, perhaps sensing its meaning as an allegory about growing up. For Rousseau, it was the only novel he would have allowed Émile to read, although other critics have not always been so keen, variously detecting within it too much encouragement towards independence in the young, an over-concentration on the possession of material goods, or latterly, an undesirable colonialist attitude towards traditionally subject races.

Succeeding robinsonnades have also illustrated the same fantasy of personal super-competence and have also gone through a period of great popularity with children, although like *Robinson Crusoe* itself, they are less read today, at least in their original versions. In

The Swiss Family Robinson by Johann Wyss, for example, it is a complete family, rather than one individual, which successfully colonises the desert island. The same is true of Captain Marryat's *Masterman Ready*, written in reaction to Johann Wyss, in whose work he found

Much ignorance, or carelessness . . . in describing the vegetable and animal productions of the island on which the family had been wrecked . . . It is true that it is a child's book; but I consider, for that very reason, it is necessary that the author should be particular in which may appear to be trifles, but which really are not, when it is remembered how strong the impressions are upon the juvenile mind. Fiction, when written for young people, *should*, at all events, be *based* upon truth.

But although Marryat may have given the greater attention to detail he promises here in his preface to *Masterman Ready*, his book still caters to the same, basic fantasy of personal self-sufficiency, come what may. If some of the real difficulties of this situation are made more evident, others have a way of disappearing as if in a daydream, culminating in the final miraculous rescue at the stockade, even though this caused the loss of poor old Ready himself, servile to the last. As with Robinson Crusoe and Man Friday, readers can enjoy both their identification with the resourceful, purposive settlers on their desert island, along with the fantasy of having the gratifying devotion of a faithful, uncritical follower.

Despite adult best-sellers since, like H. de Vere Stacpoole's romantic *The Blue Lagoon*, the most powerful twentieth-century expression of the desert-island myth is William Golding's *Lord of the Flies*. Here, the entire robinsonnade tradition is stood on its head; children, even though surrounded by a fairly beneficent nature, threaten their own lives through moral corruption rather than because of problems of physical survival. Typically, older children are often enormously taken by this story, although it was not specifically written or published for them. As in all robinsonnades, there is the fascination of seeing how characters are going to cope with fundamental problems of physical survival, but the picture of humanity conveyed here is a dark one. This image can be especially meaningful to children, however, themselves still only partly responsive to adult norms of civilised behaviour, and naturally prone to wondering how they would cope without adult control over an indefinite period. Like many good stories, *Lord of the Flies* can also be understood at various different levels. While younger children in this age-group usually respond to it in terms of what they think about the personalities of its main characters, older adolescent readers may tend to see the plot in a more abstract way. This difference in response is paralleled by children's reactions to a separate but similar situation put to them on one occasion by a psychologist, who asked them to imagine what problems people would face if they had to start a new civilisation on a deserted island. Children of twelve years still tended to personalise their answers, talking about the need for firm policemen and fair leaders. But fifteen-year-old children responded in more abstract terms, seeing the necessity for a just and universally accepted law as only one part of the general requirements of any viable civilisation.[24]

Another classic story formula can still be found in adventure comics, already discussed, or else in action-packed novels, where a normally active, athletic hero eventually overcomes the obstacles in his path, often in conditions of great physical hardship. If there is evil to fight, or danger to ward off, this presents him with technical rather than moral difficulties — how best to dispose of the opposition, for example, rather than his right to do so. With the emphasis firmly upon action rather than analysis, these stories trade in straightforward confrontations rather than in anything more subtle, with progress measured in physical achievement instead of psychological understanding. In this agreeably simplified world, readers can easily identify with a hero who presents them with such a flattering, exciting image of humanity and its capacity for brave deeds and positive action.

A once popular adventure story writer like R.M. Ballantyne could help his readers believe in the veracity of his fictional heroes by himself identifying with them so strongly as author — a tradition in adventure stories that was carried on by Ian Fleming, who incorporated his own biography and physical appearance, as well as his active fantasy life, into the character of James Bond. Ballantyne, in his turn, used to supply his own self-portrait for the engravings that illustrated his books, which is why his heroes are usually bearded stalwarts. As he wrote in his preface to *Martin Rattler*: 'All the important points and anecdotes are true; only the minor and unimportant ones being mingled with fiction.' He was, therefore, somewhat put out by discovering a mistake he made in *The Coral Island*, where he described coconuts as soft enough to be pierced by a simple poke of the finger. Like Captain Marryat, Ballantyne knew that authenticity of detail would always make his novels more

167

palatable to parents and educators otherwise often rather uneasy about the whole idea of their children coming across such full-blooded adventure stories. At the same time, any patently false detail can always threaten the whole mood of heroic wish-fulfilment and successful suspension of disbelief necessary to sustain both author and audience alike throughout the progress of any larger than life adventure story. After this experience, therefore, Ballantyne resolved never to write about things that he had not come across himself at first-hand, and in later years he served his turn as crew-member of the local fire-brigade or inside a lighthouse in his search for authentic copy. For his popular public lectures, he used occasionally to don his full trapper's hunting-kit complete with bowie knife, long-barrelled gun and leather jerkin, left over from his days working for the Hudson's Bay Company of Canada, the background to his first successful novel. Once again, this meticulous attention to detail may have pleased members of his audience in search of authenticity, but it also helped lend credence to the wilder, more immature fantasies contained in Ballantyne's stories, so popular with author and public alike.

Within the pattern set by adventure stories, however, there can always be variation towards greater subtlety. While Stevenson's orthodox melodrama *The Black Arrow*, for example, was immediately successful with the juvenile readers of the *Young Folks* magazine, there is evidence that the same audience did not initially take so enthusiastically to *Treasure Island*. This is hardly surprising, since the whole book is an attack upon the attractive fantasy of ever-resourceful man and the complaisant nature of desert islands. The Robinson Crusoe figure here is Ben Gunn, complete with parrot and goatskin, but superstitious and soft in the head. Later on, the fight at the stockade, a detail taken from *Masterman Ready*, has none of the reassuring melodramatics found in the original; instead, it is a dangerous, inconclusive and sordid affair, and in general it is no wonder that when Jim Hawkins returns to the safety of home, 'Oxen and wain-ropes would not bring me back again to the accursed island.' His desire for a quiet future is understandable if hardly heroic, but may have puzzled younger readers still expecting the simple-minded reactions of the more conventional adventure-story hero, who never seems to have enough of danger.

Once it was published in book form, however, *Treasure Island* immediately won over a large, adult audience, and very soon young readers also began to respond to this small masterpiece. Even today, children can still find themselves enjoying its stirring plot, while usually missing the satiric intention behind Ben Gunn, or the very ambiguous attitude towards that 'smooth and formidable adventurer', Long John Silver. Stevenson always had an affection for this character, who does not conform to any simple-minded definition of a villain and of course finally escapes with some of the loot — another interesting reversal for the formula adventure story. Hints that the forces of law and order — the squire and the doctor — are themselves a little corrupted by greed for the treasure may also be missed the first time round. *Treasure Island* is one of those novels that have the power to inform as well as to feed the imagination, and this was one of Stevenson's intentions. As he wrote himself:

A child should early gain some perception of what the world really is like — its baseness, its treacherousness, its thinly veneered brutalities; he should learn to judge people, and discount human frailty and weakness, and be in some degree prepared and armed for taking his part later in the battle of life. I have no patience with this fairy-tale training that makes ignorance a virtue.[25]

If this refusal to deal in easy stereotypes may, at least initially, have failed to stir some younger children expecting a more conventional treatment, the novel's success among older readers has never been in doubt (although on hearing that Mr Gladstone had enjoyed it, Stevenson retorted that he 'Would do better to attend to the Imperial affairs of England'[26] — it was also much appreciated, incidentally, by two other prime ministers, Lord Rosebery and A.J. Balfour).

This tradition of the masculine, all-action adventure story for children continued this century in comics and various light fiction. An author like Captain W.E. Johns, the creator of Biggles, for example, is a direct heir to the patriotic adventure-story writers of the nineteenth century. Once again, Johns presents an excessively simplified, flatteringly chauvinistic world to his readers, peopled by super-competent stereotypes of the Englishman as God's greatest gift to mankind. As he wrote himself, 'I teach that decent behaviour wins in the end as a natural order of things. I teach the spirit of team-work, loyalty to the crown, the Empire, and to rightful authority.'[27]

Within such a setting, children have the satisfaction of identifying with a super-hero who is virtually invincible; in this way, the excitement of vicarious danger is shared with the certainty of ultimate success. There may be occasional pauses in the action to contain Biggles's frequent mini-lectures on topics from race — where Captain Johns clearly held some of the anti-black prejudices common to his time — to the habits of seventeenth-century buccaneers; but there will be no delays when it comes to moral choice or character analysis — such things are always as clear-cut as the features on Biggles's own face. It does not matter that his friends Ginger, Algy and Bertie, with their 'By Joves!', 'Thunders!' and 'Gads!' are equally implausible stereotypes, even more so than when they were first created. The whole Biggles corpus fulfils a need for what is desirable rather than probable — a return to an uncritical world of personal wish-fulfilment.

Biggles books remain best-sellers, though they are now beginning to lose some of their former popularity, and similar adventures can also be found in various modern novels as well as in those numerous annuals published around every Christmas. Girl characters have little or no part to play in these stories, something for which Captain Johns again had a ready explanation: 'The modern boy knows what he wants and will strive to get it. Of course, this has nothing to do with sex. Boys hate the introduction of girls into these stories.'[28] This is, at best, only partly true; adolescent boys may be very interested indeed in sex, and younger children will have their share of curiosity too. But in another sense, Johns is probably right. At the stage that Freud once labelled sexual latency, roughly between late infancy and puberty, the child will be chiefly concerned with establishing what he or she feels to be a genuine masculine or feminine identity in all but the fully sexual role, by imitating some of the more adult models they find around them. Sexual fantasy may seem fairly remote at this stage of pre-puberty; a recent study of children's fantasy life suggested that while most boys and girls between the ages of ten and twelve enjoy fantasies that involve adventure and lively action, it was only when they get to thirteen and fourteen years old that their fantasies commonly begin to shift in the direction of romance and sex.[29]

With the relaxation of literary taboos in the last thirty years, however, came the arrival of the sexy fictional male hero, potent in every way, and with him one clearer division of interest between older and much younger readers. Even so, certain popular adventure stories still continue to satisfy a fairly large age-range, such as Ian Fleming's *James Bond* series. Bond has all the flattering, effortless superiority of the true British hero, and as such is an extremely satisfying character with whom to identify perhaps at any age. His name dropping, mastery of incidental technical detail, resistance to pain and amazing capacity to survive are all aspects of the same fantasy of personal supremacy, just as is his ability to attract the love of beautiful women. This side to his activities may make him even more attractive to adolescent and adult readers, if not to those younger children who still find 'love-interest' a tedious interruption to otherwise pleasantly hectic and exciting action.

More sophisticated writers, of course, have extended the conventions of the adventure story to points where it will be of little interest to a child. Voltaire, for example, surrounds a superficially exciting narrative in *Candide* with an adult cynicism few children would understand, and Conrad invests adventure stories with an introspection quite alien to quick thrills and easy wish-fulfilment. There are also major divisions in subtlety within adventure stories specifically aimed at children, since not all writers want to hand back to children their basic daydreams on a literary plate. While no author of fiction, whether for adults or children, can ever afford to get too far away from plots which echo popular personal fantasies, so that readers can easily identify themselves with certain characters and situations in stories, there are ways of developing such daydreams towards a greater sense of reality. Arthur Ransome, for example, often describes a gentle, domestic variation of the *Robinson Crusoe* fantasy in his novels, very popular with both sexes, where self-sufficient child characters manage for themselves in a generally serene atmosphere. But he also writes about the more practical problems surrounding such activities, where difficulties do not always resolve themselves neatly, and progress is accordingly sometimes slow. If the end results are still on the side of romance, children still get quite near to the real nature of sailing, camping or whatever other practical activity he is describing.

As readers mature, however, their choices of fiction will become increasingly adult, so that — for example — by the age of fourteen detective novels of the Agatha Christie type are often popular.[30] Other topics and approaches may also now have a new excitement and relevance, notably the treatment of sex and sometimes sadistic violence, or descriptions of general disenchantment with people or society to coincide with the increasing experience of personal depression often likely at this time. Some contemporary writers for older children have tried to take on these new concerns, often alongside descriptions of the social hazards open to teenagers, like drugs, abortion or suicide. Treatment of these topics in books specifically aimed at older children — an audience sometimes described by publishers as 'young adults' — has up to now usually been quite restrained. For readers who want more sensational descriptions of what may still be taboo subjects and emotions to many children, there is always the sleazy world of the adult pulp novel, like Richard Allen's *Skinhead* and its successors, published by the New English Library. Deplorable and disgusting as these novels are, as, for example, in Richard Allen's indefensible treatment of racial issues, they sometimes seem to reflect the violent, erotic, cynical and depressed aspect of many young adolescents' fantasy lives in ways that normally cannot be found in literature of more integrity. For some critics, therefore, this implies that sadistic pulp literature has a legitimate function, in that it acts as an outlet for the various fantasies of violence that are common at this age. For others, however, this literature is seen as further encouragement for such fantasies, rather than as any form of catharsis.[31]

Female teenage readers may also read similar books, yet on the whole literature aimed specifically at girls avoids violence. Adventure stories for younger girl readers, for example, concentrate instead more on personal achievement in fields where women have been allowed to excel, like ballet dancing or horse-riding, though even so the heroine of Enid Bagnold's *National Velvet* was forced by the rules then in operation to dress up as a male in order to compete in the Grand National. The milder adventures in the autobiographical novels of Laura Ingalls Wilder are also very popular with younger readers in this age-group, where a whole family rather than a single heroine is shown coping successfully with adverse conditions, and where the appeal is as much in the gentle, idealised picture of late-nineteenth-century domestic life as in any personal story of self-fulfilment.

With the general demise of the girls' school story, however, there are fewer adventure books around now aimed specifically at older girls, except for pony stories and various fictionalised accounts of young heroines taking up certain careers. Some of the other literary genres already mentioned in this chapter, however, often have a greater female than male readership, particularly as girls seem more willing to read family novels where boy characters play a bigger part than is the case with boy readers of stories that centre largely around girls. There is one distinctive 'Cinderella' fantasy in the domestic novel, however, that has always been particularly popular — first found in books like *Little Women*, then in other best-sellers like

Heidi, Rebecca of Sunnybrook Farm, The Secret Garden and *Anne of Green Gables*, and finally to be endlessly repeated in various comics and novels written for girls today. Within such stories, plucky child characters, usually of no great personal beauty, nevertheless eventually manage to win over an initially unfavourable adult world, so that in the end even the most curmudgeonly characters are like putty in their hands. Novels like these again mirror compensatory fantasies of power over formidable, sometimes frightening adversaries who in real life would be unlikely to be quite so malleable. Since young characters in these books work on the adult world by charm rather than muscle-power, their stories have generally been addressed to girls rather than boys, except perhaps in the case of another once best-seller, *Little Lord Fauntleroy*. There may also be an echo of a girl reader's Oedipal fantasies in these plots, where very often it is a gruff, distant man quite old enough to be the heroine's father, who is finally won over by a young lady very much his junior — a situation most memorably illustrated in *Jane Eyre*, another favourite novel amongst older children, and especially girls.

At the same time, however, many older girl readers will also be reading a comic or magazine when boys of the same age are beginning to turn instead to hobby or technical publications. There are, it is true, various periodicals still around for the young male market to feed immature fantasy. These carry a mixture of mild pornography, violent war stories and articles such as 'How to be a tiger in bed', 'You can have a he-man voice', or 'You can look taller in built-up shoes'. On the whole, though, these comics with their diet of compensatory fantasies for young males have smaller circulation figures than romantic magazines aimed principally at a young, female audience.

The usual ingredients for these publications, by contrast, consist of love stories, told either in prose or in strip-cartoons, numerous articles about pop singers, clothes and beauty-care, horoscopes, readers' letters and advertisements designed to lure teenagers towards various contemporary fashions. The incidental advice offered by these magazines on matters like hygiene or diet, for example, can be sensible, but other tips on personal behaviour are more questionable. In *Romeo*, for example, a publication which is now defunct but still typical of its genre, a girl reader who wanted to attract boys was advised to 'Adopt the shy, demure approach. You know, fluttering the old eye lashes when a boy speaks to you, looking at your feet when you get a compliment. Boys like a shy girl — but don't over-do it. It makes them feel like a protector which gives them the feeling of superiority that they enjoy.'

Young people, stranded between childhood and adulthood, are often confused about their personal identity and group loyalties, so it is not surprising that these comics have now arrived to underpin and inform a whole extended youth culture which once hardly existed. Magazines that take up adolescent problems and interests are certainly responding to a need, therefore, and can also have an immediacy that books will lack, since by appearing each week they can seem to be truly in the vanguard of various current teenage fashions and interests. At a time when adolescent readers may feel that it is important socially for them to appear to be absolutely up to date about such things, comics like these may at times seem like a welcome and useful support. On the other hand, there is always the suspicion that these magazines often help create certain teenage needs or anxieties so that much of any so-called youth culture is something invented and then imposed upon adolescents by the media itself. Readers' letters to these comics, for example, are sometimes rewritten by the editorial staff before publication in order to make them conform to an artificial, breathless and slangy prose style supposed to represent how contemporary teenagers talk, but only normally heard from the mouths of disc-jockeys. Again, advice to readers on the 'right' way to behave may sometimes go very much beyond what most readers' parents or indeed their own contemporaries think about certain issues.

For these reasons, teenage magazines have often been accused of having undesirable influences, but this is difficult to assess since the effect of *any* literature on readers always remains a mysterious and controversial topic. While young readers are bound to be affected by the social norms and messages that come across to them in their literature and elsewhere, how each individual receives and interprets this social conditioning will always depend upon particular circumstances. Literature that reinforces any reader's typical attitudes, for example, will probably get through to him or her more easily than literature that goes against the grain of a reader's particular upbringing. Again, a child's idea of proper standards of masculinity or femininity is more likely to be influenced by what he or she sees and is taught at home than by what books are read, although stories that persistently reinforce one particular view may eventually have an influence of their own. When it comes to literature suggesting views contrary to strongly-held attitudes, while there may be times when a particular spark is struck, on other occasions the argument will simply be rejected or even missed altogether. Just as adults who are in favour of capital punishment can watch a programme stating the opposite argument, yet still often imagine that they are being offered strong support for their own views, so can children enjoy the dramatisation on television of a story like Rumer Godden's *The Diddakoi*, which attacks the misunderstanding and persecution of gypsies, yet remain quite unchanged in their own prejudices if they happen to live in a part of Britain where gypsies are already unpopular.

On the other hand, literature cannot always be excused from passing on prejudice simply because those who respond most strongly to a particular message are those already predisposed to think in this way. There is always the possibility of planting a quite new prejudice in impressionable minds, especially when there are few or even no popular books available to suggest a contrary opinion. In common with many of my generation, for example, I was brought up thinking the French Revolution was a time when noble, disinterested aristocrats were put to death by an unprincipled mob. It does not seem necessary to look much beyond the *Scarlet Pimpernel* novels of Baroness Orczy and Charles Dickens's *A Tale of Two Cities* as sources for this idea, since there were no stories, films or television programmes available at the time to provide an alternative analysis.

It is hardly desirable for children to receive only one point of view like this in their reading and critics who have since drawn attention to such clear cases of social bias have been valuable in getting this whole issue out into the open. Today, writers and publishers are more ready to produce books which illustrate different points of view, and which libraries and schools are willing to stock. For these reasons, the social prejudice that once led to the portrayal of working-class characters in so much children's literature either as loyal servants or else as dangerous malcontents, is now on the wane. Social bias of some sort in literature will always be likely, however, and may occasionally stimulate prejudice in readers, but if children come across enough books, one can at least hope that the prejudices that come over will not always be the same. To expect any author not to press a particular viewpoint without always mentioning an alternative opinion, though, would be to reduce literature to the level of those bloodless, balanced discussions still common on television or radio.

Any further generalisations on the effects caused by literature or any other of the media are always complicated by the strong likelihood of other, intervening variables which also influence behaviour. There are cases, for example, from the history of literature when particular fictional characters, such as the Byronic hero, seem to have had powerful effects upon their audience, and it has been claimed that the publication in 1774 of *The Sorrows of Werther* was even followed by a wave of suicides. But if this was true, there must also have been other readers at the time who reacted to the thoughts or actions of Goethe's characters quite differently. Once gripped by a story, readers may find some of their feelings, ambitions or favourite fantasies either defined or reflected in the characters who are pushing the story along, but what effect this may have upon each one of them will never be certain. Nor should it even be thought that it is only fiction of a high standard that can have a positive effect upon readers' imagination; Ludwig Wittgenstein, one of this century's most eminent philosophers, once praised his favourite American detective magazines as being 'rich in mental vitamins and calories'.[32]

Most readers' persistent and perhaps formative literary memories are something of a ragbag. The more prevalent, popular literary attitudes and biases of their own time may very well have influenced them in certain predictable ways, but on the other hand, there will also be those inconsequential memories from literature that somehow lodge in the mind over the years for no easily understood reason. For example, I always remembered how the narrator in one of Somerset Maugham's stories tartly observed of a certain character that she had the typical bad skin and uncertain temper of every redhead — something I found myself believing as a fact years afterwards, however feeble the supporting evidence. For a child this statement — said with all the confidence of adult authority — was a tempting generalisation to cling on to, simply because the young are always looking for rules and ways of predicting the behaviour of others in order to crack the code that seems to separate adult worldliness from their own inevitable naivety. But quite why I should have remembered so silly a generalisation, from the host of incidental knowledge and misinformation available from all the other books I read at the time, is as mysterious as any other habitual reader's own selection of idiosyncratic memories.

176

There are, of course, many other ways in which books may seem to offer useful tips, especially to untried young readers, on what to say or how to behave in certain situations — the sort of thing a child may be curious to know, but unwilling to enquire of others for fear of ridicule. Again, after reading one of Conan Doyle's historical romances as a child, involving amongst other things much pledging of faith in scenes of great emotion, I concluded from this that there was only one suitably manly way to shake hands. This was to produce a grip so powerful that, as evidence of its sincerity, it could sometimes even produce drops of blood from beneath the recipient's finger nails — a detail that Doyle mentioned several times. For some weeks afterwards, I subjected acquaintances to my own feeble attempt at this experience, until at last told to stop. Rather more practical, perhaps, was another long-remembered if obscure quotation from Graham Greene, on the occasion where one of his typically seedy characters finds, on a coach trip, that he is the only person left by his fellow passengers with a pair of seats all to himself. He soon discovers the reason for this, though, when the bus starts. 'He was seated over the wheel. He was jarred by every unevenness on the Great North Road. They had all been more knowledgeable than he. Like the first time at anything, the novice was "done".'[33] Children too are novices at everything to begin with, but in this case, suitably forewarned, I made sure on succeeding bus trips that I was not going to be caught out in the same way, and was duly grateful to Graham Greene for this small service.

These, however, are trivial examples of how a reader can respond both to the sound and the spurious, the relevant and the irrelevant in fiction. There can also be more fundamental reactions. When a particular reader finds the right book at the right time, it can provide the shock of recognition so memorably described by William Cobbett, on first coming across Swift's *Tale of the Tub* at the age of eleven:

The title was so odd, that my curiosity was excited ... In I went and got the little book, which I was so impatient to read, that I got over into a field, at the upper corner of Kew Gardens, where there stood a haystack. On the shady side of this, I sat down to read. The book was so different from anything that I had ever read before; it was something so new to my mind that, though I could not at all understand some of it, it delighted me beyond description; and it produced what I have always considered a sort of birth of intellect.[34]

It need not be a classic work of fiction to have such dramatic results upon a reader. For Edmund Gosse, at exactly the same age:

I am quite sure, that the reading and re-reading of *Tom Cringle's Log* did more than anything else, in this critical eleventh year of my life, to give fortitude to my individuality, which was in great danger — as I now see — of succumbing to the pressure my Father brought to bear upon it from all sides. My soul was shut up, like Fatima, in a tower to which no external influences could come, and it might really have been starved to death, or have lost the power of recovery and rebound, if my captor, by some freak not yet perfectly accounted for, had not gratuitously opened a little window in it and added a powerful telescope. The daring chapters of Michael Scott's picaresque romance of the tropics were that telescope and that window.[35]

In each of these cases, a book revealed to young readers the possibility of wider and more satisfying perspectives than they could find within their own narrow lives. For some readers, it may be the content of a book that is particularly important; for others it may even be the prose style itself. The most vital literary experience for the young Forrest Reid, for example, at a lonely and depressed stage of his childhood, was the reading of a novel written in the opulent prose of Marie Corelli. For him, her *Tale of Ardath* was:

A thing of over-whelming wonder and mystery, rich and dramatic as the poetry of Keats, and far more exciting. Can I read *any* book today with just that complete absorption in it? I think not. What I got then probably was the Ardath of Miss Corelli's imagination; what I should get now would be the very much less splendid Ardath of her actual achievement. Its gorgeousness would all too likely strike me as vulgarity, its passionate adventure as melodrama, its poetry as a crude straining after effect ... Might it not be argued that in any work of art it is the emotion awakened by it that matters? ... Nor is there much use, with my recollection of it, pretending that the old pleasure was not an aesthetic pleasure at all. It was. That is the whole point. It filled my mind with beauty; a barbaric, apocalyptic beauty I dare say — streaked with lust and blood and flaming, strident colours — but still beauty.[36]

In this way, a prose style itself often conveys very different attitudes and ways of looking at the world to readers, ranging from ironic detachment to full-scale commitment, and older children in particular now often start becoming more conscious of exactly *how* an author describes a story. Readers in this position may feel that a particular prose style best reflects how they themselves would like to describe things if they were able to write novels, and this realisation can influence the way they will then attempt to frame things in their own imagination or even how they try to express themselves to other people. At other times, another prose style may suggest far more novel ways of reacting to experience, as in the case of Forrest Reid. Voracious readers often quickly move from one favourite style to another, one month trying to think and write like Ernest Hemingway and the next passing on to D.H. Lawrence, as any schoolteacher of English knows from experience. Other readers, though, will not noticeably be influenced by what they read, and there are also, of course, many less distinctive prose styles, especially where writing for children is concerned, which never have any particular effect upon anyone.

But whether the imagination is affected by the style or content of particular stories, most young people — and many older ones too — will spend some of their time in daydreams sometimes inspired or helped along by books, and sometimes suggested by different sources, according to the individual concerned. It would be wrong to see this need for fantasy always as a mere escape from reality, however, just as it is false to view literature only in terms of compensatory day-dreams. An individual can put fantasy to many uses; for children, the ability to construct or reconstruct imaginary happenings in their own mind's eye can be an important step forward in their powers to organise material consequentially in the intellect. (Those children at school who are often accused of daydreaming and so not attending to the lesson, are often — on the contrary — those who cannot con-centrate on anything much at all — even their own fantasies.)[37]

In some cases, fantasies can become important extensions of experience, where children, especially as they grow older, start to experiment with different roles and feelings, work through some emotions, and generally exercise a natural curiosity that may not always want to be bound by the here and now. For one individual, early imagination can create aspirations that may later be realised; for another, life may always be something of a disappointment com-pared with such early daydreams. It will never be possible to predict how imagination will be used, therefore, but lack of imagination can be a handicap, particularly with the already underprivileged. As Bernard Shaw has written, 'A famous German Socialist, Ferdinand Lassalle, said that what beat him in his efforts to stir up the poor to revolt against poverty was their wantlessness. They were not, of course, content: nobody is; but they were not discontented enough to take any serious trouble to change their conditions.'[38]

Today such materialist fantasies, at least, are reflected and stimu-lated by advertising, but in other ways the private, fantasy world perhaps plays a less varied part in the lives of many children than it used to. This is not always for bad reasons; many autobiographers have linked their former habits of prolonged, sometimes even obsessional, imaginative games when young with the extreme bore-dom they were once made to suffer. Long Sundays where play was

179

forbidden, boring rote-learning every day at school, or endless needle-work at home are all phenomena that children now are better off without, and some of the daydreams these situations helped to foster as a way of passing the time may occasionally have become too intense, with life itself becoming a second-rate exchange for a world of exciting fantasy. Modern children, however, sometimes have little time on their own, and when they are bored, they can usually turn on the radio or the television set. There is still opportunity for pri-vate daydream here, of course, but very often what children are exchanging will be the small, private world of individual fantasy for the public daydreams of the mass media.

Literature, however, can still have a vital role in stimulating more personal, individual fantasy in children. For one thing, the way that novels have to be reconstructed by the individual in their own mind's eye already gives the resulting experience a great deal in common with personal fantasies. Many readers, for example, have described how they sometimes used to incorporate fictional characters into their own daydreams when young, or keep a type of parallel story going alongside the main action when they were reading, where it would be they themselves who were also engaged in the plot. Once again, this sort of involvement can of course also happen when watching films or television, though usually around a rather more narrow choice of characters and situations, which do not need to be personally realised in their audience's own creative imagination in the same way.

Where literature is concerned, however, individual readers can still indulge the imagination in the widest possible way, especially when they are allowed privacy within which they can travel into this other imaginary, internal world, free from external diversion — and typically children's favourite place for reading is nearly always in bed. For younger readers, daydreams like having a make-believe friend, inhabiting an imaginary country, or possessing magical powers can all be fuelled and elaborated upon by the choice of appropriate literature, so that the result can be a fusion between books and pri-vate fantasy. An imagination stimulated in this way has every chance to grow. At the same time, children are also provided in fiction with a very wide range of characters, in whose existence they may quite literally believe up to the age of seven, and sometimes beyond. Many of these characters also represent different aspects of adult maturity, and readers still inevitably uncertain about what sort of people they themselves are going to be, may occasionally find themselves trying to identify with such characters, sometimes even looking upon them as those 'immemorial comforters and protectors' in the imagination that C.S. Lewis claimed to find in certain fairy tales.

Older children may also find stimulating support for their own particular type of fantasy life in fiction. In addition, the whole structure of any conventional novel, where author and hero alike set out to discover a meaningful resolution to certain human situations, may have a particular significance as readers approach adolescence. The novelist, simply by writing a book, is showing how someone can search for purposes and patterns in life and eventually come up with something that may seem valid, at least at the time. As E.M. Forster has written, in what is still the best defence of fiction:

Novels, even when they are about wicked people, can solace us; they suggest a more comprehensible and thus a more manageable human race, they give us the illusion of perspicacity and of power . . . In the novel we can know people perfectly, and, apart from the general pleasure of reading, we can find here a compensation for their dimness in life.[39]

This appeal, however, may be particularly important to readers at the stage of adolescence when they often become more conscious of the confusions and inconsistencies of human existence. Novels can sometimes be a help and even a comfort here, and of course, experience of fiction can be far more vivid than this on those occasions when, through reading a particular novel, all the diversity of life suddenly seems to fall into shape and take on a new, vital meaning. Such moments may not always stand up to critical scrutiny later on in the light of greater experience, but on the other hand, they may sometimes last an individual a lifetime, giving a shape and meaning to things in a way that always remains personally satisfying. For G.K. Chesterton as a boy, for example, George MacDonald's novel The Princess and the Goblins was a book that 'made a difference to my whole existence'. The idea of wickedness undermining the castle in which goodness was enthroned was for him 'A vision of things which even so real a revolution as a change of religious allegiance has substantially only crowned and confirmed.'[40]

Ultimately, most individuals have to adopt some private, individual myth in order to explain the main direction of their lives to themselves and so give meaning to their existence by replacing the mere jumble of experience with at least the appearance of something more purposive. For W.B. Yeats, this was the 'one myth for every man which, if we but knew it, would make us understand all he did and thought'.[41] Youth in particular is the time for establishing a sense of identity, looking to the future, and trying to determine by what goals an individual may wish to live. It is therefore a natural period for fantasy, and it is only when people get much older that they begin to indulge themselves in fewer, or more backward-looking daydreams, once their real-life options start to close in upon them.[42] At the same time, literature is uniquely suited to discuss or portray a very wide range of thought or feeling since — in Lionel Trilling's words — it alone can 'take the fullest and most precise account of variousness, possibility, complexity and difficulty'.

Some puritan critics of literature, however, especially in the past, have never seen fiction as anything better than mere frivolous escapism, and have often used this opinion as grounds for condemning all pleasurable fantasy that provides an alternative to the demands of real life. Behind this type of condemnation, though, there has often been the fear that literature may sometimes provoke ideas that would be inappropriate or even socially subversive if readers were to take them seriously. It is a fact, of course, that however constricted an individual may be in real life, the imagination itself can always remain free; one reason, of course, why oppressive societies have frequently tried to control literature that could risk stimulating even internal, imaginative rebellion. As Dickens's Mr Gradgrind says to the little working-class girl who dares to imagine something other than her dismal reality: 'You mustn't fancy ... You must discard the word Fancy altogether. You have nothing to do with it.'[43]

No one now would want to sympathise with this sort of bullying, but on the other hand there can sometimes be danger signals for any individual in certain ways of reading, for example when books are used as a substitute for life itself, as in the traditional image of the bookworm. There may indeed be times in anyone's life, like periods of unhappiness, personal flux or unavoidable boredom, when it is quite advantageous for them to retreat into literature. At such times, books can be important sustaining forces, as Dickens describes in his autobiographical account of the miseries of the young, disgraced David Copperfield, when it was the novels of Smollett and Fielding that 'kept alive my fancy, and my hope of something beyond that place and time'.[44] At other times, reading may be used more as a useful drug, as another author has described:

My personality can scarcely have been formed before I found it an intolerable one to live with. Left to myself, I fled my self. Either I committed temporary suicide by total immersion in a book or I became an alternative self ... I still crave daily immersion in experience other than my own (it needn't be more pleasant, exciting or illuminating — merely other) and I still fall into books as though into catalepsy.[45]

But dwelling too much and too long in the imagination sometimes makes re-entry into reality extremely hard. The Brontë children, for example, lived so intensely in their imaginative worlds, fuelled by the books and newspapers that came into the house, that they always found forming social contacts with others outside the family very difficult. Charlotte, for example, once described herself as someone who 'had never played and could not play'. Later on, of course, the three sisters were able to draw successfully upon their wonderfully vivid imaginative worlds, though without ever losing their social diffidence. In Branwell's case, however, the gap between the glories of his imaginary country Angria and the far more mundane demands of the real world may eventually have been one of the factors that proved too much for him.

A distinguished children's writer has also described the possible dangers as well as the splendours of a rich, bookish imagination. As a child, Eleanor Farjeon made up a game with her brother Harry called TAR, where he had only to say 'We are This person and That, and we instantly *were* those two.' Such a game is one thing at the age of five, however, when it was originally conceived, but a different matter when it persists for the next twenty years, to Eleanor Farjeon's later regret.

So actual, so exciting, so fascinating was this twin-gift of ours, so much more marvellous was the life we could make for ourselves than the one we had found made for us, and so fertilely did the gift develop as we grew older, that the game of childhood had no excuse for dropping away with our growth. My own development took place far more within the boundaries of TAR than within those of life. At an age, and long past it, when life's horizons should have been widening, they kept their narrow circle, while those of TAR widened increasingly. I had no desire for new adventures, friends or experience, outside this powerful game. When I should have been growing up, it was a harmful check on life itself, for its imaginative extension did not include natural knowledge.[46]

Elsewhere, the particular nature of an unrealistic, possibly book-fed fantasy may later prove something of a personal handicap. *Madame Bovary*, for example, is a convincing imaginative portrait of someone tragically obsessed with romantic daydreams, and Mayhew makes the same point in his description of nineteenth-century London prostitutes:

The ruin of many girls is commenced by reading the low trashy wishy-washy cheap publications that the news shops are now gorged with, and by devouring the hastily-written, immoral, stereotyped tales about the sensualities of the upper classes, the lust of the aristocracy, and the affection that men about town — noble lords, illustrious dukes, and even princes of the blood — are in the habit of imbibing for maidens of low degree . . . who may perhaps feel flattered by reading about absurd impossibilities that their untutored and romantic imaginations suggest may, during the course of a life of adventure, happen to themselves. Well, they wait day after day, and year after year for the duke or the prince of the blood, perfectly ready to surrender their virtue when it is asked for, until they open their eyes, regard the duke and the prince of the blood as apocryphal or engaged to somebody else more fortunate than themselves, and begin to look a little lower, and favourably receive the immodest addresses of a counter-jumper, or a city clerk, or failing those a ruffianly pot-boy may realise their dreams of the ideal.[47]

Obviously literature cannot take all the responsibility for the degradation of young women in this case, who were presumably pushed into that sort of life and a weakness for romantic fantasies by social, economic or personal circumstances as well. There is evidence, as it is, that children with little confidence in themselves often have a particular need for compensatory fantasies in their literature, and may dislike more realistic stories. Children who do poorly at school, for example, are often less willing to encounter stories about school failure than are pupils who are more academically successful.[48]

In such cases, popular 'wishy-washy' publications, then and now, may underpin rather than initiate romantic, compensatory daydreams. Even so, when any young person's favourite fantasies, possibly triggered off or reinforced by such romantic literature, become too much out of step with their actual life-chances, the results can often be bitter disillusionment, especially for those already living in deprived circumstances.[49] So while the initial deprivation that may make romantic fantasies very popular cannot be blamed on literature, totally escapist material may also have little or nothing positive to suggest to most of its readers in these situations, other than offering the temporary relief of a drugged imagination.

Whether escapist literature actually dupes young readers or else merely gives them material which they already know to be false, is another question. Patronising commentators from the middle classes like Mayhew have often been over-pessimistic on this issue, seeing the working class as pathetically easy victims for any fantasy material in the mass media. Research, however, suggests a more complex picture. As a contemporary teenage girl once said, when asked about the fictional characters in love comics, 'The girls in the stories are too lucky. They always get a lovely boy in the end. They have a bit of upsets [*sic*] in the middle, but in the end it always comes all right. In real life you never get the boy you really want.'⁵⁰ Along with her friends, she still liked romantic comics, however. Even though they all knew them to be utterly unreal, these comics did at least offer a welcome contrast to the details of their own lives. Fictional heroes were nice to read about, for example, because 'They never swear. The blokes round here never stop swearing. These others in stories take them out to nice places, keep saying nice things . . . Boys in the club are never like that. They all stick together and just want to show off in front of their mates.'⁵¹

For Connie Alderson, who conducted this research, 'The girls did not connect the love-story world with theirs. Rather, they enjoyed the escapism.'⁵² The same would also be true of the older women who also read adolescent comics, sometimes nearly making up half of their total market. On the other hand, determinedly escapist literature of this sort usually does little to inspire readers, and there may always be girls or boys perhaps more socially isolated than others and so already more prone to compensatory daydreams, who take such material, and its unreal expectations, more seriously to heart. Like the confirmed television addict, however, one may here be dealing with someone who for other reasons of personality already 'finds relationships with other children difficult and seeks companionship and security in television and the other mass media . . . The addict has less desire to do things for himself and is more often prepared to see things on television rather than in real life.'⁵³

Any freedom of thought and expression always carries with it possibilities of abuse, however, and it is never *certain* that any of the effects discussed so far will ever necessarily happen. While some individuals of any age may occasionally become almost obsessed with particular fantasy material in print, for most readers it will probably always be much more a case of simply following a story because they want to find out what is going to happen next, with the whole experience little more than an agreeable diversion from everyday reality. This can, of course, be one of the great pleasures of reading for all of us, and accordingly every novel must first possess a good, engrossing story in order to make it come alive in the imagination. In this way, even *War and Peace* could be read solely for the sake of its romantic overtones and passages of exciting action, although it would not yield to this sort of approach as easily as would more light-weight fiction.

In any kind of reading, however, it has been claimed that we best 'identify when a certain character . . . enables us to achieve a close matching of our defences within a total re-creation of our psychological processes by means of a literary work'.[54] For Norman Holland, in his admirably thorough study of responses to fiction, the reader is always trying to project his own characteristic fantasy into what he reads, even if this means that he must 'tone, split, or shape the literary work considerably to make it fit'.[55]

But while it is true that older, more established readers may largely come to prefer books which duplicate and therefore confirm their own particular ways of looking at the world, the position can be rather different where younger readers are concerned. As we have seen from various autobiographical reminiscences, books can sometimes have an almost electrifying effect on readers still on the threshold of forming impressions and making up their own minds. Encountering passages from fiction, for example, which describe a familiar, personal state of mind can sometimes provide young readers with a novel and potentially revealing experience. For one thing, there is always the fascination of noting the skill with which an author may be able to describe and even sometimes give a name to hitherto private feelings or ideas; in Pope's words, 'What oft was thought, but n'er so well express'd.' But when authors occasionally go on to consider the possible reasons and motivations behind such states of mind, young readers — caught up in these discussions — may sometimes experience the real excitement that is always associated with gaining new, important psychological insights into certain aspects of one's own or other people's personalities. At another level, as I have already mentioned, individuals can also discover in these moments that they are not necessarily alone in some of their particular ideas, anxieties or aspirations. This realisation can be a valuable one, since as C.S. Lewis once truly wrote, 'Nothing, I suspect, is more astonishing in any man's life than the discovery that there do exist people very, very like himself.' After finishing a certain novel, however, readers — especially those who sometimes feel at odds with their surroundings — may now be relieved to know that they are not the only ones to feel or think in certain ways.

When it comes to responding to new experiences in literature, readers indeed often use fiction mainly to search for confirmations of the type of personal fantasy and outlook already familiar to them in their own imagination. But the fact that such fantasies can also be placed in very varied settings in fiction also helps extend the imagination in other directions. In fiction, after all, readers are free to roam both in time and space in an infinity of different disguises, identifying one day with an ancient Roman, on another with a nineteenth-century orphan, and on a third with a contemporary child from the Third World. In this way, they can have the sensation of entering into and sometimes even learning something about quite different roles, experiences or sensations, rather as infants will try to anticipate the mysteries of adult behaviour through imitating various grown-up pursuits in their own imaginary games. Sometimes one particular fictional personality, occupation or setting can seem much more attractive than all the others, and here individuals may take away some long-lasting impressions from their reading. As it is, children occasionally develop fantasies about their own future which are not always so divorced, when the time comes, from reality itself.[56] Fiction too can contribute here in giving more particular shape to early fantasies, which can occasionally linger on into later life as important goals in the imagination. Graham Greene, for example, has written that the reading of Rider Haggard's *King Solomon's Mines* as a boy 'certainly influenced the future', in terms of his life-long obsession with exploring and living in Africa.[57] It would be interesting to know how many other future choices of career or country received similar nudges from fiction read at a formative age, or how many times, as in the case of Forrest Reid, a particular prose *style* may sometimes have proved important in revealing aspects of a reader's personality to himself that he may not previously have known before.

But even though readers may be enabled in their imagination to step outside the historical, geographic and social boundaries that normally tie them down to the here and now, it could still be argued, as Norman Holland does, that individuals will always respond to new imaginative experiences according to their already habitual psychological processes and defences. This would seem to put a limit to any chance of genuine psychological growth occurring as a result of reading, but for younger readers in particular, still at a necessarily impressionable stage of development, there is always the chance that attitudes gleaned from literature can themselves become absorbed into this more general, personal outlook. Books that offer glimpses of different ways of defining or assessing common experiences, for example, may conceivably help readers, already so disposed, to

187

further broaden their attitudes and mental sets. As it is, different nations very often have their own distinctive outlook, reflected within their most famous novels as well as elsewhere. For a British reader, brought up on the stoical, self-help examples set by many of our own national fictional heroes or heroines, the defiant, self-destroying romanticism of a Stendhal, or the perpetual questioning of a Tolstoy, may come across as something both new and stimulating. Going back in time, there may also be moments when fictional characters from the past behave in ways that are no longer easy for today's reader to predict or sympathise with. Children now, for example, sometimes become quite out of patience when a character like Jane Eyre does not always act as they themselves would think best, when, for example, she refuses to stay any longer at the house of Mr Rochester. But because Jane is such a lifelike, compelling individual, readers may eventually find themselves forced into taking her point of view, and so once again extending their own understanding of a different way of thinking beyond the preconceptions of the immediate self.

It does seem possible, therefore, that reactions to literature can sometimes extend an individual's habitual way of perceiving and assessing imaginative experience, and that under this sort of spell, readers may indeed have the sensation of sharing thoughts and emotions very different from those they normally hold. This is not to say that those who have such experiences when reading literature necessarily make use of them in order to broaden their outlook in daily life. While some psychologists have claimed to find a connection between general 'decentration' skills and practical altruism, factors governing everyday behaviour may still be quite different from those other factors which help determine sensitive, widely-embracing reactions to literature. There can also be readers who turn to the humane in literature as compensation for the nature of their own actual behaviour. While love of the arts may sometimes ennoble some individuals, elsewhere those same arts may act as a type of drug through which other people can temporarily escape from the knowledge of their own shortcomings or transgressions. As George Steiner has written of the Nazi era, 'We know of personnel in the bureaucracy of the torturers and of the ovens who cultivated a knowledge of Goethe and Rilke.'[58]

Positive messages in literature, therefore, may not always be used in a positive way. Even so, the possible enlargement of the self still remains one of the most valuable *potential* gifts available from books. In the words of C.S. Lewis, once again, 'In reading great literature I become a thousand men and yet remain myself . . . I see with myriad eyes, but it is still I that see . . . I transcend myself; and am never more myself than when I do.'[59]

7 · Selection, censorship and control

While the effects of books upon children of any age vary from one individual to another, as we have seen, there have always been claims that certain literature has the capacity to produce general, undesirable results in the young. In fact, argument over selection and censorship is inseparable from discussion of children's literature; as Plato once wrote about conditions in his ideal republic, 'We shall therefore establish a censorship over writers of such stories, and shall desire mothers and nurses to tell only the authorised fiction, moulding the mind with such tales', and similar sentiments can be found up to our own times. There are probably as many calls for censorship of children's literature today as ever before, with issues like suspected racialism, sexism or social prejudice in literature now joining and sometimes replacing more traditional concerns about bad language or sexual frankness. Adults can all find themselves involved in this debate from time to time, even those who commonly see themselves as holding moderate positions. To take a hypothetical case: few today would feel happy about the re-issue of certain Nazi publications once addressed to children, from picture-books with titles like *Never Trust a Fox or the Promise of a Jew*, to a simplified biography of Hitler, where our hero was at one stage shown sharing his last crust with three little mice in his garret, although the text hastened to reassure young readers that 'He still knew how to be harsh with his enemies.'

Adult readers, at least in a democracy, are now generally thought of as able to take care of themselves so far as most literature is concerned; the prosecuting counsel's appeal to the jury during the trial in 1960 of D.H. Lawrence's *Lady Chatterley's Lover* — 'Is it a book that you would even wish your wife or your servants to read?' — is generally considered to have been an important factor in his losing the case. Childhood, however, is an impressionable period when chil-

190

dren pick up and acclimatise themselves to the different values, norms and attitudes of their own culture.

Some of the messages that come through to children from books as part of this process may have an important formative effect later, although quite how important is still a matter under dispute. It is a fact, for example, that early independence training has always been closely related to later high achievement in children, and the American psychologist David McClelland believes that such training very often includes regular exposure to stories which show their main characters as repeatedly successful in overcoming adversity. According to McClelland's researches, folk or children's literature particularly rich in examples of this type of 'achievement motivation' is found chiefly in societies especially during, and just before, periods of economic expansion. Poorer, more apathetic societies, on the other hand, tend to produce stories which reflect less hopeful attitudes.[1]

As we have already observed in the chapter on fairy-tales, there are indeed pronounced differences of atmosphere between, say, the fatalism that runs through tales from the Middle East such as *The Arabian Nights* and the general get-up-and-go spirit of stories like *Dick Whittington*, first popular at an expanding time in our own history during the seventeenth and eighteenth centuries. The difficulty that arises from McClelland's deductions, however, lies in deciding between the exact balance of cause and effect. Does early independence training, including exposure to positive stories, lead to an energetic adult population in later years and a thriving economy? Or are there other, more important factors to consider, such as the existence of a benign environment in the first place, thereby creating conditions where optimistic folk stories and a generally outward-looking culture are logical responses to this sort of bounty?

However this argument is resolved, it is still quite natural that adults should be concerned about the kind of knowledge and attitudes which may reach the young in their books, and after social revolutions, as in Russia and China this century, new governments often make a determined effort to change the tone of existing literature, both for children and for adults, in the effort to break away from past traditions and create a new atmosphere. Whatever the success of this sort of move, though, it seems to remain true in any society that whenever adults have the freedom to choose their own reading, they often themselves are attracted by rather different, less high-minded writing than they may wish their children to read.

Children's literature, however, is generally not expected to reflect all the varied, sometimes sordid preoccupations of a society; for this reason, both child and adult characters in books for the young may often reflect somewhat idealised versions of the real thing, although comic-strip characters can be something of an exception here. But teasing out and illustrating the less attractive values and behaviour in any society has more often been seen as one of the tasks of the adult rather than of the children's novelist.

This is not simply a question of double standards, although adult hypocrisy has undoubtedly sometimes been a factor. Children are quite naturally equipped, both intellectually and emotionally, to accept a more fundamentally moral, law-abiding view of things; they may not yet be ready to start on more complex literature that questions received moral values before they have first had the chance to learn what those values are supposed to represent. Many adults thus feel it is better to act cautiously, choosing books for children that do not step too far outside conventional, contemporary values and attitudes. If these standards appear to rub off on the young, then few will complain. But if parents think they can trace their children's antisocial behaviour back to the experience of reading certain outspoken books in school or library, then there may be a lot of anger directed, whether justifiably or not, against writer, publisher or the source that made such literature available.

Most children's literature, therefore, must always take account of the adults who will first be buying and then scrutinising it to make sure of its suitability for the young. For this reason, writers and publishers of children's literature have usually been inclined to play safe when it comes to anything very controversial. Indeed, until recently children's books were often something of a showcase for the conventional opinions of the middle classes of the time, from whom most of its authors have usually been drawn, and for whose offspring — until the arrival in the 1950s of more widespread school and public library facilities — very many children's novels were written. But to dismiss most children's books simply as propaganda for preserving broad conventions and even the whole class system itself, would be superficial. In some of the most interesting children's writers, lip-service to respectability often co-exists with a more radical approach. *Alice in Wonderland* and *Huckelberry Finn* are both in some ways disturbing books, and a writer like Rudyard Kipling, while echoing many of society's most conventional ideas, also injected his own particular brand of scepticism into his fiction. Interestingly, the contemporary reviews of his school story, *Stalky & Co.*, are among the most agitated that have yet been written about what was still ostensibly a children's book. Other talented writers, like E. Nesbit or Hugh Lofting, both mildly progressive in their social views, also brought some gentle iconoclasm into their books, while elsewhere preserving the conventional approaches expected of a children's writer.

Most children's authors, however, do choose to stick to current, non-controversial standards and ideas in their fiction. These conventional values may satisfy most parents and teachers but there are others who find them more objectionable. A social critic like George Orwell in his essay *Boys' Weeklies*, already referred to, can mock some of the weaknesses in current literary orthodoxies that later become obvious to many more people; spokesmen for present minority ideas or underprivileged groups can claim in the same way that conventional children's fiction is very prejudiced in certain ways and call for changes in approach. The modern children's novel, to take just one example, contains many favourable illustrations of family life. Most adults would not question such scenes, but those few who dislike the whole idea of the family see this as undesirable social propaganda, and unfair on those children from one-parent families who, faced with this type of family story again and again, may often feel left out and deprived. Again, various critics have attacked other trends in children's literature which most of us are similarly quite happy to go along with, such as the current emphasis upon self-fulfilment as an ideal, as opposed to what are now often thought to be more old-fashioned virtues, like duty, or loyalty to community values.[2] But it is always easier to assess such criticisms when one is able — with hindsight — to see whether they are pointing at things which do eventually prove to be weaknesses in current attitudes, just as it is easier to criticise Victorian children's literature now for its sentimentality and insensitive, patronising attitudes, than it would have been at the time when most critics themselves would have sympathised with this outlook. Contemporary critics of particular trends in children's literature may one day seem to be proved right, therefore, but the opposite can also be true. All they can do, therefore, is sound a warning note; whether it is heard or not will depend both on their persuasive powers, and also on how radically they are trying to make writers step away from the conventional, contemporary wisdom which always crops up in the bulk of children's literature.

Today, children's books — taken as a whole — still reflect the current liberal orthodoxies of most of their typical writers and buyers, with stories that usually contain more progressive views on race, social class or personal psychology than would be the norm in any random cross-section of public opinion. These are values that most parents would be more or less willing to go along with, however, at least in literature if not in practice, but this tolerance would not necessarily extend to more radical departures from current attitudes. A quick look at the changing history of certain nursery rhymes, for example, can give as good an idea as any of how children's literature has always had to accommodate itself to various shifts in conventional adult taste over the centuries.

To begin with, early versions of nursery rhymes were often extremely earthy, and even the most liberated parent today might object to the original form in which *There was a Lady Loved a Swine* appeared in print, where it was coupled with a crude joke about bestiality. The first recognisable nursery-rhyme anthology, *Tom Thumb's Pretty Song Book* (1744) also included three very coarse rhymes illustrating the sort of lavatory humour that is still found amusing by children, but which in a book today would probably find few adult defenders. Some more racy nursery rhymes also found their way into the first really comprehensive collection put together by James Halliwell in 1842, more for antiquarian interest than anything else, though Halliwell still took care to omit other versions which he describes as 'Very curious, but unfortunately too indelicate to print'.

As it was, the anthology was a great success with children, and subsequent editions of it all show how Halliwell became increasingly responsive to Victorian demands for respectability where young readers were concerned. When it was reprinted, Halliwell wrote a new preface which claimed that, 'In the expectation of rendering our collection an unexceptionable contribution to the juvenile library, every allusion that could possibly offend the most fastidious reader has been carefully excluded.' Gone now, for example, were malicious verses of the *Said Moses to Aaron* variety, as well as extracts from an unpleasantly anti-semitic ballad, about St Hugh of Lincoln, fatally lured into a garden by a murderous young Jewess. But there were also some rather good rhymes that were dropped, probably because they did not now seem sufficiently genteel for children, like this one:

> Bryan O'Lin had no breeches to wear,
> So he bought him a sheepskin to make him a pair,
> With the skinny side out and the woolly side in,
> 'Oh, how nice and warm', cried Bryan O'Lin.

In another instance, Halliwell keeps the rhyme but changes one word only. Here is his original version:

> O rare Harry Parry!
> When will you marry?
> When apples and pears are ripe,
> I'll come to your wedding,
> Without any bidding,
> And lie with your bride all night.

In his second edition, Halliwell tactfully substitutes 'And dance with your bride all night', but in later years even this was obviously thought to be too indiscreet, and the line finally ended as 'And dance and sing all the night', thus reasserting prudence at the expense of the natural rhythm of the verse.

In the last edition supervised by Halliwell, which appeared in 1890 shortly after his death, a number of the other more outspoken rhymes of his earlier editions had been dropped or altered, sometimes to be replaced by pious, obviously moralistic verses, such as

> When little Fred went to bed,
> He always said his prayers,
> He kissed his Mamma and then his Papa,
> And straightway went upstairs.

Today, we are still living with some of the effects of this type of nineteenth-century clean-up of nursery rhymes: in modern versions of *Lavender's Blue, Lavender's Green*, for example, it is rare now to find references to earlier lines like

> While you and I, diddle diddle,
> Keep the bed warm.

Similarly, the little maid, courted by the little man, hardly ever promises that she will 'make a little print in your bed, bed, bed', preferring instead the altogether more respectable 'E'er I to the church will be led, led, led'. Few would probably mind now if these older lines were restored, but every generation has its own taboos so far as nursery rhymes are concerned, and today there are quite different verses that many would prefer no longer to see in print. In the rhyme *Old Mother Goose and the Golden Egg*, for example, one traditional verse runs:

> Jack sold his gold egg,
> To a rogue of a Jew,

Who cheated him out of,
The half of his due.

Although Halliwell, as we saw, purged his original nursery-rhyme collection of any anti-semitic rhymes as early as 1843, a few anthologies continued to keep this verse, including Walter de la Mare's otherwise delightful *Nursery Rhymes for Certain Times*, still in print. Others, however, usually get round the embarrassment of the second line by substituting 'a merchant untrue', or even 'a neighbour called Hugh', and these new versions seem to win most people's approval, although I did receive one protest letter, when originally discussing this topic on the BBC, from a Mrs Hughes protesting against the libel 'on behalf of my family and all Hughs'. As part of an oral culture, however, nursery rhymes have always been responsive to changes in contemporary meaning or emphasis, even though they can also retain some very ancient words and attitudes at the same time. There are some other, fairly unredeemable old shockers, however, that would seem hardly worth saving for children by whatever means, like the following rhyme, cheerfully reprinted as late as 1962:

A penn'orth of bread to feed the Pope,
A penn'orth of cheese to choke him;
A pint of beer to wash it down,
And a good old faggot to burn him.

Apart from objections to particular lines, there have always been wholesale attacks upon all nursery rhymes, but none of these have ever been successful. The last organised campaign against them was launched by a Yorkshire business man, Mr Geoffrey Hall, under the banner 'The True Aim Movement for Nursery Rhyme Reform'. Between 1948 and 1955 he attempted to clean up any reference to violence or unhappiness in nursery rhymes by providing his own anthology where, for example, three blind mice became three kind mice, and the old woman who lived in a shoe 'Had so many children, and loved them all too'.[3] The campaign was a flop, however, both with parents and children, even though there has been a reaction in this century against some of the violence found in older nursery-rhyme anthologies. Rhymes that seem designed to frighten children to go to sleep, with the image of 'Boney', the Kaiser or even Hitler coming to gobble them up if they remain awake, although still found in oral circulation, are now generally dropped from collections. Some of those savage little riddles have also disappeared now, such as this one (the answer is an orange):

When I went up Sandy-Hill,
I met a Sandy-Boy,
I cut his throat,
I sucked his blood,
And left his skin a-hanging-o.

Despite the evidence of a gradual change in nursery rhymes, however, anyone who has ever tried to push children's literature too far and too quickly in the direction of respectability has had to recognise that particular favourites under attack normally manage to survive, just as children's jokes, games, chants and folklore can last almost intact for centuries. Like nursery rhymes themselves, children's taste cannot be easily altered or improved beyond a certain limit, except perhaps over a long period of time.

Popular literature for children thus often represents something of a compromise. On the one hand, adults and children expect it to echo conventional ideas of morality, but children may also want to find within it some reflection of their unsocialised, less acceptable feelings, and here they often run into adult opposition. Some of the most successful children's popular literature, therefore, is that which manages to satisfy both sorts of expectation. Traditional rhymes and stories start with an advantage, since they have been around for so long that everyone is more or less used to them, even to the occasionally aggressive note in many nursery rhymes, in contrast to the placidity expected from most other literature ostensibly aimed at infants.

The history of the fairy-tale also illustrates this same tension between what children want and what adults allow them to have. Like Halliwell's first anthology of nursery rhymes, fairy stories too were originally collected ostensibly for the attention of folklorists rather than for children, which helps to explain why certain details were sometimes allowed to slip through in a way that later embarrassed succeeding generations and even the anthologists themselves. An amusing example of this can be found in George Dasent's 1859 translation of *Popular Tales from the Norse*, taken from the great collection by Asbjornsen and Moe. Very much the scholar, Dasent writes defiantly in his 'translator's notice' to the first edition that he

Is sorry that he has not been able to comply with the suggestion of some friends upon whose good will he sets all store, who wished him to change and soften some features in these tales, which they thought likely to shock English feeling. He has, however, felt it to be out of his power to meet their wishes, for the merit of an undertaking of this kind rests entirely on its faithfulness and truth; and the man who, in such a work, wilfully changes or softens, is as guilty as he 'who puts bitter for sweet, and sweet for bitter'.

197

The collection almost immediately sold out and in his preface to the second edition, Dasent added another notice — and by this time he was more aware of the juvenile nature of his audience. Accordingly,

Before the Translator takes leave of his readers for the second time, he will follow the lead of the good godmother in one of these tales, and forbid all good children to read the two which stand last in the book. There is this difference between him and the godmother. She found her foster-daughter out as soon as she came back. He will never know it, if any bad child has broken his behest. Still he hopes that all good children who read this book will bear in mind that there is just as much sin in breaking a commandment even though it be not found out, and so he bids them goodbye, and feels sure that no good child will dare to look into those two rooms. If, after this warning, they peep in, they may perhaps see something which will shock them.

It is hard to imagine many normal children resisting this temptation, similar to the situation in Bluebeard's castle although with rather different consequences, since the two forbidden stories, about unfaithful wives or fiancées, are not really so very shocking. Most fairy stories once in print, however, become increasingly separated in style and content from their original, oral sources, which were usually very short and abrupt. As Andrew Lang wrote in the preface to *The Orange Fairy Book*, 'The stories are not literal, or word by word translation ... but have been altered in many ways to make them suitable for children. Much has been left out in places, and the narrative has been broken up into conversations.'[4] Joseph Jacobs admitted to the same thing, and Wilhelm Grimm also rewrote many of his collected stories, bringing in more dialogue and extra detail, such as popular proverbs, all with a definite child audience in mind. In fact, some of the Grimms' best-known stories, like *Little Red Riding Hood* and *Snow White and the Seven Dwarfs* were taken from literary rather than oral sources.

Further discreet alterations have been made to Grimms' tales by later English translators. Edgar Taylor's translation in 1823, for example, which was widely used both for future editions here and for many other versions abroad, censored much of the violence and changed mentions of the devil and hell into the less controversial references to giants and caves. British children have thus been denied the interesting theological idea that the devil has a grandmother, a detail which occurs in several of the original German stories. Religious references, for example to the Virgin Mary behaving in a way that is distinctly vampirish, have also been glossed over. It is due to Taylor, too, that the magic donkey in *The Table, the Ass and the Stick* now rains gold from his mouth rather than from both ends, thus depriving the story of a good finale, where an ordinary donkey, wickedly exchanged, is led home in triumph only to rain 'what were not gold pieces' on to the clean table-cloth specially provided. Other more earthy references, for example where princesses lull their swains to sleep by delousing their hair, were changed into respectable but surely less soporific games of ball.

Some of these emendations (Joseph Jacobs consistently changing all mention of 'mid-wife' into 'nurse' in one story, for example), seem ridiculous today, but it would be a brave critic who would argue now for a completely unexpurgated version of Grimms' tales for children.

It can be argued that children need to find a reflection of their own violent feelings in their literature, of course, and fairy stories shorn of all their occasional savagery could degenerate into the bland, passionless stuff despised by Kipling, peopled by 'little buzzflies with butterfly wings and gauze petticoats, and shiny stars in their hair, and a wand like a school-teacher's cane for punishing bad boys and rewarding good ones'.[5] But the way in which more specific, sadistic details are sometimes described in certain fairy-tales is another matter, especially when narrators like the brothers Grimm so clearly appear to approve and even gloat over the idea of cruel punishment and lingering death. In their version of the Cinderella story, for example, they incorporate 'two little white doves' who fly down and peck out the eyes of the proud sisters. This is a very pointed punishment for the sin of envy, perhaps, but hardly an improvement on the oral version they drew on, where the sisters were merely humbled. Other stories in the same collection now give rise to other objections: *The Jew Amongst Thorns*, for example, is too crudely anti-semitic for comfort, and *The Dog and the Sparrow* seems quite disproportionately savage. In fact, the Grimms themselves later omitted some of their most blood-thirsty tales from their collection, such as the one where children — playing at slaughterhouses — end by killing and dismembering one of their playmates.

There are other examples where former editors omitted details that do not seem so bad today, but were less censorious over other matters that now prove more offensive. Andrew Lang once prepared an edition of *The Arabian Nights* 'with the omission of pieces suitable for Arabs and old gentlemen', and in his series of colour fairy books promised that 'In many tales, fairly cruel and savage deeds are done, and these have been softened as much as possible.' Even so, the team of ladies who edited and transcribed these tales, under Lang's direction, still included the story *What the Rose did to the Cypress* in *The Brown Fairy Book*, where a beautiful and barely clothed lady is first flogged and then made to eat dog excrement by order of her jealous husband. Crude, cautionary tales designed to terrify children into good behaviour were also once very popular, like Joseph Jacobs's *Mr Miacca*, about an ogre who devours bad boys who go out in the street against their mothers' orders. There is another, similar story in his collection *English Fairy Tales*, where a white-faced, elf-mother comes down the chimney at night in search of children who will not go to bed on time. Parents may still sometimes read or tell such stories, or variations upon them, in an attempt to frighten or generally bamboozle their offspring into good behaviour, especially at night-time, but this is a bad and possibly harmful way of trying to establish control.[6]

What one may be left with finally in any fairy-tale anthology, therefore, must always be a compromise between faithfulness to older sources and some acknowledgement of differences in contemporary standards of taste.

This argument over acceptable levels of violence in literature for children can also be found in the 1955 debate on horror comics in this country, which culminated in an Act of Parliament banning their future sale. An American psychiatrist, Dr Frederick Wertham, played an active part in this whole discussion for some years, finally writing a best-selling book called *Seduction of the Innocent*, which graphically described certain comics that were pushing their stories and illustrations to new levels of sadism. In one comic, for example, published by a firm ludicrously named 'Tiny Tots Incorporated', a sixteen-year-old girl was shown raped by a sheriff, who then framed an innocent youth who was later beaten to death with the accompanying noise of 'crunching, crushing bone'. Elsewhere, there were nostalgic reminiscences by concentration-camp guards ('Hit him some more, Franz; make him bleed more,') and Super-Duck, a self-proclaimed 'hard-guy' with a 'heart made of stone', beats a rabbit to death with a baseball bat. Meanwhile, similar sadistic fantasies were being dreamed up weekly by other rival writers and illustrators.

The notching-up of special, violent effects is nothing new in the mass media. As the producer of an American TV series called 'The Untouchables' once wrote to one of his staff, 'On page 31 of this script, I wish we could come up with a different device than running the man down with a car, as we have done this now in three different shows. I like the idea of sadism, but I hope we can come up with another approach to it.'[7] Horror comics also got steadily nastier as they looked for new approaches, and public opinion, spurred on by the National Union of Teachers who mounted a travelling exhibition of the worst examples was eventually roused against them. Cynics, however, were sometimes heard to say that the very success of the exhibition was also an example of how fascinated many people were by such comics, and that one reason Wertham's book exposing them sold so well was precisely because of its horrific illustrations.

Whatever any possible ambiguities of response, however, the House of Commons duly introduced and passed an 'Act to prevent the dissemination of certain pictorial publications harmful to children and young persons'. Previously, comics could not be prosecuted under the already existing Obscene Publications Bill, because as the Home Secretary, Major Gwilym Lloyd-George observed at the time, 'obscene has come to be regarded as being restricted to matters relating to sex'. American publishers were also eventually forced to adopt a self-imposed Comic Code of Behaviour, and for the time being the horror comic is dead, although every now and again some unpleasant specimens still work their way into newsagents' shops.

In the debate, horror comics were not able to ask for the licence granted to horrific literature, such as Shakespeare's *Titus Andronicus*, since it was generally agreed that 'literary merit is irrelevant to pictorial publications'. On the other hand, no one defended them on the grounds of their sometimes clever if twisted artwork (at this stage, comic-strip techniques had yet to become fashionable and sometimes influential amongst more respected artists). The general feeling in the House of Commons was that comic-strips, particularly in their American form, were not worth defending at any level. Many people still agree with this judgement, but it was resented then and since by enthusiasts from comic-strip art, who felt they were getting short measure from such sweeping judgements, where the rights of literature were considered far more important than those of any type of illustration.

Other critics, meanwhile, pointed out what seemed to them a different set of double standards: the government publishing the bill to ban horror comics in the same week as it produced its White Paper on defence and the H Bomb. As an American critic later put it, while adults were freely experimenting with far more serious excesses of violence themselves, there was the professed concern that 'We, the young, were being corrupted by violence in comic books.'[8] Whatever the wider issues raised by this argument, however, there is reasonable evidence that violent literature can be used by the young to stimulate what have been termed 'eerie, unhealthy fantasies'.[9] This still tells us little about any tangible effects arising from reading violent comics, however, and when young readers were asked their opinions on the most horrific moments they had yet experienced in literature, 'By way of curious example, the most frightening thing that the researchers encountered was *Jane Eyre*, which one would hardly think of as dangerous material.'[10]

In some senses, the horror comic was the direct heir to the eighteenth- and nineteenth-century Gothic fantasy, with its emphasis upon putrefaction, necrophilia and haunted graveyards. There was often an element of pastiche in such writing, and this too could be found in horror comics, with their insistent, alliterative prose styles, and heavily exaggerated effects. Those who relished this material in comics were not so different from readers who once lapped up penny dreadfuls, 'bloods' and all the other catch-penny stuff that used to thrive on highly-coloured, occasionally sadistic, dramatic content. It is difficult to say whether this sort of literature creates or satisfies a demand in readers. Havelock Ellis, for example, describes in his own life how a passion for the tamer but still 'extravagantly sensational and romantic adventures' of a penny weekly, *The Boys of England*, affected him at the age of eleven.

The fascination with which this literature held me was a kind of fever. It was an excitement which overwhelmed all ordinary considerations. My mother forbade me to read these things, but, though I usually obeyed her, in this matter I was disobedient without compunction . . . But the fever subsided as suddenly as it arose — probably it only lasted a few weeks — and left not a trace behind. It is an experience which enables me to realise how helpless we are in this matter. If this is the literature a boy needs nothing will keep him away from it.[11]

Teachers of English in the classroom today will also know how eagerly many adolescent boys react towards any suggestion of violence in literature, whether it is there deliberately to titillate or not. Havelock Ellis goes on to explain this interest in terms of 'The latent motor energies of developing youth', seeing it as merely a passing phase, of no great importance. Subsequent research on the effects of violent material in the mass media has, on the whole, both confirmed and qualified this view. It is, in fact, comparatively rare to find specific, antisocial behaviour that can be traced back directly to the influence of particular reading matter, and in general there are always other social and personality factors also at work in the making of a juvenile delinquent. But a few particular, already unbalanced individuals have seemed to become very influenced by various violent fictional or television fantasies from time to time. The argument here is usually over whether such people would have acted in this way anyhow, or whether certain stimulation from outside might have been just enough to trigger them off into specific actions they might not otherwise have considered.

At the same time, other critics have claimed that if any culture gives quite undue emphasis to certain sadistic material, like the way that American television constantly portrays scenes of violence and death, then no one can be surprised if young people in general come to accept the incidence of violence as an everyday part of adult life still to come. But as we have said before, while adults have often felt that they themselves can choose what they want to read or view without necessarily becoming contaminated by such material, and so frequently resist the idea of any censorship of their own favourite books or television programmes, they have generally felt less happy with the idea of children also having the same rights to choose exactly what they might want to read or view. The most powerful argument against horror comics was finally that their use of comic-strip techniques made them accessible even to small children who can, of course, react to pictures long before they can decode prose. It was this factor that was eventually to prove conclusive in getting such comics banned.

Horror comics, therefore, tried to push the public tolerance of sadistic material in children's publications too far, and the reaction that followed was sometimes quite fierce. The Comic Code finally adopted by American publishers, while cleaning up such publications, also worked against the development of comics in other ways. American comics have always had greater creative potential than their British counterparts, but no literature can ever flourish once it has to follow too many of the ponderous guidelines of the sort that were then imposed, where, for example, 'No story can appear in which a law-breaker makes a police officer look foolish', and 'In the comic books we approve, every attempt is made to uphold high ideals of family life.'[12] This new right to interfere was also occasionally put to political use; three cartoonists who had formerly attacked Senator McCarthy in their strips now found themselves censored.

Other interested pressure groups also became active, from the 'Mothers of America' to professional associations objecting to slurs upon their members, for example in traditional jokes about cruel dentists, inefficient laundries or explosive chemistry sets. The Comic Code was eventually forced to become less rigid, but the whole episode illustrates how difficult it can be to establish clear standards of what is thought acceptable in children's literature, and the dangers that can follow either from letting things well alone, or else from excessive interference. For this reason, most free societies prefer to interfere with literature as little as possible — a stand variously described as a belief in freedom of speech, mere indifference, or moral cowardice in the face of strong commercial interests, according to personal conviction.

Where other types of reading are concerned, however, children are sometimes quite able to act as their own, occasionally quite harsh moral censors; for example, turning away in disbelief or disgust from descriptions of behaviour that has now become unpopular, such as the wholesale slaughter of wild animals for sport. Contemporary writers and publishers often share these inhibitions and taboos, together with other, usually liberal attitudes of their own. Most children's books, for example, will now be very careful about offending the sensibilities of minority groups. In fact, children's writers' greater social tolerance today sometimes makes it hard for them to create and then put the blame on any recognisable villain at all.

Where wild animals are concerned, for example, predators — who once used to make splendid, ravaging villains in children's stories — may now instead be explained in terms of their ecological functions and for smaller children, savage lions and tigers may be transformed into more generally quiescent, misunderstood creatures, as in Louise Fatio's series about the happy lion who simply wants to live quietly away from the real villains of the piece, his human persecutors. Greater tolerance can also be found in the modern literary treatment of witches. As we have seen, psychoanalysts tend to believe that the idea of the witch, so central to human imagination, is a projection of children's darker fantasies about the mother, just as fairy godmothers represent more idealised fantasies. But the particular literary stereotype of the witch — a bent old lady with a cat — is an image that dates from one of the most inhumane episodes in European history, when confused, older women, living on their own, were picked on and tortured, particularly during the seventeenth century, as scape-goats for general discontent with society.

Modern writers have reacted against this stereotype and now show far more compassion in how they portray the elderly in every way — something frequently absent from nineteenth-century authors like Dickens or W.S. Gilbert, who were always ready to turn in comic descriptions of crabbed or decaying old age. One result, however, has been a spate of recent well-intentioned but very feeble books with titles like *The Good Witch*, *The Lonely Witch*, or in a certain comic, *Esmeralda — the Happy Witch*. As their titles suggest, evil witches seldom stay the course and usually end as friends with the child characters, who discover that they are nice old ladies after all. If they persist in trying to be wicked, they usually make a mess of it, and finish up looking ridiculous or even pathetic.

This decline of the all-purpose villain in children's fiction, whether it be witch, hump-back, rough gypsy, working-class thug, sinister Lascar, lisping Chinese or any other former target for fear or intolerance, is complemented by the gradual disappearance in children's literature of the upright fictional hero who can do no wrong, although both these stereotypes can still be found in various contemporary comics and annuals. Politically, uncritical hero-worship has resulted in disaster this century, and elsewhere modern philosophy and theology has increasingly stressed the unavoidable difficulties involved in trying to make blameless moral choices in a world of conflicting claims and values. Many modern authors, responsive to these changes in outlook, therefore find it less easy to create convincing ever-upright heroes of the old fashioned sort. Instead, true heroism is more likely now to be shown as something achieved in spite of fears and shortcomings, rather than because of special superior virtues.

For all the gains in greater understanding, this sort of treatment does not easily lend itself to the simple-minded heroics that younger children still find attractive in their literature. The same more scep-tical attitude can also be found today in popular historical writing. Gone are the days of best-sellers like Charlotte Yonge's *A Book of Golden Deeds*, where stories of 'The exposure of life and limb to the utmost peril' were designed to cause young readers' hearts to 'burn within you as you read of these various forms of the truest and deepest glory'. Today, Florence Nightingale is probably as famed for the frosty image she imposed upon future nursing practice as for her heroism in the Crimea, and Edith Cavell was described as 'dangerously naive' in a popular, mildly debunking children's book published in paperback, and typical of this more quizzical way of looking at things.[13]

Older children often welcome a more open approach to moral dilemmas, as it is easy to tire of those literary characters who are too good to be true. As Graham Greene writes about Rider Haggard's heroes, Quatermain and Curtis:

> They were men of such unyielding integrity (they would only admit to a fault in order to show how it might be overcome) that the wavering personality of a child could not rest for long against those monumental shoulders. A child, after all . . . is quite well aware of cowardice, shame, deception, disappointment. Sir Henry Curtis perched upon a rock bleeding from a dozen wounds but fighting on with the remnant of the Greys against the hordes of Twala was too heroic. These men were like Platonic ideas: they were not life and one had already begun to know it.[14]

Younger or less sophisticated readers, however, as we have already seen, still respond to the idea of absolute good and evil, and their personification in characters who are made to both look and act the part. The witch in Disney's film *Snow White*, for example, must be one of the most successful villains ever portrayed, and so convincing that legions of children are said to have wet their seats in the film's original show place in America, which eventually had to be completely re-upholstered.[15] The cheer that comes when she finally falls to her death is always wholehearted, and it takes a good villain to die in such a satisfactory way, leaving an audience in the happy state of having no second thoughts or residual pity for his or her ultimate fate. The more complex treatment of heroes and villains found in some contemporary children's fiction, however, can lead to a split between those books children read when prepared for something demanding, and the more popular material that exists to satisfy less sophisticated literary needs and expectations, found particularly in comics and annuals.

This split between the popular and the more demanding has always been present in children's literature, however, and arguments about the desirability of either can often be heard when various long-lived, sometimes even notorious characters in popular children's reading are occasionally singled out for critical attack. In 1970, for example, Frank Richards' *Billy Bunter* stories were banned by an Ipswich librarian who believed that 'Nowadays we are wiser and realise that excessive fatness is a physical disability like any other — not the result of gluttony. Bunter and his sister were gluttons, and we do not want to perpetuate this mistaken image.' There is some force in this argument, however patronisingly it was later attacked in the correspondence columns of the press by former Bunter fans, who obviously felt that any criticism of these stories was also a criticism of themselves, and the enjoyment they once derived from such things. But raising laughs from mocking a physical oddity or defect is a crude form of humour, and there would be no sympathy, for example, for any story that made fun of spastic children, although cruel jokes on this topic can unfortunately be heard in school playgrounds today. In the same way, over fifty epithets to do with excessive fatness, still in current use among contemporary children, have been listed by the Opies.[16] But the mere existence of traditional, perhaps rather defensive oral humour about individuals who look to varying degrees different from the norm, is no argument for the same type of humour appearing in literature.

One major difficulty in trying to discourage Bunter books, however, is that he is already here and still very popular. Like Mr Punch and his hump, he dates from a time when crude humour was more acceptable. Once children have got a literary character whom they find amusing, they will be unwilling to let him go, and as nostalgic adults, may continue to rise in his defence. There is, too, more to Bunter than his mere fatness: he is also a cheat, liar, braggart, coward, and at times a snob. All this, added to his distinctive clown's dress (check trousers, floppy bow-tie) makes him a natural nonconformer, and without him Greyfriars would not be nearly so entertaining a place. His massive greed is an organic part of this character, as is his rebellion against the social inhibitions that other, more law-abiding children are learning to adopt as they grow up. The humour associated with Bunter's size is inseparable from his total comic effect. When he first began his literary life, he was only a minor character, not even particularly fat — the smallest boy in the form, in fact. As his girth grew, however, so did his comic impact, and the result is someone who hardly looks human and behaves with a lack of conventional restraint that makes him, like Falstaff, both funny for himself and also for the effect he has on others.

Bunter, therefore, belongs to a long line of stout, untamed anti-heroes, who — in contrast to most of their readers — unashamedly give way whenever possible to the deadly sin of gluttony, and often break other social rules as well. The example of Bunter may still sometimes encourage the teasing of obese children, and any attempt today to build up a comic fictional character based on extreme physical oddity would probably be strongly opposed before it could take root in the popular imagination. Minority groups of any sort, once good for cheap laughs or easy prejudice, have every right to be championed by their spokesmen, of course, but it is also true that to be successful comic characters for the young must, at least to some extent, work within the broader forms of humour or social stereotypes that children can easily recognise. It is unrealistic, therefore, to expect children's literature always to avoid any reflection of its audience's immaturity, even when such reflections may sometimes seem crude and perhaps unfeeling. If all children's authors consistently write above the heads of their audience, and if the institutions which provide books for the young become over-fastidious in their selections, rather than children themselves changing, children's literature itself could become increasingly remote from those for whom it is supposed to be catering.

Anyone concerned with book provision for children is bound to come across these arguments from time to time, and they can never be resolved to everyone's satisfaction. But there are other ways in which writers can reflect popular, powerful juvenile fears or prejudices in their fiction, without always having to dress them up in traditional stereotypes. The strong emotions aroused by witches, for example, need not always centre upon the image of an old hag; C.S. Lewis was able to create an equally effective and murderous young witch in his best-selling 'Narnia' series — a lady with a face as white as snow or icing-sugar, except for her very red mouth. Another writer for children, Lucy Boston, describes a dumpy, middle-aged witch posing as an American doctor of demonology in *An Enemy at Green Knowe*, who possesses large hands like 'rooks' claws about to land'. Other stereotypes and traditional jibes can be developed into something more original and possibly challenging. In *Lord of the Flies*, William Golding creates in 'Piggy' the stock fat boy of rough school humour, and shows how mindless jeering devalues and finally destroys him, the most intelligent child there.

If parents or teachers, aware of some of these issues and anxious to make the right literary choices for children, turn to 'expert' advice, they are still unlikely to find unanimous recommendations about which books to avoid. Maurice Sendak's *Where the Wild Things Are*, for example, is one of the most striking picture-books published since the war, but it has sometimes divided both critical and lay opinion. Although Sendak won the Caldecott medal for it, the *American Journal of Education* declared: 'We should not like to have it left about where a sensitive child might find it to pore over in twilight.' It is indeed a powerful work; as Sendak himself has said, 'My object is never to lie to children' and his books recognise that the child can have very strong feelings indeed — anger and fear, as well as the need to be 'Where someone loved him best of all'.[17] The monsters, which the tyrannical boy hero Max conjures up from his imagination, may be fearsome to some children, but they are apparently less horrific than the drawings that Maurice Sendak has received from some of his young fans, with requests like 'How much does it cost to get to where the wild things are? If it is not expensive my sister and I want to spend the summer there.'[18] To protect children from books like this may help shelter them from the odd upset, but it also means that they will be denied some vital, stimulating work.

It does seem reasonable though, to avoid very terrifying or sadistic details in illustrated books, in that small children may be influenced by them, whether such books were originally designed for them or not. As it is, powerful, horrific visual effects can sometimes return to haunt a child's imagination in a way that Charles Lamb, among others, has described so movingly.[19] Where prose alone is concerned, some parents or teachers may also hesitate over the gory details in the traditional Bluebeard story, including, 'the floor . . . covered with clotted blood, in which were mirrored the bodies of several dead women, hanging on hooks around the wall'. Decisions to ban such material may turn out to be wrong in terms of possible, immediate effects; small children sometimes react calmly to horrors, while becoming more upset over ostensibly more trivial matters. But literary judgements are concerned with individual values as well as with possible after-effects; at the age when children still look to parents and teachers to be involved in the selection and reading aloud of their books, it is reasonable for adults to avoid literature that seems to them very unpleasant or immoral, whatever the impact of the literature concerned may or may not have turned out to be.

There are also more objections today to racialism in children's literature, and in a multi-racial society it is certainly wrong that black children — at least up to a few years ago — could find few books that acknowledged their existence, apart from dated stereotypes like the cannibal chief or the faithful black servant plodding along in the footsteps of his white master. Studies of the effects of this cumulative cultural bias have suggested that young black children often react by denying their own colour, for example by frequently preferring a white to a black doll when asked to 'choose a doll that looks like you', or in self-portraits picturing themselves with European features.[20] Helped by pressure from outside, however, there are today more books within which black children can recognise themselves in a modern, urban setting. The same books can also help white children to get used to this idea, whether they share their everyday environment with black children or not.

Most people would agree that books which recognise new situations in which children live are useful additions to any bookshelf, as long as their literary or artistic quality is also good, and the book is not just an attempt to jump upon a lucrative, progressive bandwagon. No reader, after all, wants to be bored or unconvinced by what he or she reads, even though it is written in a good cause. The problem is rather different, however, when it comes to deciding what to do with already existing books for children that are clearly colour-prejudiced. Forgotten literature like the Victorian favourite, *The Story of the Naughty Little Coloured Coon*, does not present a problem; and few today would even remember the 1957 version of a comic like *Chicks Own*, where Rupert — the resident 'black chum' — was still referred to as 'Nigger'. Nursery rhymes can be modified by word substitution, as they have often been changed before over the centuries, and it no longer need be ten little *nigger* boys who are decimated. This is not a trivial point: children are not to know that some phrases, whether about Jews, Negroes or any other minority group, carry deadly meanings to certain people, and it is surely right whenever possible not to pass on such dangerous material to the young for possible imitation.

The difficulty, however, is greater when it comes to the classics. *The Adventures of Huckleberry Finn* is an outstanding work, and Huck's attitudes and vocabulary are indivisible from his history and background. In one recent specially-prepared American edition of the novel, however, the phrase 'one of the servants' now replaces 'a nigger woman', and 'A young white gentleman' is changed into a mere 'young gentleman'; possible gains in race relations must be offset against the loss to literary truth. In literature more specifically aimed at children, this sort of censorship is happening all the time.

Enid Blyton's publishers, for example, are now going in for some tactful rewriting: in the Pan edition of *The Three Golliwogs* (1973), the names have been changed from Golly, Woggie and Nigger to Wiggie, Waggie and Wollie. In the same way, Roald Dahl has excised some rather patronising references to pygmies in his popular novel, *Charlie and the Chocolate Factory*. While there will always be arguments about whether it is ever right to interfere with the classics, at least where child readers are concerned, no one seems to mind occasional censorship at the less demanding level of literature for children. But the position becomes more difficult in the case of a children's book where colour prejudice plays such a central part that emendation is impossible, and the issue then turns on whether children should have these books made available to them or not. The cruel, racial humour in Hugh Lofting's *The Story of Dr Dolittle* has already been mentioned, and librarians have also sometimes decided against stocking Helen Bannerman's late Victorian classic, *The Story of Little Black Sambo*, because some black children and their parents detest what they see as its patronising attitudes, not to mention the name 'Sambo' itself, and its unhappy associations with racial abuse. For white readers, this book may seem an exciting little story, but perhaps not worth defending — at least in terms of library provision — if the cost is to be the confidence and goodwill of many other readers in the same vicinity, particularly if racial friction is already an important factor there. It is one thing for individuals to decide whether to buy a particular book or not for their children, but it is a different matter when a library or school spends public money on children's literature that may hurt or offend some young readers or prejudice the opinions of others.

Even so, it would seem desirable that whenever possible literature should remain free from political interference, and in cases where racial wounds have healed there would be little reason to continue trying to protect everyone's susceptibilities. Because we are now more conscious of the evils of anti-semitism than was once the case, for example, few would now approve of the sort of remark found in C. Day Lewis's adventure story *The Otterbury Incident*,[21] published as late as 1948, where meagre payment from a shopkeeper is described as being 'Jewed', reminiscent of the schoolboy references in Kipling's *Stalky & Co.* to 'filthy Shylocks'. On the other hand, there seems no good reason now to worry about the nursery rhyme *Taffy was a Welshman, Taffy was a Thief*, although there was a case for inter-

211

fering at a time when it was used provocatively, chanted loudly on the Welsh border on St David's Day, as was once apparently the case.[22] In the same way, a complaint recently made to the Race Relations Board against the stereotype of a mean Scotsman, Angus McScrimp, which appeared in a girls' comic *Tammy*, was rejected, surely quite correctly.[23] This tired cliché is certainly prejudiced, but children often enjoy this sort of mental shorthand, however crude, and it would be hard to see how society is seriously put at risk through permitting hoary, everyday national jokes of this sort. To ban all racial stereotypes from books would be an insult to readers often quite capable of spotting such prejudices for what they are. The existence of more savage stereotypes in older literature, however much one may regret them now, can also provide an essential historical perspective for the origin and former popularity of various intolerant attitudes.

Sexist literature for the young has also been attacked recently, and picture-books showing passive, stay-at-home females and domineering enterprising males have been accused of helping to prolong out-of-date, socially unjust stereotypes in children's minds. Publishers are now urged to scrutinise any new books they produce for such messages, and traditional fairy stories, like *Sleeping Beauty*, or nursery rhymes like *What are Little Boys made of?*, may also be condemned. Attacking ephemeral literature like reading-schemes or cheap picture-books is one thing, but to take on the best-known fairy stories, which have always had a profound appeal, is a more serious matter. It might be different if *Sleeping Beauty* could be proved without a doubt to have had sexist effects upon young readers, but children's perceptions of their sexual roles are built up from many different sources, and it seems unfair to pick on books as particular scapegoats. *Sleeping Beauty* is, in any case, not simply about sexual roles: it can also be read as a parable about different aspects of human personality — in Jungian terms, the animus and the anima, the male and the female elements, which exist within every one of us. In this sense, all readers could be said to identify with both Sleeping Beauty *and* her prince. It is thus probably always too crude to equate literary or pictorial images simply with contemporary practice. Images of passive, defenceless womanhood, for example, can also be produced by societies where women are beginning to play quite opposite roles, but where people still occasionally look to literature for fantasies of a more traditional type of femininity. Trying to suppress all such outlets in fiction may simply lead to individuals trying to realise their fantasies elsewhere.

On the question of suggesting and stimulating new literature, however, rather than merely urging the disappearance of older books, the Women's Movement has already had some positive successes. Reading schemes which once portrayed traditional sexual roles in an ossified manner, have been revised to contain more progressive attitudes. There have also been some lively, interesting, new picture-books for children, where writers and artists have taken advantage of this shake-up in attitudes. In these books, mothers may also go to work and even play football with their children, sharing the housework with a more domesticated type of husband. As it is, books for children often tend to live in the past, with writers and artists drawing upon their own childhood memories, and this sort of stimulus from a pressure group to catch up with important changes in contemporary life style is entirely welcome when it is appropriate. But the wider call that is sometimes heard against the provision for children of *any* book that could be construed as sexist in attitude is a different matter. Literature at any level is not synonymous with lessons in civics, and social interference with it should only be considered in the most extreme cases — for example where racial tension may result. Writers and publishers are bound to listen and sometimes be affected by the many different pressures on them, but ultimately they must be free to come to their own conclusions.

If, therefore, a book is published that unimaginatively trots out clichés, for example to do with extreme sexual stereotypes, then — judged by quite normal critical criteria — it is probably going to be a dull and badly written piece of work anyway. When a writer produces a book of artistic or literary merit for children, however, but which may also happen to convey an image of society that some members of a pressure group may dislike, then the author surely must be granted his or her right to picture society in this particular way. Occasionally it may seem reasonable to limit the access of certain books for children, whether written now or in the past, at least when it comes to stocking these works in schools or junior libraries, but to go any further than this would create more problems than it would ever be likely to solve. As it is, almost any story can be found offensive by someone, although certain groups and causes can certainly claim to have suffered more in this way than others. Even so, dentists have already objected to all the sweets eaten in children's

213

books, environmentalists have taken issue with fictional paper-chases that spread litter, farmers have complained about the sentimentality towards rabbits encouraged by Beatrix Potter's stories, and Labour Councils have sometimes wanted to rid their public library shelves both of Biggles, for his imperialist attitudes, and of Enid Blyton for her snobbishness.

Clearly, taking all these and other pressures into account when writing a book would be impossible, and there is in any case a limit to the extent that any literature can be expected, let alone required, to set a consistently noble, responsible example. To take just one example from a series of books by Monica Dickens that has always sold very well (although it has never been a critical success): 'Rose Arbuckle was Aunt Valentina's drippy friend, a drag, a moaner, a failed person, who had once announced that she should have been drowned at birth. No-one had disagreed.'[24] Adult readers may flinch at this sort of prose, with its callous lack of understanding or charity, but on the other hand it gets close to the way an opinionated, slightly rebellious child may think or speak, just as the rest of this novel goes on to recognise and reflect a host of pre-adolescent fantasies and prejudices at a uniformly undemanding and facile level. Children's books that consisted of nothing but writing of this kind would be shallow and unstimulating, but without it, there would be the risk of writing above the heads and hearts of many young readers, and so eventually leaving them behind.

Children's literature, however, will always be picked on more often than adult books for its possible bad effects, reflecting society's desire to produce future generations in the mirror of its own more positive values, but without its faults. Any children's literature that challenges these values too radically is always liable for censorship, either gradually, in the way that various nursery rhymes or fairy stories have been modified over the years, or else by the process of law, as in the case of horror comics. On the other hand, unless there is also comparative freedom for authors to write as they wish, if necessary defying neat categorisations of what should or should not generally be spoken about in front of the children, then it seems doubtful whether many good authors will ever want to write for the young, unless it is going to be customer-oriented works like reading primers or school textbooks. The special freedom that has, after so many battles, been won for creative literature to express itself in its own way — still of course denied in totalitarian countries — is now

214

generally recognised for most children's literature as well. While there are complex rules dictating what should be avoided in television drama and advertisements where children are the main audience, there are as yet no statutory commands that any writer or publisher of books for young readers is forced to follow.

It is inevitable, in any free society, that children's literature will sometimes use this freedom to suggest values and examples that may appear questionable or even downright bad to various concerned adults. If such values always seem to be biased in the same direction, with no books available to suggest alternative examples, then pressure groups can reasonably try to get other sorts of literature published — perhaps always a more positive policy than merely urging censorship or repression. When it comes to less ideological examples of possibly bad or unwise behaviour, however, there have always been plenty of these in children's literature to alarm older readers. Taking one deservedly well-loved author out of many, Arthur Ransome created very appealing child characters in his fiction, whom readers have often sought to imitate — perhaps by trying to build their own outdoor camps or makeshift rafts. Almost inevitably, however, when a writer describes lively, authentic-sounding children in fiction, there may be less desirable activities that readers may also choose to take up. Arthur Ransome characters can be very free with the bows and arrows which in real life continue to put so many children into hospital with eye injuries, and they constantly sail their boats without wearing lifejackets in a way that seems horrifyingly casual today. Child readers follow these examples in their own lives at their peril, but to deny them the books for this reason would also be to rule out all the pleasant and positive examples which are also available in these novels. On a quite different level, there is a scene in a Ransome story where a girl from a rival gang is first captured and then tied up, and more than one reader has later admitted to finding this erotically arousing.[26] In these cases, it seems likely that reading this chapter simply revealed already existing masochistic fantasies, rather than suggested them, and it would be impossible for any parent to try to shield children from all such innocently suggestive passages in their literature. Even so, one can never be entirely sure how certain unexpectedly stimulating imaginative material may sometimes affect children at an impressionable age, and it would be disingenuous to try to explain away every example of literary influence, whether good or bad, in terms of a reader's predisposition to be

215

so influenced. Imitation simply out of curiosity is always a possible response, especially in a young reader; almost every year, for example, there are newspaper stories of children who try to fly as a result of first encountering *Peter Pan.*

In their reading, as in their life, however, young readers must always make the choice between the behaviour they most admire and wish to emulate and the behaviour they want to avoid. E. Nesbit's child characters often do positive things, like bringing out their own family newspaper, and when readers imitate this sort of thing parents are usually very pleased. But it would be a different matter if the same child readers tried to follow other wilder examples set in her books. In *The Phoenix and the Carpet,* for example, one child is shown throwing paraffin over an indoor firework which at least up to that point, appeared not to be working. This incident is something that would never be tolerated, say, in a television film for children. In *The Story of the Amulet,* however, the same author specifically warns children against the appalling dangers of fire, with one character claiming that 3,000 children are burned to death every year. It would certainly be much better if child readers chose the good examples to follow when given the choice, but ultimately, an author's freedom to describe both good and bad examples, and a child's freedom to choose between them, are both necessary if society wants to preserve the type of liberty that makes any literature worth its name possible in the first place. An occasionally outspoken freedom of expression in children's literature may also, of course, constitute one of its chief attractions to young readers, who will certainly not always want to hear about good examples and be told what is the right thing to do. Literature should not always be expected to make for comfortable reading; a good book, like *Huckleberry Finn,* can often be a subversive book — no-one who reads thoughtfully the dialectic of Huck's great moral crisis will ever again be wholly able to accept without some question and some irony the assumptions of the respectable morality by which he lives, nor will ever again be certain that what he considers the clear dictates of moral reason are not merely the engrained customary beliefs of his time and place.[26]

Children have as much right to be in on this kind of discussion, when they are ready for it, as anyone else, and they must always eventually make their own choices from the multiplicity of literature at their disposal, and read the books in their own, individual way — however much adults may wish to direct them away from particular books or attitudes towards different ones. This is not to say, however, that everything always works out for the best in any ostensibly *laissez-faire* system of publishing for children. Certain themes and values are already very fully represented in children's literature, reflecting the norms and style of the particular social class who still tend to produce and control it, rather than any more truly cross-sectional span of interests. Again, while any pressure group has the right to argue for changes in children's literature, some groups may be far more vocal than others, and therefore take on a disproportionate importance in the views of publishers. Such issues inevitably affect the whole question of just what sort of an audience children's literature is written for. Throughout this book, I have referred to 'children' or 'the child' as if somehow this included every young person, whereas some perfectly literate children may hardly ever read a book at all. Whether this is the fault of the fiction available to children, or whether it is due to the development of a generally dismissive attitude towards all literature, will be one of the points discussed in the next and last chapter.

8 · Who reads children's books?

Any survey of children's reading is bound to be concerned with broad trends rather than individual cases, and on the whole working-class children always emerge from such surveys as reading many fewer books than their middle-class counterparts. It is, of course, quite true that avid readers may still come from backgrounds where there has never been any encouragement for books, while nearly one-third of fourteen-year-old boys with good intelligence and from middle-class homes never read any books for pleasure at all.[1] Nevertheless, the trend of research always suggests an opposite pattern, where children of low ability seem to read less than those of high ability, children from working-class homes seem to read less than children from other social classes, and boys seem to read less than girls.

When it comes to trying to explain this last sexual imbalance, it is true, for example, that boys commonly have more difficulty in learning reading skills than girls do. This difference sometimes persists into later life, but even so, over two-thirds of the boys who later show no interest in literature are assessed by their teachers as of average or above average in general school attainment.[2] Nevertheless, the fact that boys often have more initial reading difficulties than girls still helps to label reading, in the eyes of the young, as a predominantly female activity, and this may also be reinforced by a child's perception of the role book-reading seems to play among adults. In their own homes it will be mothers who read to them more than fathers. In the infant and primary-school classroom, reading and books will again be associated with school-teachers who will usually be female. Here as elsewhere, girl pupils may take to most aspects of what has sometimes been called the 'feminised' primary school more readily than is often the case with boys. They, on the other hand, may feel that they assert their masculinity by turning away from

218

what seems to them to be 'female' values, including reading and various social skills, in favour of science or sports, more often seen as special 'masculine' preserves. Even when there are male teachers in primary schools to take an interest in books and reading, boy pupils may still look upon them not as truly masculine figures to be imitated, but just further victims of a fundamentally matriarchal set-up where conformity, cleanliness and obedience tend to be valued at the expense of more rugged virtues.[3]

The only literature that is always popular with boys is comics, especially those in the *Beano* and *Dandy* tradition, which as we have seen portray many figures who are often very tough and badly behaved. This particular characteristic, however, and the resulting disapproval that comics sometimes produce among parents and school-teachers, may be one important reason why small boys feel that they can enjoy this type of reading in the open without fear of censure from their friends. An interest in books can otherwise seem somewhat suspect in the minds of boys when it comes to the all-important business of establishing a truly masculine persona in the opinion of one's peers. As it is, male pupils who are lower than average in their academic attainments are often rated highly by their fellow pupils in terms of other stereotyped masculine attributes. The more academically successful boy pupil, however, who may also be a fluent and enthusiastic reader, is frequently rated less highly by his peers in terms of being a 'proper' boy.[4]

In the home, there is often a connection between enthusiasm for reading in a boy and a strong relationship with the mother. In studies done on families where fathers had gone away from home during the war, it was found that children were often stronger in the arts side of their studies in school than was the case with those children who still had both parents at home. Interest in maths, science and more generally technical subjects, however, occurs more often in children who have close relationships with their father.

There is also the possibility that sex differences in reading interests, however buttressed by convention, may originate from basic biological differences between male and female. Girls may prefer the passive reading experience, while boys may be happier active, playing football or tinkering with their bikes, because they are made that way. From quite early on, boys explore their environment more than girls do, and later, are far less in the house than their sisters. Whether this is attributable to innate differences or to artificially imposed social conventions is still a controversial issue in psychology. The existence of these sex differences in behaviour, however, whatever their possible causes, still has important implications for the establishment of reading interests in boys and girls, and their perceptions of their own social roles.

Such sex differences also tend to be more rigidly expressed in working-class families, where the reading of books may be seen as 'unnatural' in someone who ought instead to be out playing with friends. In fact, parents' negative attitudes to reading may influence both sexes from quite early on; while many middle-class mothers often feel that reading aloud at bedtime is part of their educational duty, some working-class mothers are more likely to see it as a diversion, or at best a childish indulgence, to be resisted as the child gets older with arguments like, 'You're getting a bit too old for stories.'[5] In fact, while 56 per cent of the middle-class mothers in the Newsons' survey regularly read to their children at bedtime, this was only true of 14 per cent of mothers from working-class backgrounds.

At school, conditions may not favour working-class children, who are more likely to have inappropriate and inadequate books to read, given that generous provision and care of books today are things that comparatively well-heeled parent—teacher associations are best equipped to help out with.[6] Even if there is an adequate stock of books, school is not usually a good place for private reading; surveys suggest that children prefer to read in reasonable comfort, curled up in an armchair, perhaps, or lying on the bed. The hard chairs and general bustle of the classroom cannot rival this sort of cosy intimacy, nor can homes where, for reasons of space or economics, children are packed together in one room with the family, making the privacy that can be important when it comes to reading difficult to achieve. Even so, it is probably those negative, parental attitudes towards books, found more frequently in working-class homes than elsewhere, that eventually prove most important in determining a child's reactions to literature later on at school. This is not to say that children particularly from the unskilled sections of the working class are always backward in the technical skills of reading; in fact, for every ten poor readers from this background, there are also seven good ones.[7] But while there is clearly no such thing as a uniform working-class attitude to book-reading, there remains a greater *probability* of less interest in literature among children from the unskilled working class than elsewhere, and this could still represent a direct inheritance from the days when reading of any kind was often considered a frivolous occupation for people living in straitened circumstances. ' "Put that book down!" a mother would command her child, even in his free time, "and do something useful." '[8] And some fifty years after the times that Robert Roberts describes so well in his autobiography, other social surveys still discover very similar attitudes.[9]

There can also sometimes be the wrong sort of encouragement for reading, especially in homes unused to books, and therefore more prone to misunderstandings in this area. As it is, about half the books given to children are bought by parents and others just around Christmas, sometimes with only the vaguest idea of their suitability. It is difficult to account, otherwise, for the huge sales of unabridged nineteenth-century classics like R.D. Blackmore's *Lorna Doone* or Fenimore Cooper's *The Last of the Mohicans*, still on offer at low prices in various chain stores, which hold out a promise on their illustrated covers too often belied by the stodgy prose within. Choosing suitably interesting and attractive books for uncertain readers is never easy, and all parties can be quickly put off if the first, uninformed choices turn out to be unpopular. Children may also be nagged into finishing unsuitable books, once started, under the mistaken impression that this will do them good in the long run. In fact, children who are already good readers often start and then reject a number of books before finding one that really seems to suit them.[10] A wide choice of books, and the confident attitude that there will, somewhere, be a title that the reader can really enjoy, are both obvious advantages.

In another quarter, the public-library system exists to encourage young readers from all types of social background, but once again working-class parents and their children are under-represented in proportion to other borrowers. This may indicate an alienation from what is seen as the middle-class world of 'book-learning', coupled perhaps with an inability to make use of a library to full advantage. Some children's librarians have gone to great lengths to bring the idea of their library home to every potential user, sometimes by stocking books in unorthodox settings such as sports centres, and by putting on public story-telling sessions for children in parks and recreation centres.[11] Even so, an aura of self-improvement is still evident in public libraries, given their original commitment in the mid-nineteenth century 'to lead the labouring portion of the population from animal to intellectual pursuits'. In terms of limited space and money, this means that more will be spent on quality books, often those useful for study or reference, and less on ephemeral, popular literature, like romantic novels or cowboy stories. Inevitably, such an atmosphere means more to readers, young or old, who see books in terms of their own self-improvement and continuing education. Those who want the instant pleasure of an undemanding read may feel out of place in an institution so clearly given over to higher educational goals, which may seem remote from readers with few such ambitions for themselves.

In sum, then, the prospect for many a working-class child reader remains unpromising, when they may well come from homes where there are only five books or less in the house — the figure found in 1966 by the Plowden Report in 29 per cent of British homes — and live in areas containing few, if any, specialised children's bookshops. At the same time, the authors of children's books are sometimes still accused of aggravating this basic situation by concentrating on backgrounds and characters that are often alien to a working-class readership, particularly in the sort of books a child may encounter when first learning to read. This view has been put forcefully by Leila Berg, who by way of contrast devised and edited the 'Nipper' series of early readers, all of which are set very firmly in working-class backgrounds. These have been popular with many children, and there is an obvious value, particularly where illustrations are concerned, in portraying familiar, contemporary urban scenes; early books which illustrate nothing but pleasant, lawn-surrounded houses would certainly be less meaningful to most working-class children, who will naturally sometimes want to find pictures in their books which they can recognise from their own experience. But the popularity of Miss Berg's stories themselves with young readers of all social classes may simply be because they are funny and well-written, centering around fantasies and situations — like getting lost — that are relevant to every child. In fact, the social background to stories often has relatively little to do with their popularity with younger readers, when Enid Blyton, writing from an upper-middle-class background, and Leila Berg, at pains to stress aspects of working-class life, both end up appealing to a large audience of all children. Each writer, after all, offers something exciting and out of the ordinary: in Enid Blyton's case, there may be a concentration upon a romantic, never-never land, and with Miss Berg it is more a question of making a familiar environment seem exciting and interesting by thinking up

222

situations that are also funny or memorable — and therefore once again out of the ordinary.

The social background to fiction is more important, however, when young teenage readers are concerned. Their greater capacity both for introspection and for distancing themselves from the material in front of them, can make them more inclined to be critical of fiction which describes a world that is unreal or even alien to them. As Robert Roberts has written about his own working-class childhood, at a stage of adolescent disillusion with the formerly much-loved adventures of Greyfriars School in the *Magnet* comic, 'It came as a curious shock to one who revered the Old School when it dawned upon him that he himself was a typical sample of the "low cads" so despised by all at Greyfriars. Class consciousness had broken through at last.'[12] Today, teachers still sometimes report similar sentiments coming from older working-class children in particular, occasionally faced by a succession of set books for public examinations all embodying particular middle-class assumptions and backgrounds. Black adolescent readers, too, may also quite understandably become resentful with a diet of fiction which only seems concerned with white characters.

But while there may still be a shortage of good novels which feature black children, there has been a very pronounced shift in children's fiction recently away from the previous concentration upon purely middle-class characters and backgrounds. Instead,

The settings of realistic stories have moved rapidly down the social scale from nice old houses in the country to the dimmer suburbs, the back streets and the council estate. The school story, dependent as it was on the closed world of the boarding school, has virtually died; fictional children still go to school, but school is only a part of their daily lives. In historical novels, the protagonist is now more likely to be a member of a downtrodden class than a young aristocrat or clean-limbed empire-builder.[13]

Even with this change of emphasis, however, it would still be simple-minded to imagine that older working-class readers will necessarily always prefer books set in backgrounds with which they may be more familiar. The chance to identify with those who are leading more luxurious, even sometimes profligate existences, has always been one of the main appeals in reading novels. For that reason, there are very few popular fictional heroes and heroines, at least in escapist literature, who remain stuck in the modest circumstances in which, like Cinderella, they may originally have been situated. Besides this, it may still often be the case that it is the psychological

223

rather than the surface similarities of fictional characters that eventually most appeal to readers. Where younger children are concerned, novels about naughty boys either in prep schools (Bunter and Jennings) or else living somewhere in the stockbroker belt (William) have always remained popular with everyone, and Jennings' adventures also sell very well in France today — a country without any tradition of prep school education at all. Obviously, in such cases, these stories embody particular, broadly classless, fantasies or aspirations common to a great many children. In the same way, later on, although James Bond may be a member of the British upper classes and William Golding's novel *Lord of the Flies* concerns marooned choir boys rather than children from any less selective type of education, this is far less important to many working-class adolescents than the fact that the adventures of these characters seem to act out in print fantasies that are significant to almost everyone.

A more important factor when it comes to putting off many young people from reading, however, may lie in the very nature of the more formal verbal style generally adopted by all but the simplest fiction, whatever the characters or situations found in such stories. As we have seen, some children will soon become used to the typical structures and conventions of written English through hearing their own parents read to them from an early age, and also through living in homes with a 'greater emphasis on the use of language in socializing the child into the moral order, in disciplining the child, in the communication and recognition of feeling'.[14] To that extent, children from these backgrounds may tend to feel more at home with forms of literature which also make use of similarly complex vocabularies and grammatical structures.

Children from some, although of course by no means all working-class homes, however, may not have had much previous experience of hearing stories, and their habitual level of verbal communication may anyhow be more concerned, in Bernstein's phraseology, with 'particularistic meanings which are closely tied to a given context and so do not transcend it'.[15] More complex fiction therefore, may already be communicating in ways which seem unfamiliar or even alien, once basic dialogue or the description of action in a novel becomes overlaid with verbal analysis and discussion. As Bernstein always stresses, this does not mean that working-class children necessarily differ from their middle-class counterparts in their *understanding* of language. Rather, the more complex verbal contexts in which much literature is written may simply appear increasingly unnatural to them, and to that extent may stand less chance of creating the sense of personal involvement where a reader's initial curiosity is always more likely to be triggered off.

Even so, there are still many cases where young readers, often from very deprived backgrounds, have eventually found in fiction exactly the stimulating, questioning spirit that they seemed to have been looking for. Particularly gifted teachers and librarians have also often been able to overcome initial cultural barriers in many of their pupils through the compelling force of their own belief in literature. Eleanor Farjeon, for example, has described one such headmistress, who before the last war ran

A remarkable L.C.C. 'Infant and Junior mixed' school in Bethnal Green, some of whose six hundred pupils came to their classes almost shoeless and in rags. The headmistress, Mrs Mary Dean, had fired her staff, and so the children, with her passion for imaginative education, and had divided her pupils into four houses, namely Rudyard Kipling, Laurence Housman, Walter de la Mare, and Eleanor Farjeon. Each house had its flag and colours, and a motto from its author.[16]

In due course, a fancy dress Christmas party there was attended by Eleanor Farjeon and Walter de la Mare at the request of the headmistress, who wrote, 'Do come and let the children see and *touch* you, and know you are *real*.' It would be surprising if this imaginative enthusiasm and involvement did not result in more children becoming interested in literature than might normally be the case. The Department of Education and Science has also noted the general improvement in the quality of reading at school when a particular teacher is given the encouragement and opportunity to develop a special interest in children's books,[17] and this is borne out by the Schools Council report, which found that, 'A vital factor (sometimes the most important factor of all) was the degree to which individual teachers and teacher-librarians brought to bear upon their pupils' reading an informed and sympathetic concern and interest.'[18]

Such enthusiastic teachers, who have always been so important, now have far better facilities at their disposal than would ever have been the case in Eleanor Farjeon's day. There are, for example, many more school and public libraries available for children than before, and some schools are also experimenting successfully with their own bookshops or with one of the mail-order book clubs for children. More pupils now stay on at school after the school-leaving age, with greater opportunity to read the attractive, still fairly cheap paperbacks that have come on the market during the last twenty years. Where young readers are concerned, the 'Books for your children' movement often acts as an effective pressure group, and the literature its members are now bringing to the attention of many parents is usually far better than that published between the two world wars, when children's books — with some honourable exceptions — tended to be in the doldrums.

Despite all this progress, however, many children of all social classes still seem uninterested in reading fiction, and this proportion increases in size after the age of ten. Sometimes schools themselves help contribute to this lack of interest, with libraries kept locked during most of the day, or teachers who are themselves reluctant readers may push dull and unsuitable books at their pupils. Even where teachers have keen literary interests and are full of enthusiasm, the standard of their reading aloud to pupils can often be disappointingly inept — equivalent, say, to hearing fine music played on an old, scratchy record with a worn needle. The skill and confidence that once enabled performers to dominate their audience in public readings has practically disappeared today; something well worth trying to resurrect if teachers are ever going to make more demanding books accessible and attractive to pupils who may not yet be up to reading such material for themselves.[19]

But even if these handicaps were overcome, and bright, well-stocked children's bookshops appeared in every area, this would still not affect all the factors that lead some children away from fiction. The fascination most human beings seem to find, in some form or other, with stories can be satisfied without opening a book at all — through accounts of football matches or murder trials in newspapers, for example, or from jokes swapped in convivial surroundings. Interest in longer stories can also be easily satisfied by watching television, which spends at least half of its available time on broadcasting plays and serials which usually appear at peak-viewing times. Television viewing may not have led to a decline in all kinds of reading — it often seems to stimulate interests that are later followed up in books, but it has certainly led to less reading of popular fiction. In Canada, for example, it has been estimated that an average student about to enter college may now have seen more than 500 full-length films, and viewed some 15,000 hours or television but read perhaps only fifty books on his or her own initiative.[20]

Some of the ways in which television viewing has replaced reading in terms of popularity may not be very significant, since watching a popular television serial or reading an undemanding novel satisfies similar imaginative needs, and there may be little to choose between the two experiences. The most popular television comedies, serials and plays broadly contain and project the same repetitive, common needs and fantasies once found in folk-tales and later in popular fiction; there will be some interesting, attractive or amusing characters to become involved with, set in plots that ultimately reinforce the *status quo* while offering *en route* glimpses of rebellion against it. When it comes to viewers' preferences, it is those television plays or films which embody stereotyped fantasies and conventional social values which so often find particular favour, for example, the various popular crime series, where rebellion against the accepted order of things is always condemned and shown not to succeed.[21] There is, of course, more demanding, original material on television too, but this seldom has so many faithful viewers.

Popular television, then, is fulfilling a need that popular fiction once satisfied, and it is now unlikely that fiction will ever regain its former ascendancy. Reading itself is always going to be a difficult technique for some people to master, and it would be optimistic to imagine that authors find it easy to write gripping stories 'of high interest and low vocabulary' — requirements once demanded by an American publisher for readers of limited ability. Even for people with no reading problems, watching television after a day's work involves less effort than reading a book, given that viewers are presented with ready-made images, whereas readers have to construct their own pictures imaginatively from the words on the page. When faced with the choice of a very easy as opposed to what may be only a slightly more taxing alternative, it is not really surprising that even good readers devote more time to television than to books. The British public actually spends about five times as many hours now watching television as reading, and the average number of books read in a year has dropped to sixteen per head. Even this number would be too much for some children and adults, however, who can read perfectly well and may have a high intelligence, but who simply have no interest in novels, although they may be happy with other forms of story-telling on television or elsewhere.

While some of the reasons for not liking novels may indeed reflect inadequacies in cultural or educational background, though, it would be absurd to argue that this is always the case. Individuals in any social class who are 'thing-oriented' rather than 'person-oriented' may simply not find the analysis of personality and the interplay of characters in novels interesting or convincing, while others may get more excitement and satisfaction from a sport or craft or indeed one of the other creative arts. While all children should be given an equal chance to enjoy fiction, therefore, there will always be those who will never take to its particular conventions. One person's right to read, though, must be balanced by another's right eventually to reject fiction, after a period of trial and error, without then being condemned by bookish people, unable to comprehend that their enthusiasm is not shared by everyone else.

The case for always bringing literature to the attention of the imaginative, potentially enthusiastic individual however, has already been made in previous chapters, and is one that I hope will never go by default. To recapitulate: it may be true that people can get equally involved in a good story whether it is presented on television or in a book, but television, because of the huge audiences for which it has to cater, deals very often in stereotyped material in a way that tends to follow 'the law of optimum inoffensiveness'. Stock reactions, therefore, are often drawn out of an audience by long-favoured, cinematic techniques, such as the musical crescendo at an emotional climax, or the zooming in on to a suspicious look or significant gesture as a way of underlining an obvious dramatic point. Because it is also more difficult to convey introspection or indirect speech in visual terms, characters in popular films or in television plays are always more likely to wear their hearts on their sleeves, articulating their desires and acting out their essential characteristics in an obvious way, to make sure that every viewer gets the point.

This crudity is not, of course, found in all television plays, but is more likely to be associated with popular programmes, where millions of viewers are provided with material whose appeal has to rest on well-tried, common factors that exist in the public imagination. Contemporary best-selling novels may also, of course, be doing very much the same thing. But unlike television, within literature there are always going to be other books available at the same time which dwell on less fashionable ideas, drawn from different times and cultures or else simply from a more individual view of things. Apart from the screening of various old films, television on the whole presents its viewers with strictly contemporary fare; books, on the other hand, can satisfy individuals who may also find what they want in descriptions of various former values and attitudes. As we saw in the previous chapter on censorship, a few such attitudes can sometimes embarrass modern, more liberal readers; at other times, though, individuals of any age may find that certain more positive but no longer current concerns or behaviour in fiction from the past can strike chords within them in a way that would be unlikely to happen when reading typical samples from today's literature. It can, of course, be equally stimulating at other times to discover moods and attitudes in older literature that are exactly similar to some of our contemporary preoccupations.

There are other potential differences between reading from the whole range of novels available and watching television programmes. Stories on television have to be viewed at particular times, with no possibility — except for those with expensive video recording equipment — of turning back the programme once it has begun, or deferring the end until a more convenient moment. Unless children have private sets, they will often be viewing in the company of others, and their responses will be conditioned by those around them, as well as by the way television attempts to build in a particular audience response, such as using canned studio laughter in even the feeblest comedy show. A book, on the other hand, is usually read in a more private way, very much according to the whim of the reader. One child may peep at the last page before starting the book, to make sure that everything is going to end happily, while others will have their own habits of skipping, re-reading or pausing over the text. The individual nature of this experience is also reflected in the decision as to what books to read or re-read, and it is usual to find as much divergence as overlap at any age between one reader's choice of favourite books and those of others. Whereas television, comics or pop music tend to weld all their consumers into Marshall McLuhan's concept of a global village, where everyone knows the gossip about the personalities of the moment, literature offers a more particular experience, the nature of which is more likely to change from individual to individual.

In fact, many people can and do enjoy fiction in books and on television, while others — given the choice between the two — may be quite happy never to read a novel again. But this can only be an informed choice if individuals have first had a reasonable chance to weigh up the principal attractions of each medium. Certainly, films and television are sometimes very stimulating for viewers, in the sense that, like fiction, screen material also reflects and defines certain personal experiences and aspirations in what can seem like a significant and sometimes even a formative way. But as I have already stated, there is less chance here of more individual, unstereotyped material appearing on the screen than is the case with certain books, and this could be important for individuals sometimes searching for something which may be in marked contrast to the more repetitive conventions of their own culture.

In sum, therefore, the case to be made for children's literature today is slightly different from one that might have been argued thirty years ago. It is no longer a question of simply advocating the importance of any imaginative experience for an otherwise constricted and under-stimulated child audience, since children today receive from television a greater quantity of ready-made fictional material than at any other time in history. But this outpouring of what is very often stereotyped and repetitive material can eventually start to impose its own restrictions upon the imagination. One strong argument for literature now, therefore, is that it often has the potential to offer a different, far more individual imaginative experience to the child, in which he or she may sometimes discover important personal meanings unavailable to them elsewhere.

Two twentieth-century authors have given memorable accounts of the way that certain books seemed to offer them as children a more satisfactory vision of life than they could find within the normal conventions and constraints of their own culture — which today would also include the sort of television shows that, in Richard Hoggart's words, largely 'reinforce the given life of the times' and consequently 'dare not genuinely disturb or call into question the *status quo*'.[22] The negro writer Richard Wright, for example, recalled in his autobiography what books meant to him during his own wretchedly deprived childhood, at a time when

The impulse to dream had been slowly beaten out of me by experience. Now it surged up again and I hungered for books, new ways of looking and seeing. It was not a matter of believing or disbelieving what I read, but of feeling something new, of being affected by something that made the world different . . . It had been only through books — at best, no more than vicarious cultural transfusions — that I managed to keep myself alive in a negatively vicarious way. Whenever my environment had failed to support or nourish me, I had clutched at books.[23]

It need not, however, only be deprivation that can produce this thirst for stimulation from certain individual writers and their unique, sometimes apparently subversive ways of looking at things. All sorts of children, for many different reasons, long for other worlds and experiences, whether they were born in high estate, slums or the suburbs of Kathleen Raine's childhood, where,

My father gave me, instead, books; and with books, access to inner vistas, to the 'realms of gold'. But — this he did not realise — he was all the time, by placing in my hands the means of knowledge to ways of life and thought other than any accessible to me, unfitting me for Ilford, sowing the seeds of unrest, of great unhappiness; for I was developing the ways of thought and modes of feeling of people who had lived in worlds where fine sensibilities were sheltered in walled gardens, and high thoughts in old libraries; where imagination led naturally to action in terms of existing possibilities. Shakespeare may be a fine education for a ruling class, but in the suburbs to think Shakespeare's thoughts is to be filled with energies, desires, impulses, which because they can have no outlets, no expression in the real, generate only fantasies and discontent. It was well I did not know how far removed I was from those worlds which had created the poetry I fed upon, how many ranges of hills remained to be crossed, or I might have despaired of escape, which seemed to me then an easy matter.[24]

As we saw in previous chapters literature can create aspirations or escapist fantasies that later may not be realised, but this risk is always present when opening up children's minds to possibilities well outside their immediate experience, ambitions and concepts of self. The case *for* alerting individuals to their own and the world's potentialities has probably best been stated in a famous passage by Coleridge, taken from a letter to a friend in 1797:

Should children be permitted to read Romances, and Relations of Giants and Magicians and Genii? I know all that has been said against it; but I have formed my faith in the affirmative. I know no other way of giving the mind a love of 'the Great' and 'the Whole'.[25]

The desire to find patterns in life, and the continuing search for the Great and the Whole, is still with us today, and — as always — particularly among younger people. This desire may only play a small part in any individual's conscious or unconscious reasons for reading books, and there has probably always been a preference among all ages for light reading, whether it be thrillers, horror, romance, adventure or detective stories. This sort of writing, as well as providing relaxation, may also have a formative effect in helping to set social norms or suggest particular models of behaviour. There may be other times, however, when individuals want to discover some more profound, private meaning in the bewildering volume of experience that makes up their lives, and it is then that other, rather different books, perhaps with a greater capacity to understand or reflect personal, complex emotions or aspirations, can sometimes take on the role of genuine friends and allies, on the side of the reader against the straitening uniformity of vision that might exist in family, school, community or mass media. In whatever way young people finally decide to make use of literature, therefore, the existence of this potential treasure-trove at their disposal is something that should surely, at some stage, be brought to their attention. To do this most effectively it is as well first to understand some of the general factors most likely to affect children's reactions to literature at different ages. If this present book can help towards gaining such understanding, however incomplete, then one of its main purposes will have been served.

Notes

(*The place of publication is London unless otherwise stated.*)

Introduction

1 *Jane Eyre*, chapter 3.
2 Pat D'arcy, *Reading for meaning*, vol. 2, *The reader's response*, Hutchinson, 1973, p. 78.
3 See A.H. Thompson, *Censorship in public libraries in the United Kingdom during the twentieth century*, Bowker, 1975, p. 137. See chapter 4 where the work of Enid Blyton is discussed in greater detail.
4 See Frank Whitehead, A.C. Capey, Wendy Maddren and Alan Wellings, *Children and their books*, Macmillan, 1977, p. 114.
5 G.K. Chesterton, *William Cobbett*, Hodder and Stoughton, 1925, p. 116.
6 See D'arcy, *Reading for meaning*, vol. 2, p. 182.
7 Quoted in James Sutherland (ed.), *The Oxford Book of Literary Anecdotes*, Oxford: Oxford University Press, 1975, p. 71.
8 Quoted in *Books for your children*, edited by Anne Wood, vol. 12, no. 1, Winter 1976, p. 3.
9 Joan Aiken, 'A thread of mystery', in *Children's literature in education 2*, July 1970, p. 44.
10 Compton Mackenzie, *My Life and Times. Octave one, 1883–1891*, Chatto and Windus, 1963, p. 101.
11 J. Reid, *Children's comprehension of syntactical features of extension readers*, University of Edinburgh Occasional Papers, 1972.
12 Harriet Graham, *The Lucifer Stone*, Collins, 1977.
13 There is a further discussion of this point in my book, *Suitable for children? Controversies in children's literature*, Sussex University Press, 1976, pp. 113–52.
14 See, for example, 'The fairy Pickwick', in *Selected essays of G.K. Chesterton*, chosen by Dorothy Collins, Methuen, 1951.
15 Natalie Babbitt, 'Happy endings? Of course, and also joy', reprinted in Virginia Haviland (ed.), *Children and literature, views and reviews*, Bodley Head, 1975, pp. 156–7.

1. First books (ages 0—3)

1 William James, *Principles of psychology*, vol. 1, Macmillan, 1890, p. 488.
2 Jean-Paul Sartre, *Words*, Penguin Books, 1967, p. 34.
3 Quoted in Antonia Fraser, *A history of toys*, Weidenfeld and Nicolson, 1966, p. 244.
4 Michael Pollard, 'Picture reading an additional skill to be learned', *Times Educational Supplement*, 31 January 1969.
5 Gwen Dunn, *The box in the corner: television and the under-fives*, Macmillan, 1977, p. 23.
6 *Ibid.* p. 24.
7 M.D. Vernon, *The psychology of perception*, Penguin Books, 1962, p. 26.
8 See Joyce Irene Whalley, *Cobwebs to catch flies: illustrated books for the nursery and schoolroom, 1700—1900*, Elek, 1974, pp. 103—4.
9 Quoted in M.D. Vernon, 'The development of visual perception in children', in D. Brothwell (ed.), *Beyond aesthetics; investigations into the nature of visual art*, Thames, 1976, p. 72.
10 See Anthony Booth, 'Drawing status and picture preferences of primary school children', *Educational Studies*, vol. 1, no. 1, March 1975.
11 Walter Crane, quoted in B. Mahony Miller, *Illustrators of children's books 1744—1945*, Boston: Horn Book Inc., 1947, p. 221.
12 Discussed in M.D. Vernon, *Perception through experience*, Methuen, 1970, p. 191.
13 *The Puffin Book of Nursery Rhymes*, Penguin, 1963, p. 7.
14 See, for example, *The teaching of reading*, Association of Assistant Mistresses, April 1978, p. 9.
15 Quoted in C. Fitzgibbon, *The life of Dylan Thomas*, Dent, 1965, pp. 367—8.
16 I. and P. Opie, *The Oxford Dictionary of Nursery Rhymes*, Clarendon Press, 1951.
17 *The life of Dylan Thomas*, p. 368.
18 See I. and P. Opie, *The Oxford Dictionary of Nursery Rhymes*, p. 2. As with anyone writing about this subject, my debt throughout this chapter to this authoritative work is a large one.
19 *The Oxford Book of Nursery Rhymes*. Assembled by Iona and Peter Opie, Oxford University Press, 1955.
20 *The Oxford Dictionary of Nursery Rhymes*, p. 365.
21 *Ibid.* p. 357.
22 Ardell Nadeson, 'Mother Goose — sexist', in *Elementary English*, vol. 51, no. 3, Illinois, March 1974, p. 375.
23 See Geoffrey Handley-Taylor, *A select bibliography of literature relating to nursery rhyme reform*, 1952, published privately, available in Manchester Public Library, reference section.
24 J. Piaget, *The language and thought of the child*, Routledge, 1926, p. 178.
25 James Reeves, *The everlasting circle*, Heinemann, 1960.
26 Quoted in Nicholas Tucker, *Mother Goose lost*, Hamish Hamilton, 1971.
27 I. and P. Opie, *The Oxford Dictionary of Nursery Rhymes*, p. 248.
28 I. and P. Opie, *The Puffin Book of Nursery Rhymes*, p. 197.

29 Louise Jean Walker, 'Moral implications in Mother Goose', *Education* (USA), vol. 80, no. 5, January 1960.

2. Story and picture-books (ages 3–7)

1 Pat Hutchins, *Rosie's Walk*, Bodley Head, 1968.
2 A. Berry, *Art for children*, Studio Publications, 1942.
3 See Edward Ardizzone, 'Creation of a picture book', in S. Egoff (ed.), *Only connect: readings on children's literature*, Toronto: Oxford University Press, 1969, p. 349.
4 James Reeves, *Titus in Trouble*, Bodley Head, 1969.
5 Quoted in Nat Hentoff, 'Among the wild things', in *Only connect*, pp. 328–9.
6 Quoted in Beryl Geber, 'Towards a developmental social psychology', in Beryl Geber (ed.), *Piaget and knowing*, Routledge, 1977, p. 226.
7 Quoted in Michael Chandler, 'Social cognition: a selective review of current research', in W.F. Overton and J.M. Gallagher (eds.), *Knowledge and development*, vol. 1, New York, Plenum Press, 1977, p. 130.
8 See Elaine Moss, ' "Them's for the Infants, Miss": some misguided attitudes to picture books for the older reader', in *Signal*, vol. 26–7, May–September, 1978.
9 Jean and Gareth Adamson, *Topsy and Tim's Monday Book*, Blackie, 1960.
10 G.F. Vaughan, 'Children in hospital', *The Lancet*, vol. 1, 1957, pp. 1117–20.
11 Lindsey March, 'Adopting a child', *Where?*, no. 88, Cambridge, January 1974, p. 13.
12 See Nicholas Tucker, 'Comics for Infants', *Where?*, no. 48, Cambridge, March 1970, p. 39.
13 See also Nicholas Tucker, 'Who's afraid of Walt Disney?', *New Society*, 4 April, 1968, pp. 502–3.
14 See Margery Fisher, *Who's who in children's books*, Weidenfeld and Nicolson, 1975, p. 361.
15 Leslie Linder, *A history of the writings of Beatrix Potter*, Warne, 1971, p. 187.
16 *Ibid.* p. 146.
17 *Ibid.* p. 146.
18 Beatrix Potter, *The Tale of Samuel Whiskers*, Warne, 1908, p. 19.
19 Linder, *A history of the writings of Beatrix Potter*, p. 192.
20 *Ibid.* p. 258.
21 *Ibid.* p. 110.
22 Quoted in Margaret Lane, *The tale of Beatrix Potter*, Warne, 1947, pp. 82–3.
23 Lane, *The tale of Beatrix Potter*, p. 130.
24 See John Bowlby, *Separation; anxiety and anger*, The Hogarth Press, 1973, p. 198.
25 See 'Beatrix Potter', in *The Lost Childhood*, Eyre and Spottiswoode, 1951, p. 106.

26 Arthur N. Applebee, *The child's concept of story*, University of Chicago Press, 1978, p. 105.

3. Fairy stories, myths and legends

1   From Mrs Trimmer, *The Guardian of education*, vol. 2, January 1803, quoted in Nicholas Tucker (ed.), *Suitable for children?*, p. 38.
2   K. Chukovsky, *From two to five*, Berkeley: University of California Press, 1966, p. 116.
3   *Ibid.* p. 120.
4   Susan Isaacs, *Intellectual growth in young children*, Routledge, 1930, p. 18.
5   G.K. Chesterton, 'The ethics of Elfland', in *Orthodoxy*, Bodley Head, 1909, p. 94.
6   Applebee, *The child's concept of story*, p. 49.
7   *Ibid.* pp. 41—50.
8   Joseph Jacobs, Preface to *English fairy tales*, 1890, p. viii.
9   C.S. Lewis, *Of other worlds*, Geoffrey Bles, 1966, pp. 36—7.
10 Piaget, *Language and thought of the child*, p. 178.
11 For a further discussion of this point, see Nicholas Tucker, *What is a Child?*, Open Books, 1977, pp. 78—9.
12 Jean Piaget, *The moral judgement of the child*, Routledge and Kegan Paul, 1932, pp. 250—1.
13 Piaget, *Language and thought of the child*, p. 174.
14 See, for example, Gustav Jahoda, *The psychology of superstition*, Allen Lane, 1969.
15 I. and P. Opie, *The classic fairy tales*, Oxford University Press, 1974, p. 15.
16 John and Elizabeth Newson, *Toys and playthings*, Penguin Books, 1979, p. 106.
17 W.H. Auden, 'The Quest Hero', in Neil D. Isaacs and Rose A. Zimbardo (eds.), *Tolkien and the critics: essays on J.R.R. Tolkien's 'The Lord of the Rings'*, University of Notre Dame Press, 1968, p. 46.
18 D. Elkind, *Child development and education: A Piagetian perspective*, New York: Oxford University Press, 1977, p. 150.
19 Evelyn Goodenough Pitcher and Ernst Prelinger, *Children tell stories: an analysis of fantasy*, New York: International Universities Press, Inc., 1963.
20 Quoted in R.M. Dorson, *The British Folklorists*, Routledge and Kegan Paul, 1968, p. 175.
21 Joseph Campbell, Folklorist commentary to *The Complete Grimms' Fairy Tales*, Routledge and Kegan Paul, 1975, p. 860.
22 *Ibid.* p. 846.
23 Ernest Jones, 'Psychoanalysis and folklore', in Alan Dundes (ed.), *The study of folklore*, New Jersey: Prentice-Hall, 1965, p. 100.
24 Preface to P.M. Pickard, *I could a tale unfold: violence, horror and sensationalism in stories for children*, Tavistock, 1961, p. ix.
25 Carl Jung, *Man and his symbols*, New York: Dell Publishing Co., 1968, p. 68.
26 Michael Hornyansky, 'The truth of fables', in S. Egoff (ed.), *Only connect*, p. 128.

27 Dundes (ed.), *The story of folklore*, p. 109. This remark can also be found, this time attributed to me, in *The Private Eye Book of Pseuds* (Deutsch, 1973). My use of inverted commas round such a statement, which I realised could seem to have certain comic possibilities for the irreverent, went unheeded.

28 Erich Fromm, *The forgotten language*, New York: Grove Press, 1957, p. 240.

29 Bruno Bettelheim, *The uses of enchantment*, Thames and Hudson, 1976, pp. 166—83.

30 Melanie Klein, *Our adult world and its roots in infancy*, Tavistock, 1960, p. 4.

31 Richard Wright, *Black Boy: a record of childhood and youth*, New York: Harper, 1945, p. 35.

32 Quoted in Bettelheim, *The uses of enchantment*, p. 23.

33 Norman Holland, *5 Readers Reading*, New Haven: Yale University Press, 1975, p. 40.

34 S. Freud, *Introductory lectures*, Allen and Unwin, 1933, p. 134. Quoted in C.S. Lewis, *They asked for a paper*, Geoffrey Bles, 1962, p. 127.

35 I. and P. Opie, *The classic fairy tales*, p. 16.

36 Matthew Hodgart, 'The Witch's secret', in *New York Review of Books*, vol. 9, p. 20.

37 'The novel and the fairy tale', in Virginia Haviland (ed.), *Children and literature, views and reviews*, p. 224.

38 S. Ferenczi, *Sex in psychoanalysis*, Boston: Richard Badger, 1916, p. 238.

39 See L. Snyder, *German nationalism: the tragedy of a people*, New York: Kennikat Press, 1969, pp. 44—74.

40 C.S. Lewis, *Of other worlds*, p. 31.

4. Early fiction (ages 7—11)

1 See Whitehead *et al.*, *Children and their books*, p. 214.

2 See Applebee, *The child's concept of story*, p. 122.

3 Quoted in Colin Welch, 'Dear Little Noddy', *Encounter*, vol. 10, no. 1, January 1958.

4 William Empson, *Some Versions of Pastoral*, Chatto and Windus, 1935.

5 Quoted in Peter Green, *Kenneth Grahame, 1859—1932*, John Murray, 1959, p. 197.

6 Quoted in Green, *Kenneth Grahame*, p. 274.

7 I have written more about Toad in 'The children's Falstaff' in *Suitable for children?*

8 Patricia Beatty, *The Sea Pair*, New York: Morrow, 1970.

9 Mary and Conrad Buff, *Forest Folk*, New York: Viking, 1962.

10 'Nature stories — unrealistic fiction', in *Elementary English*, Illinois, vol. 51, no. 3, March, 1974, p. 348.

11 Piaget, *Language and thought of the child*, p. 258.

12 D. Elkind, *Children and adolescents*, New York: Oxford University Press, 1970, p. 57.

13 See Margaret Sutherland, *Everyday imagining and education*, Routledge and Kegan Paul, 1971, p. 91.

14 Enid Blyton, *The story of my life*, Pitkin, 1952, p. 38.

15 Quoted in Geoffrey Trease, *Tales out of school*, Heinemann, 1964, p. 116.

16 Enid Blyton, *Five go to Demon's Rocks*, Hodder and Stoughton, 1961, pp. 134—5.

17 Blyton, *Secret Seven on the trail*, Leicester: Brockhampton Press, 1952, p. 19.

18 *Ibid.* p. 88.

19 *Ibid.* p. 105.

20 Blyton, *The Mountain of Adventure*, Macmillan, 1949, p. 91.

21 *Five go to Demon's Rocks*, p. 20.

22 *Ibid.* p. 74.

23 *Ibid.* p. 69.

24 *The Mountain of Adventure*, p. 17.

25 *Five go to Demon's Rocks*, p. 87.

26 Quoted in Trease, *Tales out of school*, p. 22.

27 See Barbara Stoney, *Enid Blyton*, Hodder and Stoughton, 1974, p. 172.

28 Blyton, *Five go to Mystery Moor*, Hodder and Stoughton, 1954, p. 146.

29 *The Mountain of Adventure*, pp. 172—3.

30 Quoted in I. and P. Opie, *The lore and language of school children*, Oxford University Press, 1959, p. 2.

31 'Books your children read', *Where?*, 73, Cambridge, October 1972, p. 276.

32 Penelope Gilliat, colour supplement, *The Observer*, 4 July 1965.

33 'William's truthful Christmas', in Richmal Crompton's *Still William*, George Newnes, 1925, p. 136.

34 Crompton, *William The Ancient Briton*, Armada, 1965, pp. 5—6.

35 Quoted in *The collected essays, journalism and letters of George Orwell*, vol. 1, Penguin Books, 1970, pp. 537—8.

36 See interview with Dr Eurfron Gwynne Jones, *The Guardian*, 28 Feb., 1978.

37 Quoted in Colin Alves, 'Moral education in the middle years', in Michael Ragget and Malcolm Clarkson (eds.), *Teaching the eight to thirteens*, vol. 2, Ward Lock Educational, 1976, p. 164.

38 D. Graham, 'Moral development: the cognitive-developmental approach', in V.P. Varma and P. Williams (eds.), *Piaget, psychology and education*, Hodder and Stoughton, 1976, pp. 105—6.

39 Quoted in Peter McKellar, 'Thinking, remembering and imagining', in J.G. Howells (ed.), *Modern perspectives in child psychiatry*, Part 1, Edinburgh: Oliver and Boyd, 1967, p. 171.

40 Quoted in Beryl Geber, 'Towards a developmental social psychology', in Geber (ed.), *Piaget and knowing*, p. 227.

41 Margaret Donaldson, *Children's minds*, Fontana, 1978, p. 121.

42 Michael Chandler, 'Social cognition: a selective review of current research', in W.F. Overton and J.M. Gallagher (eds.), *Knowledge and Development*, vol. 1, New York: Plenum, 1977, p. 138.

43 Donaldson, *Children's minds*, p. 55.

44 Colin Rogers, 'The child's perception of other people', in Harry McGurk (ed.), *Issues in childhood and social development*, Methuen, 1978, p. 110.
45 *Ibid.* p. 122.
46 Dorothy Edwards, *My Naughty Little Sister*, series published by Puffin Books, from 1970.
47 See Whitehead *et al.*, *Children and their books*, p. 214.
48 Rogers, 'The child's perception of other people', p. 109.
49 A.L. Baldwin and C.P. Baldwin, 'Children's judgements of kindness', *Child Development*, vol. 41, USA, 1970, pp. 29—47.

5. Juvenile comics (ages 7—11)

1 *The children's market*, IPC, 1970.
2 Whitehead *et al.*, *Children and their books*, p. 161.
3 Peter Dickinson, 'A defence of rubbish', in Virginia Haviland (ed.), *Children and literature*, p. 101.
4 Quoted in George Perry, *The Penguin Book of Comics*, Penguin Books, 1971, p. 17.
5 Jules Feiffer, *The Great Comic Book Heroes*, The Penguin Press, 1967, p. 186.
6 Quoted in E.S. Turner, *Boys will be boys*, Michael Joseph, 1975, p. 67.
7 I have written more about this great figure in *Anti-Superman*, in Tucker (ed.), *Suitable for children?*
8 K. Wolfe and M. Fiske, 'The children talk about comics', in *Communications Research, 1948—9*, edited by P.F. Lazarsfield and F.N. Stanton, New York: Harper, 1949.
9 Sartre, *Words*, pp. 72—3.
10 *Ibid.* p. 71.

6. Literature for older children (ages 11—14)

1 See Derek Wright, *The psychology of moral behaviour*, Penguin, 1973, p. 169.
2 See Hans G. Furth, 'Young children's understanding of society', in Harry McGurk (ed.), *Issues in childhood and social development*, Methuen, 1978, p. 249.
3 George Eliot, 'The sad fortunes of the Rev. Amos Barton', in *Scenes from Clerical Life*, chapter 4.
4 Mrs Molesworth, *The Ruby Ring*, Macmillan, 1904, p. 121.
5 Mrs Molesworth, *A Christmas Child; a sketch of boy-life*, Macmillan, 1880, pp. 72—3.
6 Nina Bawden, *Squib*, Victor Gollancz, 1971, p. 123.
7 Bawden, *The White Horse Gang*, Victor Gollancz, 1973, p. 55.
8 Bawden, *A Handful of Thieves*, Victor Gollancz, 1971, p. 7.
9 J.R.R. Tolkien, *Tree and Leaf*, Allen and Unwin, 1964, p. 38.
10 Quoted in Frances Kingsley (ed.), *Charles Kingsley: His letters and memoirs of his life*, vol. 2, 1877, p. 266.

11 Quoted in R.L. Green, *Tellers of tales*, Kaye and Ward, 1969, p. 129.
12 See Gustav Jahoda, 'Children's concepts of time and history', *Educational Review*, vol. 15, 1962, pp. 95—6.
13 Geoffrey Trease, *A whiff of burnt boats*, Macmillan, 1971, p. 145.
14 Louise Bates Ames, 'The development of the sense of time in the young child', *The Journal of Genetic Psychology*, USA, vol. 68, 1946, pp. 97—125.
15 Jahoda, 'Children's concepts of time and history', p. 93.
16 See Susan Chitty, *The lady who wrote Black Beauty*, Hodder and Stoughton, 1971, p. 235.
17 *Ibid.* p. 185.
18 Ruby Ferguson, *Jill Enjoys her Ponies*, Hodder and Stoughton, 1954.
19 Diana Pullein-Thompson, *Ponies on the Trail*, Fontana, 1978.
20 René Guillot, *The Wild White Stallion*, Harrap, 1961.
21 Monica Dickens, *The Horses of Follyfoot*, Heinemann, 1975.
22 A. Morrison and D. McIntyre, *Schools and socialisation*, Penguin, 1971, p. 126.
23 Paul Hazard, *Books, children and men*, Boston: The Horn Book Inc., 1960, p. 58.
24 J. Adelson, 'The political imagination of the young adolescent', in *Daedalus*, vol. 100, 1971, pp. 1013—50.
25 Quoted in Lloyd Osbourne, Preface to *Treasure Island*, Heinemann, 1924, p. xv.
26 Quoted in J.C. Furnas, *Voyage to windward*, New York: William Sloane, 1951, p. 198.
27 Trease, *Tales out of school*, p. 80.
28 Quoted in Trease, *Tales out of school*, p. 146.
29 See Jerome Singer, *Daydreaming and fantasy*, Allen and Unwin, 1975, p. 151.
30 Whitehead *et al.*, *Children and their books*, p. 149.
31 See, for example, Don Salter, 'The hard core of children's literature', in *Children's literature in education*, vol. 8, July 1972.
32 See Norman Malcolm, *Ludwig Wittgenstein, a memoir*, Oxford University Press, 1958, p. 35.
33 Graham Greene, 'Across the border', in John Lehmann (ed.), *The Penguin new writing*, vol. 30, Penguin Books, 1947, p. 83.
34 *The autobiography of William Cobbett*, William Reitzel (ed.), Faber, 1967, p. 18.
35 Edmund Gosse, *Father and son*, Penguin Books, 1949, pp. 161—2.
36 Forrest Reid, *Apostate*, Constable, 1928, p. 183.
37 Singer, *Daydreaming and fantasy*, p. 180.
38 George Bernard Shaw, *The intelligent woman's guide to socialism and capitalism*, Constable, 1928, pp. 41—2.
39 E.M. Forster, *Aspects of the novel*, Penguin Books, 1962, pp. 70—1.
40 Greville MacDonald, Preface to *George MacDonald and his wife*, Allen and Unwin, 1924, p. 9.
41 Quoted in Holland, *5 Readers Reading*, p. 51.
42 Singer, *Daydreaming and fantasy*, p. 59.
43 Charles Dickens, *Hard Times*, chapter 2.

44 *Ibid.* chapter 4.
45 Brigid Brophy's contribution to *Bookmarks*, edited by Frederic Raphael, Quartet Books, 1975, p. 24.
46 Eleanor Farjeon, *A nursery in the nineties*, Oxford University Press, 1960, p. 318.
47 Quoted in Peter Quennell (ed.), *London's underworld*, Spring Books, 1960, pp. 101—2.
48 See D.C. McClelland, J.W. Atkinson, R.A. Clark and E.L. Lowell, *The achievement motive*, New York: Appleton-Century-Crofts, 1953, p. 88.
49 See Singer, *Daydreaming and fantasy*, p. 60.
50 Connie Alderson, *Magazines Teenagers read*, Pergamon Press, 1968, p. 98.
51 *Ibid.* p. 99.
52 *Ibid.* p. 99.
53 See H. Himmelweit, Oppenheim, A. and Vince, P., *Television and the child*, Oxford: Oxford University Press, 1962, pp. 394—5.
54 Holland, *5 Readers reading*, p. 205.
55 *Ibid.* p. 285.
56 Singer, *Daydreaming and fantasy*, p. 31.
57 Graham Greene, *The lost childhood*, p. 14.
58 George Steiner, *In Bluebeard's Castle*, Faber, 1971, p. 63.
59 C.S. Lewis, *An experiment in criticism*, Cambridge: Cambridge University Press, 1961, p. 141.

7. Selection, censorship and control

1 See D.C. McClelland *et al.*, *The achievement motive, passim.*
2 See, for example, Fred Inglis, 'The lesser great tradition', in *Children's literature in education*, vol. 9, no. 2, 1978.
3 I have written more about Hall and his campaign in Derwent May (ed.), *Good talk 2*, Gollancz, 1969, pp. 246—62.
4 The new edition of Andrew Lang's *Fairy Books*, however, published by Kestrel and edited by Brian Alderson, is very much more outspoken than its Victorian original.
5 Rudyard Kipling, *Puck of Pook's Hill*, Macmillan, 1906, p. 14.
6 See, for example, J. and E. Newson, *Seven years old in the home environment*, Allen and Unwin, 1976, p. 362.
7 Quoted in Otto N. Larsen (ed.), *Violence and the mass media*, New York: Harper and Row, 1968, pp. 43—4.
8 'The great comic book heroes', Mordecai Richler, *Encounter*, vol. 28, no. 5, May 1967, p. 46.
9 Larsen (ed.), *Violence and the mass media*, p. 277.
10 *Ibid.* p. 277.
11 Havelock Ellis, *My Life*, Heinemann, 1940, p. 60.
12 Quoted in Larsen (ed.), *Violence and the mass media*, p. 246.
13 Richard Garrett, *Piccolo book of heroines*, Pan Books, 1974.
14 Greene, *The lost childhood*, p. 15.
15 See Richard Schickel, *Walt Disney*, Weidenfeld and Nicholson, 1968, p. 220.

16 I. and P. Opie, *The lore and language of schoolchildren*, p. 168.
17 Maurice Sendak, *Where the Wild Things Are*, Bodley Head, 1967.
18 Quoted in 'Lovable horrors', Nicholas Tucker, *Psychology Today*, January 1976.
19 See Charles Lamb, 'Witches and other night fears', in *Essays of Elia*.
20 See David Milner, *Children and race*, Penguin Books, 1975. p. 120.
21 C. Day Lewis, *The Otterbury Incident*, Pitman, 1948.
22 See I. and P. Opie, *The Oxford Dictionary of Nursery Rhymes*, p. 400.
23 See Bob Dixon, *Catching them young*, vol. 2, *Political ideas in children's Fiction*, Pluto Press, 1977, p. 16.
24 Monica Dickens, *Spring Comes to World's End*, Heinemann, 1973, p. 76.
25 See Gillian Freeman, *The undergrowth of literature*, Panther Books, 1969, p. 156.
26 Lionel Trilling, *The liberal imagination*, New York: Holt, Rinehart and Winston, 1950, pp. 112–13.

8. Who reads children's books?

1 Whitehead *et al.*, *Children and their books*, pp. 62–4.
2 *Ibid.* p. 53.
3 See Patricia Sexton, *The feminised male*, New York: Random House, 1969.
4 *Ibid.* pp. 58–9.
5 John and Elizabeth Newson, *Four years old in an urban community*, Allen and Unwin, 1968, p. 259.
6 Joyce Morris, *Standards and progress in reading*, NFER Publishing Company, 1966, p. 229.
7 James Maxwell, *Reading progress from 8–15*, NFER Publishing Company, 1977, p. 90.
8 Robert Roberts, *The classic slum; Salford life in the first quarter of the century*, Penguin Books, 1974, pp. 50–1.
9 See, for example, Brian Groombridge, *The Londoner and his library*, Research Institute for Consumer Affairs, 1964, p. 50.
10 G. Fenwick, 'Junior School Pupils rejection of school library books', *Educational research*, vol. 17, no. 2, February 1975, p. 143.
11 See Janet Hill, *Children are people*, Hamish Hamilton, 1973.
12 Roberts, *The classic slum*, p. 161.
13 John Rowe Townsend, *25 years of British children's books*, National Book League, 1977, introduction.
14 Basil Bernstein, 'Education cannot compensate for society', David Rubinstein and Colin Stoneman (eds.), *Education for democracy*, Penguin, 1972, p. 111.
15 *Ibid.*
16 In Marcus Crouch (ed.), *Chosen for children*, Library Association, 1957, p. 48.
17 Department of Education and Science, 'Half a million books', in *Trends in Education*, vol. 24, October 1971.
18 Whitehead *et al.*, *Children and their books*, p. 283.

19 See Nicholas Tucker, 'Are you sitting comfortably? The sadly underestimated art of story-telling', *Times Educational Supplement*, 14 July 1978.
20 Peter Worsley, 'Keeping up with the culture', *The Guardian*, November 1972, p. 17.
21 See J.S.R. Goodlad, *A sociology of popular drama*, Heinemann, 1971, *passim*.
22 Richard Hoggart, *Speaking to each other*, vol. 1, *About society*, Chatto and Windus, 1970, p. 145.
23 Wright, *Black Boy: a record of childhood and youth*, pp. 218—26.
24 Kathleen Raine, *Farewell happy fields*, Hamish Hamilton, 1973, pp. 113—14.
25 Quoted in J.B. Beer, *Coleridge the visionary*, Chatto and Windus, 1959, p. 32.

Bibliography

(The place of publication is London unless otherwise stated.)

1. Children's literature in general

Blishen, Edward (ed.), *The thorny paradise: writers on writing for children*, Kestrel Books, 1975.

Crouch, Marcus (ed.), *Chosen for children*, Library Association, 1957.

Darton, F.J. Harvey, *Children's books in England: five centuries of social life*, Cambridge: Cambridge University Press, 1958.

Egoff, Sheila (ed.), *Only connect: readings on children's literature*, Toronto: Oxford University Press, 1969.

Ellis, Alec, *How to find out about children's literature*, Pergamon, 1966.

Eyre, Frank, *British Children's books in the twentieth century*, Allen Lane, 1971.

Fisher, Marjory, *Intent upon reading: a critical appraisal of modern fiction for children*, Hodder and Stoughton, 1964.

Who's who in children's books, Weidenfeld and Nicolson, 1975.

Ford, Boris (ed.), *Young writers, young readers. An anthology of children's reading and writing*, Hutchinson, 1967.

Green, Roger Lancelyn, *Tellers of tales, children's books and their authors from 1800–1968*, Kaye and Ward, 1969.

Haviland, Virginia (ed.), *Children and literature: views and reviews*, Bodley Head, 1975.

Hazard, Paul, *Books, children and men*, Boston: Horn Book Inc., 1960.

Hildick, Wallace, *Children and fiction*, Evans, 1974.

Hurlimann, Bettina, *Three centuries of children's literature in Europe*, Oxford: Oxford University Press, 1967.

Meek, Margaret, Warlow, Aidan, and Barton, Griselda, *The cool web: the pattern of children's reading*, Bodley Head, 1977.

Townsend, John Rowe, *A sense of story: essays on contemporary writers for children*, Allen Lane, 1971.

Trease, Geoffrey, *Tales out of school: a survey of children's fiction*, Heinemann, 1964.

25 years of British children's books, National Book League, 1977.

244

2. Developmental psychology: some related aspects

Ames, Louise Bates, 'The development of the sense of time in the young child', in *The Journal of Genetic Psychology*, vol. 68, USA, 1946, pp. 97—125.

Applebee, Arthur N., *The child's concept of story*, Chicago: University of Chicago Press, 1978.

Baldwin, A.L., *Theories of child development*, New York: Wiley, 1967.

Baldwin, A.L. and Baldwin, C.P., 'Children's judgements of kindness', *Child Development*, vol. 41, USA, 1970, pp. 29—47.

Bradley, N.C., 'The growth of knowledge of time in children of school age', in *The British Journal of Psychology*, vol. 38, 1947, pp. 67—78.

Britton, James, *Language and learning*, Allen Lane, 1970.

Brown, J.A.C., *Freud and the post-Freudians*, Penguin, 1963.

Bruner, J.S., *On knowing*, Allen and Unwin, 1962.
The relevance of education, Allen and Unwin, 1972.

Chukovsky, K., *From two to five*, Berkeley: University of California Press, 1966.

D'arcy, Pat, *Reading for meaning*, vol. 2, *The reader's response*, Hutchinson, 1973.

Donaldson, Margaret, *Children's minds*, Fontana, 1978.

Elkind, D., *Child development and education*, New York: Oxford University Press, 1976.
Children and adolescents; interpretive essays on Jean Piaget, New York: Oxford University Press, 1970.

Fraiberg, Selma, 'Tales of the discovery of the secret treasure', in *The Psychoanalytic Study of the child*, vol. 9, New York: International Universities Press Inc., 1954, pp. 218—41.

Friedlander, Kate, 'Children's books and their function in latency and prepuberty', in *New Era*, vol. 39, 1958.

Geber, Beryl A. (ed.), *Piaget and knowing*, Routledge, 1977.

Gesell, Arnold, *et al.*, *The child from five to ten*, Harper and Row, 1974.

Harding, D.W., 'Psychological processes in the reading of fiction', in *The British Journal of Aesthetics*, vol. 2, no. 2, 1962.

Holland, Norman, *5 Readers Reading*, New Haven: Yale University Press, 1975.

Isaacs, Susan, *Intellectual growth in young children*, Routledge, 1930.

Jahoda, Gustav, 'The development of children's ideas about country and nationality', in *British Journal of Educational Psychology*, vol. 33, 1963, pp. 47—60.
'Children's concepts of time and history', in *Educational Review*, vol. 15, 1962, pp. 87—104.

Klein, Melanie, *Our adult world and its roots in infancy*, Tavistock, 1960.

Landau, Elliott, Epstein, Sherrie, and Stone, Ann, *Child development through literature*, New Jersey: Prentice-Hall, 1972.

Lesser, Simon, *Fiction and the unconscious*, New York: Vintage Books, 1962.

McClelland, D.C., Atkinson, J.W., Clark, R.A., and Lowell, E.L., *The achievement motive*, New York: Appleton-Century-Crofts, 1953.

McGurk, Harry (ed.), *Issues in childhood and social development*, Methuen, 1978.

BIBLIOGRAPHY

Overton, W.F. and Gallagher, J.M. (eds.), *Knowledge and development*, vol. 1, New York: Plenum, 1977.
Piaget, Jean, *The child's conception of the world*, Routledge and Kegan Paul, 1929.
The language and thought of the child, Routledge and Kegan Paul, 1926.
The moral judgement of the child, Routledge, 1932.
Pitcher, Evelyn Goodenough and Prelinger, Ernst, *Children tell stories: an analysis of fantasy*, New York: International Universities Press, 1963.
Reid, J., *Children's comprehension of syntactical features of extension readers*, University of Edinburgh Occasional Papers, 1972.
Rosen, Connie and Rosen, Harold, *The language of primary school children*, Penguin, 1973.
Singer, Jerome L., *Daydreaming and fantasy*, Allen and Unwin, 1975.
Sutherland, Margaret, *Everyday imagining and education*, Routledge and Kegan Paul, 1971.
Tucker, Nicholas, *What is a child?*, Open Books, 1977.
Varma, V.P. and Williams, P. (eds.), *Piaget, psychology and education*, Hodder and Stoughton, 1976.
Vernon, M.D., 'The development of imaginative construction in children', in *The British Journal of Psychology*, vol. 39, 1948, pp. 102—11.
'The relation of cognition and fantasy in children', part 1, in *The British Journal of Psychology*, vol. 30, 1940, pp. 273—94.
Whiteman, Martin, 'Children's concepts of psychological causality', in *Child Development*, vol. 38, USA, 1967, pp. 143—55.
Wright, Derek, *The psychology of moral behaviour*, Penguin, 1973.

3. The growth of perceptual skills

Booth, Anthony, 'Drawing status and picture preferences of primary school children', *Educational Studies*, vol. 1, no. 1, March 1975.
Hochberg, Julian and Brown, Virginia, 'Pictorial recognition as an unlearned ability', *American Journal of Psychology*, vol. 75, 1962, pp. 624—8.
Pollard, Michael, 'Picture reading an additional skill to be learned', *Times Educational Supplement*, 31 January 1969.
Tucker, Nicholas, 'Looking at pictures', *Children's literature in education*, vol. 14, 1974.
'Ways children see', in *Times Educational Supplement*, 3 November 1978.
Vernon, M.D., 'The development of visual perception in children' in Brothwell, D. (ed.), *Beyond aesthetics: investigations into the nature of visual art*, Thames, 1976.
Perception through experience, Methuen, 1970.
The psychology of perception, Penguin, 1966.

4. Picture-books

Alderson, Brian, *Catalogue for an exhibition of Pictures by Maurice Sendak, at the Ashmolean Museum, Oxford*, The Bodley Head, 1975.
(compiler), *Looking at picture books, 1973*, National Book League, 1973.

246

BIBLIOGRAPHY

Feaver, William, *When we were young. Two centuries of children's book illustrations*, Thames and Hudson, 1977.
Hurlimann, Bettina, *Picture-book world*, Oxford University Press, 1968.
Kingman, Lee, Foster, Joanna and Lontoft, Ruth Giles, *Illustrators of children's books, 1957–1966*, Boston: Horn Book Inc., 1968.
Kingman, Lee, Hogarth, Grace and Quimby, Harriet, *Illustrators of children's books, 1967–1976*, Boston: Horn Book Inc., 1979.
Miller, B. Mahony, *et al.*, *Illustrators of children's books, 1744–1945*, Boston: Horn Book Inc., 1947.
Morris, Charles, *The illustration of children's books*, The Library Association, 1969.
Moss, Elaine, ' "Them's for the Infants, Miss"; some misguided attitudes to picture books for the older reader', in *Signal*, vol. 26–7, May–September 1978.
Tucker, Nicholas, 'Edward Ardizzone', in *Children's literature in education*, vol. 3, November 1970.
Viguers, Ruth Hill, Dalphin, Marcia, and Miller, Bertha Mahoney, *Illustrators of children's books, 1946–1956*, Boston: Horn Book Inc., 1958.
Whalley, Joyce, *Cobwebs to catch flies: illustrated books for the nursery and schoolroom*, Elek, 1974.

5. Early reading, 0–7 years

Bell, Hazel, *Situation books for under-sixes: A guide to books for reading to children when Mummy has another baby, the child is going to hospital, and so on*, Kenneth Mason Ltd, 1970.
Berg, Leila, *Reading and loving*, Routledge, 1977.
Cass, Joan E., *Literature and the young child*, Longman, 1967.
Chesterton, G.K., 'The romance of rhyme', in *Fancies versus fads*, Methuen, 1930.
Daiken, Leslie, *The lullaby book*, Edmund Ward, 1959.
Lane, Margaret, *The tale of Beatrix Potter*, Warne, 1947.
Linder, Leslie, *A history of the writings of Beatrix Potter*, Warne, 1971.
Opie, Iona and Peter, *The Oxford Book of Nursery Rhymes*, Oxford: Clarendon Press, 1955.
   The Oxford Dictionary of Nursery Rhymes, Oxford: Clarendon Press, 1951.
   The Puffin Book of Nursery Rhymes, Penguin, 1963.
Petty, Thomas A., 'The tragedy of Humpty Dumpty', in *The psychoanalytic study of the child*, vol. 8, New York: International Universities Press Inc., 1953, pp. 404–12.
Reeves, James, *The everlasting circle*, Heinemann, 1960.
   The idiom of the people, Heinemann, 1958.
Singer, Dorothy, 'Piglet, Pooh and Piaget', in *Psychology Today*, USA, June 1972.
Smith, Lillian, *The unreluctant years. A critical approach to children's literature*, Chicago: American Library Association, 1953.
Tucker, Nicholas, 'Nursery rhymes', in May, Derwent (ed.), *Good talk*, vol. 2, Gollancz, 1969.
White, Dorothy, *Books before five*, Oxford University Press, 1954.

6. Fairy stories

Auden, W.H., 'The Quest Hero', in Isaacs, N.D. and Zimbardo, R.A. (eds.), *Tolkien and the critics: essays on J.R.R. Tolkien's 'The Lord of the Rings'*, University of Notre Dame Press, 1968.

Bettelheim, Bruno, *The uses of enchantment: the meaning and importance of fairy tales*, Thames and Hudson, 1976.

Chesterton, G.K., 'The ethics of elfland', in *Orthodoxy*, Bodley Head, 1909.

Cook, Elizabeth, *The ordinary and the fabulous: an introduction to myths, legends and fairy tales for teachers and storytellers*, Cambridge: Cambridge University Press, 1976.

Davis, Robert Graham, 'Art and anxiety', in Phillips, William (ed.), *Art and psychoanalysis*, Cleveland: Meridian Books, 1963.

Fromm, Erich, *The forgotten language: an introduction to the understanding of dreams, fairy tales and myths*, New York: Holt, Rinehart and Winston, 1951.

Jones, E., 'Psychoanalysis and folklore', in Dundes, A. (ed.), *The study of folklore*, NJ: Prentice-Hall, 1965.

Jung, C.J., *Man and his symbols*, New York: Dell Publishing Co. Ltd, 1968.
The phenomenology of the spirit of fairy tales, Collected works, vol. 9, Routledge, 1953.

Lewis, C.S., *Of other worlds*, Geoffrey Bles, 1966.
They asked for a paper, Geoffrey Bles, 1962.

Lurie, Alison, 'Witches and fairies', in *New York Review of Books*, 2 December 1971.

Michaelis, Jena R., *The Brothers Grimm*, Routledge, 1974.

Opie, Iona and Peter, *The classic fairy tales*, Oxford: Oxford University Press, 1974.

Tolkien, J.R.R., *Tree and leaf*, Allen and Unwin, 1964.

7. Reading from 7–11

Blount, Margaret, *Animal land: the creatures of children's fiction*, Hutchinson, 1974.

Field, C. and Hamley, D.C., *Fiction in the middle school*, Batsford, 1975.

Gardner, Martin (ed.), *The annotated Alice*, Penguin, 1965.

Green, Peter, *Kenneth Grahame*, John Murray, 1959.

Jones, Antony and Buttrey, June, *Children and stories*, Oxford: Basil Blackwell, 1971.

Peel, Marie, *Seeing to the heart. English and imagination in the junior school*, Chatto, 1967.

Phillips, R. (ed.), *Aspects of Alice. Lewis Carroll's dream child as seen through the critics' looking glass, 1865–1971*, Gollancz, 1972.

Stoney, Barbara, *Enid Blyton*, Hodder and Stoughton, 1974.

Welch, Colin, 'Dear little Noddy', in *Encounter*, vol. 10, no. 1, January 1958.

8. Juvenile comics

Chesterton, G.K., 'In defence of the penny dreadful', in *The Defendant*, Dent, 1918.

Daniels, Les, *Comix. A history of comic books in America*, Wildwood House, 1973.

Feiffer, J., *The Great Comic Book Heroes*, Allen Lane, 1967.

Orwell, George, 'Boys' Weeklies', in *The collected essays, journalism and letters of George Orwell*, vol. 1, Penguin, 1970.

Perry, G., *The Penguin Book of Comics*, Penguin, 1971.

Report of debate on Children and Young Persons (Harmful Publications) Bill, 22 February 1955, *Hansard*, HMSO (see also Second Reading, 24 March 1955, and Committee Stage, 28 March 1955).

Richler, Mordecai, 'The Great Comic Book Heroes', in *Encounter*, vol. 28, no. 5, 1967.

Tucker, Nicholas, 'Juvenile Comics', in *Where*, Cambridge, nos. 122, 123, November, December, 1976.

Turner, E.S., *Boys will be boys*, Michael Joseph, 1975.

Wolfe, K. and Fiske, M., 'The children talk about comics', in Lazarsfield, P.F. and Stanton, F.N., *Communications Research, 1948–9*, New York: Harper, 1949.

9. Reading from 11–14

Alderson, Connie, *Magazines teenagers read*, Pergamon, 1968.

Amis, Kingsley, *The James Bond Dossier*, Jonathan Cape, 1965.

Cadogan, Mary and Craig, Patricia, *You're a brick, Angela: a new look at girls' fiction from 1840 to 1976*, Gollancz, 1976.

Cameron, E., *The Green and burning tree*, Boston: Little Brown, 1969.

Chambers, Aidan, *Introducing books to children*, Heinemann, 1973.

    The reluctant reader, Pergamon, 1969.

Chesterton, G.K., 'Books for boys', in *The common man*, Sheed and Ward, 1951.

    'The fairy Pickwick', in *Selected essays of G.K. Chesterton*, chosen by Dorothy Collins, Methuen, 1951.

Chitty, Susan, *The lady who wrote Black Beauty*, Hodder and Stoughton, 1971.

Fielder, Leslie, *No in thunder. Essays on myth and literature*, Boston: Beacon Press, 1960.

Freeman, Gillian, *The schoolgirl ethic: the life and works of Angela Brazil*, Allen Lane, 1976.

Freud, Anna, *The ego and the mechanisms of defence*, Hogarth, 1937.

Green, Roger Lancelyn, *Kipling and the children*, Elek, 1965.

Marshall, Margaret, *Libraries and literature for teenagers*, Deutsch, 1975.

Moore, Doris Langley, *E. Nesbit. A biography*, Benn, 1967.

Pearson, John, *The life of Ian Fleming*, Jonathan Cape, 1966.

Peller, Lili E., 'Daydreams and children's favourite books, psychoanalytic comments', in *The Psychoanalytic study of the child*, vol. 14, New York: International Universities Press Inc., 1959.

Quayle, Eric, *Ballantyne the brave. A Victorian writer and his family*, Rupert Hart-Davis, 1967.

The collector's book of boys' stories, Studio Vista, 1973.

Raphael, Frederic (ed.), *Bookmarks*, Quartet Books, 1975.

Tucker, Nicholas, 'Adolescent comics and magazines', *Where*, no. 51, Cambridge, September 1970.

10. Selection, censorship and control

Dixon, Bob, *Catching them young*, vol. 1, *Sex, race and class in children's fiction*, vol. 2, *Political ideas in children's fiction*, Pluto Press, 1977.

Freeman, Gillian, *The undergrowth of literature*, Panther Books, 1969.

Husband, Charles (ed.), *White media and Black Britain. A critical look at the role of the media in race relations today*, Arrow Books, 1975.

Inglis, Fred, 'The lesser great tradition: carry on, children', in *Children's literature in education*, vol. 9, no. 2, 1978.

Larsen, Otto (ed.), *Violence and the mass media*, New York: Harper and Row, 1968.

Leeson, Robert, *Children's books and class society*, Writers and readers publishing cooperative, 1977.

Milner, David, *Children and race*, Penguin, 1975.

Pickard, P.M., *I could a tale unfold: violence, horror and sensationalism in stories for children*, Tavistock, 1961.

Thompson, A.H., *Censorship in public libraries in the United Kingdom during the twentieth century*, Bowker, 1975.

Tucker, Nicholas, *Suitable for children? Controversies in children's literature*, Sussex University Press, 1976.

Wertham, Frederick, *Seduction of the innocent*, Museum Press, 1955.

A sign for Cain. An exploration of human violence, Hale, 1968.

11. Who reads children's books?

Department of Education and Science, 'Half a million books', in *Trends in Education*, vol. 24, October 1971.

Department of Education and Science, *A language for life. Report of the committee of inquiry appointed by the Secretary of State for Education and Science under the chairmanship of Sir Alan Bullock*. HMSO, 1975.

Ellison, Tom and Williams, Gerald, 'Social class and children's reading preferences', in *Reading*, June 1971.

Fenwick, G., 'Junior school pupils' rejection of school library books', in *Educational Research*, vol. 17, no. 2, February 1975.

Hill, Janet, *Children are people. The librarian in the community*. Hamish Hamilton, 1973.

Leng, I.J., *Children in the library: a study of children's leisure-reading tastes and habits*, Cardiff: University of Wales Press, 1968.

250

BIBLIOGRAPHY

Mann, Peter H., *Books, buyers and borrowers*, Deutsch, 1971.
Mann, Peter H. and Burgoyne, Jacqueline, *Books and reading*, Deutsch, 1969.
Maxwell, James, *Reading progress from 8—15*, NFER Publishing Co., 1977.
Report of the Central Advisory Council for Education (England), *Children and their Primary Schools*, (Plowden Report), HMSO, 1966.
Tucker, Nicholas, 'Are you sitting comfortably? The sadly underestimated art of story-telling', in *Times Educational Supplement*, 14 July 1978.
'Books children read: a report', in *Where*, nos. 73, 74, Cambridge, October, November, 1972.
Whitehead, Frank, Capey, A.C., Maddren, Wendy, and Wellings, Alan, *Children and their books*, Macmillan, Schools Council Research Studies, 1977.

12. Reviews and periodicals about children's literature

Books for Keeps, School Bookshop Association, 1 Effingham Road, Lee, London SE12 8NZ.
Books for your children, edited by Anne Wood, 90 Gillhurst Road, Harborne, Birmingham 17.
Children's Book Bulletin: for news of progressive moves in children's literature, Children's Rights Workshop, 4 Aldebert Terrace, London W8.
Children's literature in education, 150 Fifth Avenue, New York, NY 10011. (British subscribers: 2 Sunwine Place, Exmouth, Devon.)
The Horn Book Magazine, Horn Book Inc., 31 St James Ave, Boston 02116.
Junior Bookshelf, Marsh Hall, Thurstonland, Huddersfield, Yorks.
School Librarian, School Library Association, Victoria House, 29—31 George St, Oxford OX1 2AY.
Signal: approaches to children's books, Thimble Press, Lockwood, Station Road, South Woodchester, Glos. GL5 5EQ.

The National Book League also produces pamphlets on all aspects of children's literature, including the invaluable annual selection edited and annotated by Elaine Moss, *Children's Books of the Year* (published in association with Hamish Hamilton and from 1980 in association with Julie Macrae Books).

Index

Adams, Richard, *Watership Down*, 8, 160—1
Adamson, Jean and Gareth, *Topsy and Tim* series, 52, 54—5, 57
Adamson, Joy, *Born Free*, 161
Aiken, Joan, children's responses to language, 13
Alderson, Brian, 241, 246
Alderson, Connie, 249; on adolescent comics, 185
Allen, Richard, *Skinhead*, 172
Andersen, Hans, upsetting stories, 12, 71; *Eleven Wild Swans*, 155; *The Emperor's New Clothes*, 119; *The Little Mermaid*, 156
animals as fictional characters, in Enid Blyton's stories, 107; in comics, 55, 137; in fairy stories, 75, 77; as human symbols, 84; in nursery rhymes, 43—4; in picture-books, 26; in Beatrix Potter's stories, 62—5
Anne Frank's Diary, 163
Anne of Green Gables (L.M. Montgomery), 173
Applebee, Arthur, 236—7, 245; on children's belief in fiction, 70
Arabian Nights, The, censorship of, 199; fatalism in, 191
archetypes in literature, 6, 24, 157
Ardizzone, Edward, on illustrating children's books, 48, 257; *Tim Books*, 49, 55—6
Auden, W.H., 236, 248; definition of poetry, 34; on fairy stories, 79
Austen, Jane, *Cinderella* plots, 16
Awdry, Revd W., illustrated books for children, 65

Babbitt, Natalie, universal themes in children's literature, 19
Bagnold, Enid, *National Velvet*, 172
Balfour, A.J., liking for *Treasure Island*, 169
Ballantyne, R.M., *The Coral Island*, 165, 167—8; *Martin Rattler*, 167
Bannerman, Helen, *The Story of Little Black Sambo*, 211
Barrie, J.M., on *The Coral Island*, 165; effects of *Peter Pan*, 216
Bawden, Nina, *A Handful of Thieves*, 149, 151; *The Peppermint Pig*, 148; *The Runaway Summer*, 147, 149—50; *The Secret Passage*, 147, 149; *Squib*, 148; *The Witch's Daughter*, 149; *The White Horse Gang*, 147, 149
Baxendale, Leo, *The Bash Street Kids*, 133—6
Beeton, Samuel Orchard, on children's letters to comics, 141
Belloc, Hilaire, *Cautionary Tales*, 117
Beowulf, influence on J.R.R. Tolkien, 156
Berg, Leila, 65, 247; working-class backgrounds to stories, 222; *Little Pete* series, 55
Bettelheim, Dr Bruno, psychoanalytic interpretation of fairy stories, 89, 92; the value of Grimms Tales, 195
Bevan, Aneurin, on *The Gem*, 140
Bible, the, animal sacrifice in, 62; animal speech in, 75
Blackmore, R.D., *Lorna Doone*, 16, 221
Blyton, Enid, 248; adventure stories, 113—15, 125, 149; adult dislike of,

253